Surveillance society

Monitoring everyday life

DAVID LYON

OPEN UNIVERSITY PRESS
Buckingham • Philadelphia

303.483 LYO

Open University Press
Celtic Court
22 Ballmoor
Buckingham
MK18 1XW

email: enquiries@openup.co.uk
world wide web: www.openup.co.uk

and
325 Chestnut Street
Philadelphia, PA 19106, USA

First Published 2001
Reprinted 2002 (twice)

A catalogue record of this book is available from the British Library

ISBN 0 335 20546 1 (pb)   0 335 20547 X (hb)

Library of Congress Cataloging-in-Publication Data
Lyon, David, 1948–
    Surveillance society: monitoring everyday life / David Lyon.
        p.   cm. — (Issues in society)
    Includes bibliographical references and index.
    ISBN 0-335–20547–X — ISBN 0–335–20546–1 (pbk.)
    1. Electronic surveillance.   2. Electronic surveillance—Social aspects.
    3. Computers and civilization.   4. Information technology—Social aspects.
    I. Title.   II. Series.

TK7882.E2 L965 2001
303.48′3—dc21
                                                                00–044119

Typeset by Graphicraft Limited, Hong Kong
Printed in Great Britain by Biddles Ltd, www.biddles.co.uk

Contents

Series editor's foreword   vii
Preface and acknowledgements   xi

Introduction   1
   Surveillance has two faces   3
   Key themes   5
   How this book works   8

Part one Surveillance societies   13

1 Disappearing bodies   15
   Reconfiguring time and space   17
   Blurring public and private   20
   Recombining technology and society   23

2 Invisible frameworks   28
   Commonalities and variations   30
   Surveillance diffused through society   33
   Social orchestration   35

3 Leaky containers   37
   Policing by surveillance   39
   Watching workers   40
   Covering consumers   43
   Deregulation and risk   44

Part two The spread of surveillance   49

4 Surveillant sorting in the city   51
   Social control in the city   52

SimCity and urban realities   55
Urban surveillance   56
Under the camera   60
SimCity and the real world   66

5 Body parts and probes   69
    The body from site to source   71
    Identity, identification and modernity   72
    Body surveillance technologies   75
    Body surveillance in different sectors   77
    Movement, action and risk   81

6 Global data flows   88
    Globalization and surveillance   90
    Global security: Comint   94
    Global security: controlling borders   97
    The world wide web of surveillance   101
    Globalized surveillance   103

Part three Surveillance scenarios   105

7 New directions in theory   107
    Computers and modern surveillance   109
    Superpanopticon and hypersurveillance   114
    New surveillance in theory   118
    Returning the body   123

8 The politics of surveillance   126
    Regulative responses   128
    Mobilizing responses   131
    Resistance in context   134
    Why resistance is limited   135

9 The future of surveillance   141
    Modern and postmodern surveillance   141
    Toward a new approach   149
    Re-embodying persons   151

Notes   155
Bibliography   174
Index   181

Series editor's foreword

Collectively, the social sciences contribute to a greater understanding of the dynamics of social life, as well as explanations for the workings of societies in general. Yet they are often not given due credit for this role and much writing has been devoted to why this should be the case. At the same time, we are living in an age in which the role of science in society is being re-evaluated. This has led to both a defence of science as the disinterested pursuit of knowledge and an attack on science as nothing more than an institutionalized assertion of faith with no greater claim to validity than mythology and folklore. These debates tend to generate more heat than light.

In the meantime the social sciences, in order to remain vibrant and relevant, will reflect the changing nature of these public debates. In so doing they provide mirrors upon which we can gaze in order to understand not only what we have been and what we are now, but to inform possibilities about what we might become. This is not simply about understanding the reasons people give for their actions in terms of the contexts in which they act and analysing the relations of cause and effect in the social, political and economic spheres, but also concerns the hopes, wishes and aspirations that people, in their different cultural ways, hold.

In any society that claims to have democratic aspirations, these hopes and wishes are not for the social scientist to prescribe. For this to happen it would mean that the social sciences were able to predict human behaviour with certainty. One theory and one method, applicable to all times and places, would be required for this purpose. The physical sciences do not live up to such stringent criteria, whilst the conditions in societies which provided for this outcome, were it even possible, would be intolerable. Why? Because a necessary condition of human freedom is the ability to have acted otherwise and thus to imagine and practice different ways of organizing societies and living together.

It does not follow from the above that social scientists do not have a valued role to play, as is often assumed in ideological attacks upon their place and function within society. After all, in focusing upon what we have been and what we are now, what we might become is inevitably illuminated: the retrospective and prospective become fused. Therefore, whilst it may not be the province of the social scientist to predict our futures, they are, given not only their understandings and explanations, but equal positions as citizens, entitled to engage in public debates concerning future prospects.

This new international series was devised with this general ethos in mind. It seeks to offer students of the sciences, at all levels, a forum in which ideas and topics of interest are interrogated in terms of their importance for understanding key social issues. This is achieved through a connection between style, structure and content that aims to be both illuminating and challenging in terms of its evaluation of those issues, as well as representing an original contribution to the subject under discussion.

Given this underlying philosophy, the series contains books on topics that are driven by substantive interests. This is not simply a reactive endeavour in terms of reflecting dominant social and political pre-occupations, it is also pro-active in terms of an examination of issues which relate to and inform the dynamics of social life and the structures of society that are often not part of public discourse. Thus, what is distinctive about this series is an interrogation of the assumed characteristics of our current epoch in relation to its consequences for the organization of society and social life, as well as its appropriate mode of study.

Each contribution contains, for the purposes of general orientation, as opposed to rigid structure, three parts. First, an interrogation of the topic that is conducted in a manner that renders explicit core assumptions surrounding the issues and/or an examination of the consequences of historical trends for contemporary social practices. Second, a section which aims to 'bring alive' ideas and practices by considering the ways in which they directly inform the dynamics of social relations. A third section then moves on to make an original contribution to the topic. This encompasses possible future forms and content, likely directions for the study of the phenomena in question, or an original analysis of the topic itself. Of course, it might be a combination of all three.

David Lyon's *Surveillance Society: Monitoring Everyday Life* reflects this ethos. There is no doubt that our lives are now subject to ever-greater means of surveillance that takes a variety of forms. Closed circuit television is a routine feature of shopping centres and appears not only within banks, but also the shops themselves. It is often portrayed as being in the 'interests' of staff and customer comfort and security and to call attention to such justifications, or even to question the motivations that underlie their presence, may be castigated as indicative of the act of a guilty mind.

Those who question these developments, according to ideas of protecting the human right to privacy, may themselves be open to the criticism that it is the very presence of such instruments of surveillance that ensures such rights in the first place! In the face of such important issues and the spread of these practices, clarity of thinking about their modes of operation, rationale for implementation and consequences for human actions and society as a whole, is often in short supply and even absent. Who better, then, to fill this gap than one of the leading scholars in this area who has dedicated many years to the study of these developments?

One way in which these transformations affect our everyday lives is via changes in our interactions. That great observer of everyday life – Erving Goffman – spoke of places in which two persons interacted in situations of physical co-presence. Now, however, emails, faxes and mobile phones have transformed, with varying consequences our perception of each other and ourselves. Matters relating to time and space alter in the process and bodies 'disappear' from view. This, in turn, creates new opportunities for surveillance of routine activities with global flows of personal data playing their role in the coordination and control of human activities. The divisions between the public and private aspects of our lives then become blurred as the forms in which knowledge about persons is transformed.

These changes in knowledge may be considered by employing and adding to, a distinction used by Bertrand Russell. Here we can speak of a transition from knowledge enabled through acquaintance in the physical presence of others, to that obtained by description as mediated through new technologies. Workplaces have changed and so the boundaries between the private individual and public organizational person have begun to break down or even evaporate. In a global age, these modes of surveillance move across boundaries and track movements of people via, for example, their use of airline tickets and their purchase using credit cards. Classificatory schemas are then used for commercial purposes that enable profiles of consumers to be built up and targeted for marketing purposes. Similarly, it is possible to track, via such techniques as 'clickstream monitoring' and 'collaborative filtering', the preferences of those who use the Internet in order to exploit the resultant data for marketing purposes.

Important issues concerning the classificatory power of these technologies in relation to human rights then arise through such question as who owns such data and are there any limits to its uses for state and commercial purposes? This, in turn, raises questions about the scope and limits to human privacy. David Lyon illuminates such matters in a practical manner and achieves this by addressing them in relation to the growth of the surveillance society. In so doing, he does not succumb to the ethnocentric, gendered and individualistic forms of thought that so often inform these debates.

To more fully comprehend these issues we need to understand how these new technologies have evolved, for what reasons and with what effects? Here David Lyon provides us with a fascinating and illuminating account that does not simply view these technologies as determining, nor as mere additions to the social fabric of societies. Instead they interact and are weaved together in ways that are contradictory and which may depend upon the prediction of human behaviour which, itself, is problematic. They can also produce unintended consequences: for example, the use of genetic screening by employers to determine the susceptibility of employees to disease can lead people to avoid such tests. As a result, effective medical intervention in the name of prevention or amelioration may be considerably diminished. Surveillance, in this sense, is two-edged in that it can provide benefits, whilst also preventing people from realizing their ambitions.

David Lyon discusses these issues in ways that draw upon a variety of examples to illustrate his points and the themes that underpin the book itself. There is no doubt that we are only just beginning to realize the potential consequences of the growth in new technologies. A more participatory debate is required in the face of these changes in terms of their implications for how we lead our lives and who holds and exploits the knowledge that is generated as a result. Without doubt, this book is a major contribution to that process.

Tim May

Preface and acknowledgements

This is the second book that I have written about surveillance, and it bears a close relation to the first. *The Electronic Eye* focused especially on the rise of surveillance society, showing how electronically based communications and information technologies intensify surveillance practices and processes already familiar in modern societies. *Surveillance Society* assumes much of that historical development and explores further the ways that everyday life is today closely monitored by a myriad of means and devices. The two books are thus complementary and readers of this book may wish to fill out the picture with the examples and arguments offered in *The Electronic Eye*.

Surveillance Society looks at some emerging trends in surveillance, and pushes further certain explanations, but it relies on similar analytical, political and ethical frameworks as *The Electronic Eye*. In particular, I still stress the ways that some basic ambiguities of surveillance may be traced to religious sources in western cultures, and above all the fateful split that proceeded from Jeremy Bentham's panoptic proposals, between 'control' and 'care' motifs. Bentham's privileging of accurate vision, and his obsession with classification, has been increasingly channelled towards control in contemporary surveillance, thus marginalizing and obscuring the dimension of care. An ontology of violence ultimately lies behind such dominative dynamics, against which may be counterposed an ontology of peace, deriving as I see it from the power-refusing ethics of Jesus.

Work towards chapters in this book has been tested in various places and with a number of people. Some of the book's central theorems were aired at two seminars where I found the discussion very stimulating, one in the School of Social and Political Inquiry, Monash University, Australia, and the other at the Centre for Criminology and Criminal Justice at Hull University, UK. I thank my colleagues Robyn Eckersley and Clive Norris, respectively, for their invitations and support. Sections of Part 1 were given as a lecture at

Korea University in Seoul, and I thank Kim Mun-Cho for his hospitality and collegial comments. Other sections formed the basis of a lecture in the School of Communications at Nanyang Technological University, Singapore, and also at Hankuk University in Seoul, Korea. I am grateful to Hwang Sung-Don and to Eddie Kuo for these opportunities. An earlier version of Chapter 4 was delivered as a public lecture at the Triennale di Milano, Italy, where Fabrizio Gallanti was both host and helpful critic. Similarly, the themes of Chapter 5 were discussed at a seminar in the sociology department of the National University of Singapore, hosted by Nirmala Purushotam, and some of the material also appears in a collection of essays entitled *Documenting Individual Identity: The Development of State Practices Since the French Revolution* (forthcoming from Princeton University Press). The editors of the latter, Jane Caplan and John Torpey, gave timely and judicious advice. Some ideas that appear in Chapter 9 were discussed at a workshop on technology and modernity at Twente University in the Netherlands. Philip Brey, Andrew Feenberg, Thomas Misa and Arie Rip were the organizers, and they also gave useful comment, along with Paul Edwards and Hans Achterhuis.

A number of friends and colleagues have read the book in draft and to these I am indebted. They not only saved me from some slipshod ideas but offered many fine suggestions, references and insights without which the book would be poorer. They are Colin Bennett, Philip Brey, Yolande Chan, Lynsey Dubbeld, Steve Graham, Paul James, Gary Marx, Jolyon Mitchell, Clive Norris, Jenn Poudrier, Bart Simon, Alison Wakefield, policy staff at the Information and Privacy Commission, Toronto, and Tim May, series editor. I take responsibility for what I have written, very aware of my fallibility and finitude. Others, including Jen Dening and Tim Lyon, kindly supplied news clippings. Zoë Ezinga was my research assistant, Josh and abi lyon helped with the index. I am also grateful to Queen's University for the sabbatical leave that gave me time for writing, to my kind hosts at Monash University and the University of Melbourne and to members of the community at St Jude's Carlton. Editors at Open University Press have again proved supportive and encouraging. A final thanks to Sue and our children. Nothing could ever match the joy of working within a family that both takes my work seriously and helps me not to take it too seriously. The mountains, the gum trees and the surf played their part in the latter as well.

David Lyon

Introduction

Suddenly, you realize that someone – or something – is watching. You are enjoying a quiet drink in the bar, when you see the small camera, unobtrusively observing the scene. Why is the camera watching you? Are you a threat to public order? In another context, you are in a hurry, and accelerate through the changing traffic signals, wrongly thinking there is just time to cross the intersection before the red light. A few days later, a notice of a fine for running a red light appears in the mail. Such events occur, with increasing frequency, and usually we take them for granted. Everyday life is subject to monitoring, checking, scrutinizing. It is hard to find a place, or an activity, that is shielded or secure from some purposeful tracking, tagging, listening, watching, recording or verification device. These are all examples of surveillance, which is what this book is all about.

All societies that are dependent on communication and information technologies for administrative and control processes are surveillance societies. The effects of this are felt in ordinary everyday life, which is closely monitored as never before in history. Of course, human beings have always kept an eye on each other and this has both deflected danger and induced fear. But until modern times the scale was generally small and the watching unsystematic. Today, routine, mundane surveillance, usually mounted by agencies and organizations that are geographically remote from us is embedded in every aspect of life. Part of life it may be, but is its extent well known, and its meanings understood? I think not, which is why sociological investigation is called for, and ethical and political action required.

Surveillance sometimes surfaces by mistake and we wake up to what is happening. In February 1999 a routine online search at the University of Michigan Health System brought up confidential medical records in a patient scheduling log. Names, addresses, social security numbers, employment status and treatment records were revealed, relating to renal failure, colon cancer, pneumonia and hundreds of other illnesses. Human error meant that the data was mistakenly present on a non-password protected site.[1] In Canada, at about the same time, Air Miles collectors who registered online found that they had free access to the personal details of 50,000 other online registrants. These included names, addresses, phone numbers, email addresses, types of credit cards held, numbers of vehicles owned and other customer loyalty programmes subscribed to (such as frequent flyer clubs). For many, the fact that Air Miles collected and resold such data came as a surprise.[2] Surveillance systems are less and less obvious and overt, but more and more systematic and subtle. Thus they tend to be visible only when by mistake or misdemeanour we fall foul of them or when they fail publicly. They are, in a sense, best seen in the breach.

What is surveillance? In this context, it is any collection and processing of personal data, whether identifiable or not, for the purposes of influencing or managing those whose data have been garnered. Notice immediately that I used the words 'personal data'. The surveillance discussed here does not usually involve embodied persons watching each other. Rather, it seeks out factual fragments abstracted from individuals. Today, the most important means of surveillance reside in computer power, which allows collected data to be stored, matched, retrieved, processed, marketed and circulated.[3] Even if the data go beyond mere numbers or names to DNA (deoxyribonucleic acid) codes or photographic images, the technologies that enable surveillance to occur involve computer power. It is the massive growth in computer application areas and technical enhancement that makes communication and information technologies central to surveillance.

Such surveillance is a key feature of modern life, upon which we depend for the efficiency and convenience of many ordinary transactions and interactions. This important point should not be overlooked in what follows. The growing density of surveillance practices in everyday life is not the product of some capitalist conspiracy or the evil effects of a plutocratic urge. No, it is the outcome of the complex ways in which we structure our political and economic relationships in societies that value mobility, speed, security and consumer freedom. However, as part of my purpose in writing this book is to alert readers to some unintended consequences and negative dimensions of surveillance, I shall not spend a lot of time elaborating its benefits. In any case, plenty of politicians and advertisers of new technology products may readily be heard extolling the virtues of surveillance for efficiency or public order. Few people need further persuasion about these.

This way of understanding surveillance at once takes us beyond – but still includes – the purposeful watching of specific individuals who have aroused suspicion through their activities or words. The whole point of this generalized, routine, everyday surveillance is that you may well have done nothing out of the ordinary, let alone violated some rule or broken some law, yet your transactions, exchanges, conversations, movements and calls still come to the attention of agencies and organizations for whom these activities are significant. To make a call using a cellphone or to send an email may seem entirely innocent until someone traces your whereabouts and contacts you, using the traces that you left in the course of communicating with others.

Surveillance has two faces

The ordinariness of these activities also alerts us to another pertinent feature of surveillance. As I have just hinted, it always has two faces. Literally, the (French) word means to 'watch over'. I may ask you to 'watch over' my child to ensure that she does not stray into the street and risk being hit by a car. In this case, I have protection primarily in mind so that the child is shown care in a context where she can flourish. Or I may ask you to 'watch over' the same child to ensure that she does not get up to mischief. Now I am appealling to moral criteria, where other elements enter the picture, to do with direction, proscription, perhaps even control. The same process, surveillance – watching over – both enables and constrains, involves care and control.

The two faces of surveillance may be experienced, for example, in everyday encounters with email. What is sold as a great enabler and as a means to new-found freedoms also displays another facet which may be less welcome. The medium of email allows for very flexible forms of communication that overcome simultaneously obstacles of distance and time. From Canada I can contact colleagues in Japan or Singapore almost instantly. They can read my words during their waking day, even though their time zones do not coincide with mine. But the same medium makes it far easier to intercept our messages than was the case with paper letters. The international ECHELON system, for instance (see Chapter 6), screens electronic messages for keywords, which permits detailed scrutiny of selected messages by persons who also take advantage of the time and space transcending aspects of the same medium. I may wonder what the National Security Agency would ever find interesting in my emails. But the transparency of the medium gives me pause.

Surveillance always carries with it some plausible justification that makes most of us content to comply. The convenience of the telephone or the credit card means that we seldom think twice about the fact that our calls and transactions are traceable and that others profit from using these data. The fact that the camera is installed in the bar or at the intersection in order to reduce rowdiness or road accidents seems reasonable enough. No one wants trouble when relaxing at the bar and no one wants to end up in hospital because someone ran a red light. Much public attention today is focused on tax revenues that are used fraudulently for the health care or unemployment benefits of those who are ineligible, or are 'double-dipping' – collecting additional benefits by registering under more than one identity. If such suggestions seem plausible we may cheerfully concede that a health card with a magnetic stripe and photo identification seems like a good plan. The advantages of surveillance for its subjects are real, palpable, and undeniable.

But as I say, surveillance has more than one face. For some, this has to do with the fear of things going wrong. Clearly, mistakes are bound to occur sometimes when personal data is handled, and they may be serious ones. Surveillance in every conceivable sphere of social life is expanding so rapidly that it is hardly surprising when breaches of security occur, and personal data spills out into open, public space. For others the question of privacy is paramount, even when systems are working fine. Privacy is the concept that comes most readily to most minds – at least in the West – when the processing of personal details is under consideration. This, too, is very important, but concern with privacy can often deflect attention from other aspects of surveillance. Above all, privacy tends to reduce surveillance to an individual matter rather than an inherently social concern. My argument about surveillance goes beyond both these aspects, however.

The question of surveillance is seen here as an issue of sociological interest because it contributes to the very ordering of society. And thus the 'other face' of surveillance arises from its capacity to reinforce social and economic divisions, to channel choices and to direct desires, and even, at its sharp end, to constrain and control. In some contexts this is uncontroversial and unremarkable. We readily see and accept the point of it, or we are resigned to what seem like innocent if sometimes annoying attempts to influence us or to verify our identity. We do not often object that companies using the Internet collect from our hard drives information about which websites we visit so that they can send us customized advertising materials. And we seldom think to protest against high-tech national border controls which, among other things, are installed in the belief that we can prevent terrorists from puncturing the peacefulness of society.

Since the later part of the twentieth century countries across the world have been falling over themselves to establish advanced information infrastructures. This means that their surveillance capacities have grown at an exponential rate, easily outstripping all legal and political efforts to keep abreast of their social implications. Those surveillance capacities are used to sort and sift populations, to categorize and to classify, to enhance the life chances of some and to retard those of others. Surveillance systems do these things because they are so designed and programmed. But their net effect is to strengthen the regimes behind their design and programming, whether for good or ill. It is these effects that have been insufficiently explored and are at present so little understood.

Here then is the prime reason for studying surveillance sociologically: it is a key issue in contemporary society. While terms like 'postmodern', 'globalized' or 'information society' are invented to try and highlight the major social transformations of the present, the notion of 'surveillance society' points up some singularly significant social processes caused by and contributing to such transformations. In a previous book on this theme – *The Electronic Eye* – I explored the rise of surveillance society and some of its major dimensions. In this book I rehearse but also go beyond its origins and contemporary characteristics to examine in a different way some central trends that characterize surveillance today. Developments in video, encryption and biometric techniques raise new questions about the technological direction of surveillance, while general issues such as worldwide economic restructuring or specific ones like the commercialization of the Internet hint strongly at both the globalization *and* the localization of surveillance.

Surveillance practices are growing at an accelerating rate wherever information infrastructures and knowledge-based economies are established. One intrinsic aspect of all so-called information societies is that they are, by the same token, surveillance societies. But to start with this point could be misleading. It could easily lead to yet another high-tech society scenario, in which facial recognition technologies or encrypted smartcards each appear in turn to determine the next wave of the future. Such scenarios are misleading at best and dangerous at worst. The direction of technological development is ever unstable and unpredictable. Nothing about Internet technologies inevitably compelled the trajectory taken from military to academic to commercial uses. And no surveillance technique on its own will shape the future.

Key themes

Four key themes reappear throughout this book. They indicate why surveillance has expanded and hint at the part new technologies have played. The four recurring themes are coordination, risk, privacy and power. Of course, put like that these themes sound very abstract. But I argue that the coordination of social activities in time and space, the growing perception and production of risk, the role of privacy in generating as well as trying to contain surveillance, and the question of how power is redistributed in surveillance societies are all very practical issues. They each relate to the monitoring of everyday life which we all experience to greater or lesser extents. And they also point up the need for fresh ways of not only understanding but of responding ethically and politically to surveillance.

Coordination refers to the ways that social relations are being reshaped through the increasing use of new technologies. Until the late twentieth century modern social relations were organized and coordinated mainly using schedules and timetables, as well as the direct supervision that took place in many factories and offices. They ensured people were in the right place at the right time, say, to catch a train, or in the same place at the same time to work the factory assembly line or to study in school. Of course we still use schedules and timetables, but the use of new technologies means that activities can be coordinated over much larger geographical areas and in asynchronous time. Today's sought-after worker is nothing if not flexible. This means both geographical mobility and flexitime hours, even though close contact is maintained with management and other workers via email, fax and phone. Shopping, too, becomes less tied to place and time, and with the anticipated growth of electronic commerce this trend will intensify. At the same time, corporations' awareness of the whereabouts and day-to-day activities of both workers and customers has never been more complete.

This is where surveillance comes in. Coordinating social activities in space and time is achieved today courtesy of computers. It is not just that schedules and timetables are electronically available but that the very processes of coordination are computer assisted. Whether walking a shopping cart in the grocery store, driving a freight truck on the highway, or entering the airport to catch a flight, the chances are that your movements are monitored. The aim of such monitoring is to guide the shopper to the bargains, to check the trucker's route and speed, or to ensure that the person identified at the check-in reaches the gate in time. Such coordination depends on devices for locating, tracking and verifying activities, and these normally involve the active engagement of the person under surveillance as well. Our movements and transaction details are fed back into the system such that we constantly collude with the coordination of our activities.

This extensive computer-assisted coordination does not take place solely for the benefit of those surveyed, however. The agencies and organizations that keep track of our daily activities are trying to manage risks. This second theme connects surveillance practices with another major characteristic of contemporary societies, the desire to reduce uncertainties and to control outcomes. This is not a new development but it has been intensified since the 1960s. Calculating probable trends and market behaviours is part of the positive risk involved in classic capitalist entrepreneurialism. Minimizing the hazards of investment or expansion is another aspect of the same process. However, processes like these have now expanded into many other areas of life. Insurance companies have become increasingly important to the process, demanding to know more and more about situations and persons so that they can calculate costs and assess probabilities.[4] They thus set the standards and determine the categories within which surveillance practices operate.

Everyday governance in contemporary societies tilts towards the management of risks and especially risks associated with obtaining compliance or containing threatening behaviour. Surveillance is the means whereby knowledge is produced for administering populations in relation to risk. No one evades surveillance although some surveillance sectors touch certain lives more heavily than others. Those whose risk histories reveal mental instability, brushes with the law, or an inability to provide for dependants are unlikely to find their lives closely monitored by Air Miles or frequent flyer point systems. But they will discover that they are targets for fairly intensive police and health and welfare surveillance. In a quest for security, all institutions in whatever sector seek to minimize risk by finding out as much as possible about as many factors as possible. As Ericson and Haggerty rightly say, 'Institutionalized risk communication systems form the foundation of contemporary society and provide the governing basis of social life'.[5]

In societies where risk management has burgeoned it is hardly surprising that people in daily life become more conscious of risks. Dangers of drought, storm, fire or flood have been joined by manufactured risks of all too human origin.[6] How the applications of new technology have devastated the environment or depleted non-renewable resources is a commonly repeated theme.

But in a curious twist, the applications of technology to risk management in the social sphere may themselves be read as a risk. Privacy – the third theme – is thus counterposed to surveillance. This is one reason why privacy is significant: it serves to mobilize opinion regarding surveillance risks. Another reason is that privacy points to the personal dimension that is so easily lost or sidelined by surveillance practices. But privacy is far from straightforwardly defined or debated.

What constitutes the private sphere is open to question. A shifting sense of time and space, the fluidity of global communications and the increasing dependence of surveillance on 'body data' rather than on questioning the person (see Chapter 5) have all contributed to this fuzziness. Although what is in the 'private' sphere is always a culturally relative matter – in Japan, for instance, there is much more openness about salaries than would be the case in the USA – new surveillance regimes tend radically to destabilize the public/private boundary. Employers have the capacity to find out about the domestic and other non-work life of their employees. Marketers engage interactive styles of selling within the home, far beyond what any doorstep salesperson ever used to achieve. Government departments can probe behind the front door to discover what lifestyles obtain. The private sphere is far from being the realm of autonomous anonymity that once featured strongly in the western bourgeois dream.

Even if privacy could be pinned down it would form an inadequate platform from which to analyse surveillance. The language used to portray surveillance often refers to 'Big Brother' or to the 'panopticon' and these terms appropriately raise questions of power. This is the fourth theme and it takes us well beyond 'privacy'. George Orwell's fictional benevolent dictator who could spy out the most uncooperative citizens and command or cajole them through the 'telescreen' is routinely invoked in today's very different surveillance situations. And Jeremy Bentham's prison architecture in which prisoners supposed that they were under the all-seeing gaze of an inspector is often thought to be a sort of antetype for electronically enhanced societal incarceration. But while power is a vital theme it may rightly be asked how far these metaphors help us understand surveillance today.

Within surveillance societies power seems to flow along a variety of channels. No central watchtower dominates the social landscape, and few people feel constrained, let alone controlled, by surveillance regimes. Most of the time, most people comply cheerfully with requests to show their identification, or acknowledge that they divulge personal data to companies, believing that the benefits are greater than the costs, or that if they have done nothing wrong they have nothing to hide or to fear. I shall suggest that this compliance with surveillance systems can be seen as participation in a kind of social orchestration. For those who are not for some reason marginalized or excluded, social participation generally means active involvement in the mechanisms that keep track of and monitor their everyday lives. Conductors try to ensure that different sections of the social orchestra play together at the appropriate moment. But they still depend on the willing and usually conscious activity of the social 'players', whose participation ensures that the system as a whole works and is perpetuated.

How this book works

I have organized the material in this book into three parts. The first, 'Surveillance societies', sets the scene. In Chapter 1 social relationships in today's world are seen as more and more abstract. Whereas face-to-face contacts have characterized all previous human history, today they no longer predominate. While some remain, of course, most relationships are now mediated by many means. Email is again an obvious example. Interfaces intervene. Bodies are disappearing. The first sense in which surveillance societies exist is that techniques have emerged to compensate for the missing bodies. Tokens of trust are needed when we lack embodied persons to display signs of trust in speech or body language. Surveillance is produced to validate and corroborate our everyday actions as truly ours. It distinguishes between the bona fide and the phoney and classifies us according to criteria that include and exclude.

Chapter 2 looks at another sense of 'surveillance societies': the extent to which common frameworks hold these monitoring activities together. These 'invisible frameworks' are more precisely information infrastructures. They enable the whole panoply of surveillance practices to operate and to relate to one another. Although this book notes the rise of some apparently non-digital developments such as video and biometric surveillance, they are shown to depend nonetheless on a complex electronic software system. By means of the information infrastructure, surveillance pervades every aspect of society. But it is not just that each social sector can now enhance its surveillance capacities. As I explain in Chapter 3, surveillance data now flows more freely in and out of what I call 'leaky containers'.

My daughters recently obtained temporary jobs overseas, in Australia rather than Canada where they normally live. Nonetheless, this also entailed some other relationships. They needed a tax file number to comply with Australian law and their employers also required them to open bank accounts in which to deposit their pay. So two institutions as well as their employers now knew of their financial standing. Given the common mode of communication within information infrastructures, however, it is perfectly possible that other agencies also learned about their earnings. The Department of Immigration may have sought access because they were on a temporary visa. And the bank where their electronic transactions occur warns customers that personal information may be shared with other companies. Those data are used to inform customers about financial products. In the USA such data are often sold to outside marketing companies unless the customer specifically 'opts out' of such data-sharing arrangements.[7] Once, it was safe to assume that government departments, police, employers and marketers kept fairly discrete records. No more. Such leaky containers have far-reaching consequences that justify further the use of the 'surveillance society' concept.

Part 2 examines the current spread of surveillance in three different ways. It shows how everyday life experiences involve surveillance at several levels. In Chapter 4 the city is viewed as a crucially significant surveillance site. In urban contexts the web of surveillance networks is most dense. One layer is superimposed on another as video and closed-circuit television are added to community policing and neighbourhood watch schemes, and even buildings and roads reveal the activities of their occupants and users. Surveillance in the city is also seen to relate to overall social ordering, often through city planning but also through the reshaping of the enviroment by marketing companies. Thus surveillance in a sense produces the city, just as much as the city generates surveillance opportunities. This idea is explored by an analogy with the game of 'SimCity'.

In Chapter 5, attention turns to the human body as a source of surveillance data. This is not a contradiction of the 'disappearing bodies' thesis. Rather, yet more bits of data – such as DNA traces, thumbprints and voice scans – are now extracted from the body to verify identities and determine eligibilities. You may need to present a handprint or speak into a machine to cross international borders. Your urine may be analysed or your DNA tested before you can start a new job. Embodied persons are no more in view than in the case of bureaucratic files or digital documents. But the results also produce classifications rather like those portrayed in the film *GATTACA*, where constant blood tests divide the population between the acceptable members of society and the genetically impaired 'invalids'.

If probing the body for data seems like a micro-scale project, Chapter 6 enlarges the picture dramatically to look at globalized surveillance. The planet is not so much a site or a source of surveillance as a space across which surveillance data now flows. To purchase an airline ticket is to consign one's personal details to conduits that carry them round the world, sometimes much further than the flight itself. Surveillance is globalized as, for example, corporations extend their activities around the world, setting up plants here, introducing new product markets there. It may also be experienced in novel ways because of globalization. British car workers in a new Toyota plant in England were surprised to discover that urine analysis was routine and automated in the washrooms.[8]

In the final part of the book, three 'surveillance scenarios' are outlined. Chapter 7 considers new ways of explaining surveillance. While much may still be learned from classical theories of capitalism and bureaucracy, the argument must be taken further to account for current developments. How, in particular, does surveillance power operate? Given the range of surveillance sectors and sites, can one theoretical resource serve for all? I argue that theoretical resources must be found that do justice both to the concerns of a Karl Marx or a Max Weber but also to those of the so-called poststructuralists. Neither tendency seems able to account adequately for surveillance, yet both offer helpful insights. Embodied personhood offers some grounds for critique that helps to weigh the contributions of other theories.

The theoretical discussion also lays the groundwork for assessing the prospects for regulating or resisting surveillance. This question is further taken up in practical ways which are the substance of Chapter 8. Once the primary mode of resisting surveillance was thought to be legal. Today the struggle is taken up on numerous fronts. Just to mention one arena, surveillance contests, like surveillance practices and processes, have been globalized. The battle against a new Intel chip with its built-in unique identifier, for instance, became a transnational electronic boycott on the Internet. And during the 1990s, Privacy International lauched its Greenpeace-like campaigns to publicize the dangers of today's snowballing surveillance systems. A cynic might say, of course, that public concern with privacy has only emerged as a political issue to clear the way for electronic commerce. But if opportunities for debate are thus prised open, who knows what consequences will follow?

Finally, surveillance is situated as a central feature of postmodern, global information societies. There can be little doubt that surveillance should today be considered as a central means of social ordering or social orchestration. Information societies are surveillance societies. The means of social management currently available and in use serve variously to classify, coordinate and control populations in ways that transcend older, modern divisions based on class location or paper-file based bureaucratic sorting processes. We are just starting to understand how the biographical profiles, population data and biometric information are emerging as dynamic sources of power in the mutating social and global environment. How they augment already existing – particularly capitalist – arrangements, and what effects they have on already existing divisions based on income, gender, ethnicity and region, have yet to be fully explored. But it is quite clear that surveillance data flows are crucial to the life chances of all who live in today's global information society.

All this means that surveillance should be a topic, not merely of some supposedly detached sociological investigation, but also of ethical and political concern. I address this in the concluding chapter. It is commonly argued that the more societies are administered as it were by remote control – which is precisely what happens in global information societies – the less appeal is made to moral criteria. Zygmunt Bauman, for example, explores the ways in which areas of social life are removed successively from the reach of moral critique. He rightly cautions that this situation should be countered by the development of serious and relevant ethical criteria by which to confront today's dilemmas, differences and divisions (Bauman 1993). But it should be noted that in fact some subtle pseudo-moralities actually abound within the very surveillance systems that on the surface appear to have been cleansed of moral content. The risk management approach, to take the key example, is based on a profoundly utilitarian moral calculus that effectively displaces other moral criteria such as generosity, guilt or fairness. The denial of insurance cover or an increase in premiums in the inner city make the point well. One's life chances then depend upon probabilities – rates of consumption within each socioeconomic bracket, or comparative success at evading detection in the violation of rule or law, for example.

As I argued in *The Electronic Eye*, surveillance systems should be thought of not only in terms of undesirable, avoidable futures, but also in the light of desirable, possible worlds. At worst, the undesirable future is a nightmare of possibly hyper-Orwellian proportions. But by focusing on the avoidable, the dominant risk management approach itself does little more than perpetuate a negative if not dystopian outlook. I am committed to the view that relevant ethical criteria are available that appeal to notions of social justice and embodied personhood. These criteria speak to the issues raised by surveillance societies today and offer modes of practial engagement with them. Such criteria are transcendent and, of course, contestable. But the default position is to permit surveillance systems to continue to reinforce both social divisions themselves and the belief that risk management is an appropriate new morality. Counterposing such criteria to the pseudo-moralities of risk management is one task. Working out their implications in the politics and policies of corporations and governments is another. The escalating monitoring of everyday life demands urgent and sustained commitment to both tasks.

PART ONE

PART ONE

Surveillance societies

1

Disappearing bodies

The rise of surveillance societies has everything to do with disappearing bodies.[1] Bodies disappear when we do things at a distance. Making a phone call means communicating by voice alone, but when we email even that trace of embodiment is gone. Hence the typed symbols like smileys that are meant to stand in for the invisible face. Great effort is expended today in attempting to make distant bodies reappear, as for example in a videoconference. Politicians, business executives or scientists may simulate a meeting by remote video communication in which they can not only hear each other but also catch those physical gestures and eye movements that make up body language. But for the vast majority of relationships, especially those dependent on computer-based communication of data, embodied persons have vanished.

Disappearing bodies is a basic problem of modernity that has been accentuated with the growth and pervasiveness of communication and information technologies. To compensate for the growing difficulties of embodied surveillance that watches visible bodies, social agencies have arisen that keep track of personal traces. These try to hold together or at least to coordinate that which is now fragmented, ephemeral, almost inconsequential. These agencies use surveillance practices as a means of making visible that which is being lost from their sight; our bodies and the bodies of those with whom we relate. Such practices offer reassurance to those agencies that we are appropriately related to them at least until further notice.

While disappearing bodies may sound like something out of a spy thriller or a detective story, the reality is much more mundane. In traditional societies, people are typically available to each other in person – that is, in their physical bodies. Being in the same place with someone else is called 'co-presence'. For most of human history such co-presence has been the context in which social interaction and exchange have taken place. What holds people together in social relationships is the trust emanating from 'looking each other in the eye', from the deal sealed with a handshake, and so on.

Modes of integration began to alter radically in modern times, as transport and communication allowed people to be more mobile, and social institutions helped to mediate their relationships. So the signature, for instance, became more important as a guarantee of legitimate identity and was accepted by organizations such as banks. These organizations extended the range of human actions, as did artefacts such as the telephone, so that more and more could be done at a distance without the co-presence of bodies in relation. A token of trust, such as a personal identification number, became a proxy for the kind of trust that arises from an ongoing relationship of co-present persons.

Since the 1960s bodies have been disappearing at an accelerating rate. Communication and information technologies enable not only fax and fixed phone communication, but also email, credit card transactions, cellphones and the Internet. This means that many other relationships become possible without co-presence. Bodies and personal experience part company, and a significant portion of that personal experience is social.[2] The ties that bind are not electronic cables or satellite signals themselves, but they are increasingly *mediated* by electronic means. As the spread of such relationships picks up speed, so too does the quest of substitutes for traditional modes of integration. Disembodied and abstract relationships are maintained not so much in human memory as in databanks and networked computer systems. The focused and purposeful attention to personal details that we think of as surveillance is a major means of holding together disembodied relationships.

This point is worth stressing because it points to the historical and social structural reasons why surveillance is increasingly widespread, and why everyday life is increasingly monitored. It does not immediately draw attention to the negative aspects of surveillance or even to the interests and power relationships of those agencies that establish and operate surveillance systems. It simply stresses the ways that surveillance has developed as a structural response to emerging social conditions.

Powerful interests are often involved, of course – including those of spying and intelligence gathering – and the purposes behind surveillance include the desire to influence, manipulate or control those whose personal details are recorded and processed. In much of what follows I shall highlight the kinds of power relation involved in contemporary surveillance and their socially negative aspects. This is because I want to alert readers to what is frequently obscured. But surveillance itself, while it always expresses purposes, values and power relations, is not inherently negative, malign or antisocial.

What I have just said about surveillance deserves exploration in several other ways as well. First, we do not inhabit an entirely disembodied social world. Thankfully, everyday life continues to entail plenty of co-presence in the home, at work, at play. It is just that, superimposed on the face-to-face contacts of daily life are a multiplying number of relations that are electronically mediated and these have a direct and indirect bearing on our life chances and opportunities.[3] Each of us has a limited number of family members, friends, fellow workers and leisure time acquaintances that we see each week. But we are all part of a widespread web of relationships with other persons, agencies and departments with whom we may never have direct contact or whose existence we are only aware of in tax returns, invoices and unsolicited advertising. How far this varies with factors like region, country and level of technological development is something about which all too little is currently known.

Second, one consequence of disembodied relationships is that modern notions of 'public' and 'private' are challenged. The boundaries between them are blurred when all manner of once 'private' life details circulate within very 'public' computer systems. Part of the problem is the shift from physical to electronic space. The fiction that the inside of a home is a haven from outside demands and pressures is subverted by the ways in which electronic devices take data into and out of the house, sometimes without our knowledge. Even our bodies, often thought in modern times to be 'our own', and thus private, become a source of surveillance data. Paradoxically, the embodied person is still not in view. Only the image or the trace counts. The disappearing body makes an exclusive focus on privacy less salient to surveillance. This too is insufficiently understood.

Third, if I do not wish to give the impression that our social world is one of unrelieved abstraction, then neither do I want to imply that communication and information technologies are the cause of social disembodiment. They are indeed its primary means, but how this occurs is a complex matter of social-technological relationships. New technologies are the products of particular social patterns and purposes that in turn affect those patterns and purposes. A subtle process of co-construction takes place. But that process depends as much on economic ambitions and cultural drives as it does on electronic circuits and software programs. This is an area that has only recently become the focus for social scientific analysis.

Reconfiguring time and space

Although we talk of 'time and space' it is perhaps more accurate to speak of 'time-space'. The two really belong inseparably together as key dimensions of social life. We have already begun to see why the reconfiguration of time-space is an issue here. The growth of surveillance societies may be seen as the development of new time-space relations. In earlier modernity, space was rationally conceived as bounded territory and time as measurable duration. Social life could be organized in new ways within such structures of feeling[4] or frameworks of experience. Using the factory site, the clock and the schedule, for example, capitalist enterprises could exert considerable control over their workers. They were spatially congregated for fixed time periods. Increasingly, as sociologist Anthony Giddens has argued, artefacts such as the clock and the timetable came to dominate modern life as the means of coordinating social activities. Transport and communications were affected, but so were schools, hospitals and other bureaucratic organizations.

In the later part of the twentieth century, computer regimes began to challenge clocks and timetables as means of coordination and control. Of course, this no more implies that the computer was the *cause* of this shift than the clock had been before. But these devices are nonetheless deeply implicated in the changes that are taking place today. It is helpful to think of technological artefacts as serving to hold together or 'bind' time-space in different ways. This insight was first applied by Harold Adams Innis[5] to contrast the face-to-face relations of oral cultures with the possibilities of more remote relations enabled by writing. In this case, writing served to 'bind' time, holding together past and present in a new medium. Printing, on the other hand, lent itself to binding space. Relationships – for example, in legal systems – could be held together more readily then before, over distance. Space could further be bound by use of the telegraph and telephone, technologies that also facilitated the split of transport and communication. Once this had occurred, remote relationships could become a reality for mass populations, which they did in Europe and North America by the mid-twentieth century.

The accent during the late twentieth century was increasingly on the speed of computation and of communications, such that reduced time in a sense annihilates the distances of space. Time-space can henceforth be bound much more easily using the power of new technologies. The emergent social experience, argues cultural geographer Nigel Thrift, is now characterized by mobility.[6] This has implications for the greater proportion of relations that are remote and technologically bound together. They tend to produce ephemerality and to loosen their moorings to history and tradition. The focus of relationships is now much more immediate, and behaviours are foregrounded more than beliefs or time honoured values.

When it comes to the focused attention paid to persons within surveillance-specific situations, behaviours are much easier to monitor than beliefs and premeditated actions. So it is these kinds of data that are tracked by much computer-based surveillance. A case in point is transactionally generated information, the traceable components of commercial or other exchanges that is sought everywhere from supermarkets to the Internet. It is above all our shopping *behaviour* that companies wish to trace and track. What was bought where, when and for how much? Our attitudes to consumption or beliefs we may hold about protecting the environment are of much less interest to marketers, unless of course they can be associated with market segments identified as 'green'.

Nigel Thrift argues that since the nineteenth century speed, light and power have been important aspects of modern structures of feeling and that now they are collapsing into each other. Rapidity of movement gave travel new meaning as a value in itself, just as it made possible the circulation of items such as greetings cards. Artificial light gave new meanings to the night but also allowed for new levels of surveillance, locating and arranging bodies in space. Power, especially in the flick of an electrical power switch, provided evidence for absent presence, lent daily life new metaphors and demonstrated society's dependence on integrated networks of power. By the late twentieth century, suggests Thrift, these three merge and coalesce as 'mobility'. Electronic technologies have massively increased the volume of direct and indirect communication, just as improved transportation has hugely added to tourist travel, business trips and migration. Perception itself has been automated[7] such that the 'machinic complex' of light allows for vision where there is no human observer. Such 'panspectric surveillance' originates in military technologies. Its simulations include actual bodies and artificial vision with images that are neither visible nor viewed.

Fresh configurations of time-space have implications for surveillance beyond those in Thrift's fascinating account. Mobility creates a world of nomads and unsettled social arrangements, so it is not surprising that in transit areas, such as airports, surveillance practices are intense. In 1997 British Airways tested a smartcard system that locates every passenger at each moment, starting at Victoria train station in central London.[8] The idea was to try to improve the smoothness of flow, through the rail transport system and the airport gate corridors, of otherwise anonymous bodies.

Indirect communication, of which surveillance is a burgeoning type, is another relevant feature of everyday life today.[9] A world that is unstable, uncertain and deterritorializing raises questions about conventional conceptions of subjectivity, bodies and places. In contemporary surveillance situations, the digital persona seems to pass as a representation of the subject for some purposes, the body can be genetically or biometrically interrogated without speech, and places are only fleetingly occupied. Thus traces rather than tradition are what connects body with place. Boundaries between one place and another, or even between the inside and outside of the body itself, are more indeterminate, which means that surveillance comes to depend on dispersed power. French theorist Gilles Deleuze calls these 'societies of control'. He contrasts previous spaces of enclosure with today's experience of being 'undulatory, in orbit, in a continuous network'[10] What counts now '. . . is not the barrier but the computer that tracks each person's position – licit or illicit – and effects a universal modulation'.

Questions of time-space are thus central to surveillance, raising as they do issues of bodies in motion, and of vision. What is 'seen', by whom, or by what, and for what purposes? In a fast world, instantaneous communication within global flows of data permits personal information to travel far more quickly than any airline can deliver tourists to distant destinations. But that same personal data may include details of medical histories or may be identified using a body part such as a retina or a fingerprint rather than the word of the data subject. New surveillance methods thus locate and coordinate human behaviours on both macro and micro time-space levels as well as allowing for interaction between the two. Leaving on one side for a moment the further question of how technology and society now relate, we turn to the matter of how 'public and private' might be conceived in the world of mobility.

Blurring public and private

The unprecedented growth of surveillance practices and systems during the twentieth century was greeted, among those who cared, by calls for the protection of privacy. This concept dominates debate in North America, whereas in Europe the demand is more for the protection of personal data. Many, frankly, did not and do not care. But this, paradoxically, may be related to the fact that privacy was – and still is – the 'value' appealed to.

The problem of privacy arose within the fixed time-spaces of modernity. It was carried over into the new, more mutable – perhaps postmodern – structures of feeling characteristic of the late twentieth century. Power relations had altered and the 'right to be left alone' in 'private spaces' was not always the central issue. Despite this, concern with privacy was mobilized as a means of questioning the appropriate extent of computer-based surveillance. Thus it is worth viewing the issues through this lens, however blurry it turns out to be.

Some notion of privacy probably exists in all cultures, but how it is viewed varies with period and with place. The private is a 'zone of immunity' in Georges Duby's words,[11] where retreat and relaxation are the order of the day. It is often, though not always, domestic and thus is more than simple solitude. In modern times in the West the division between public and private is also a distinction between gendered spaces. Women are primarily associated with the private, and men with the public sphere. Inequality of access is thus built into the concept. This is seen again in the related concept of 'private property' where trespassing and transgressing is prohibited. Distinguishing between public and private has much to do with the growth of modern cities and their anonymous, impersonal relations.[12] Such a 'society of strangers', as Georg Simmel called it, helped to create the realm of the private, the intimate, the secluded, in contradistinction to it. Here at least the agencies of the state and even the travelling salesperson had to wait at the door. Over this threshold at least the individual had a large measure of control.

In the West, then, modernity was marked by the emergence of the 'sovereign individual' of capitalism and the nation state. Persons were distinguished from each other and from family, clan and city so that they might participate freely and effectively in the new democratic order. This is how the discourse of the 'individual' appeared. Paradoxically though, the same move entailed the gathering of information on such individuals.[13] Persons were more clearly unique as their individual identities were established but by the same token they became easier to control.[14] Thus a transition occurred, noted by Bertrand Russell[15] in the early twentieth century, from knowledge by acquaintance to knowledge by description. Others come to be known by mediated information rather than through direct co-presence.

Individualism, on the other hand, does not seem to be essential to capitalism as such, only to capitalism in certain manifestations. Japanese capitalism is highly corporate, for example, and even German capitalism is not as individualistic as North American capitalism. This has implications for privacy, in that the 'private individual' has never been completely sovereign, and in some societies such individuals are scarcely sovereign at all. Having said that, it should be recalled that the doctrine of what C.B. Macpherson called 'possessive individualism' is rather pervasive in western cultures. By this is meant that the individual is considered as the 'proprietor of his own person' such that 'the human essence is freedom from the wills of others'.[16] This has important implications for the debate over privacy. At any rate, the culture of consumer capitalism which may be observed today is markedly individualistic which means that strong incentives remain to defend the private individual.

In the USA particularly, privacy is highly valued. Indeed, as Steven Nock rightly observes, in that country at least the desire for privacy may be seen to give rise to surveillance.[17] The society of strangers is a private society, Nock argues, because strangers have been denied access to our personal affairs. When we make a purchase, for example, we do so from strangers, who need some token to show that we can be trusted and have the resources to pay. But this raises acutely the question of who can be trusted if the stranger – or the institution – has not had the opportunity personally to check the reputations, credentials and credibility of those with whom they must nonetheless interact from day to day.

Organizations generally satisfy themselves about trustworthiness by producing surveillance data on strangers. These are derived from credentials (such as driving licences) and ordeals (such as urine checks) that establish reputations. Lacking the chance to allow individual strangers to prove themselves personally, we rely on surveillance systems to generate sufficient trust to maintain or increase our rate of exchanges with a range of agencies. Of course, through a perverse feedback loop, privacy once again seems to be endangered by the spread of such surveillance systems, but this does not invalidate Nock's basic insight – that surveillance is the paradoxical product of the quest for privacy.[18]

Already one can see how this discussion is slipping from the realm of relationships in public and private spaces to those on paper, in files and increasingly in electronic environments. But it is important to remember that both realms remain significant. There are public places (above all the street) where, if Nock is to be believed, people wish to retain their privacy. We wish to be private in public. If street cameras can capture identifiable images of passers-by then those persons may be justified in seeking reassurances about who will use the images, for what purposes, and how long they will be kept. Equally, if similar devices are placed in workplace washrooms, employees are unlikely to acquiesce cheerfully to their presence. Even if the premises are in another sense 'private property', does this necessarily mean that nothing they do while there is, in the first sense, private?

Current technological shifts complicate matters further. The security camera system might not merely be watched by its operator. The images obtained may be digitized. Once they take the form of electronic data they are subject to other uses. The soccer fan may not wish to be caught by a commercial television camera from which his wife could see on the sports news at home that he was not, in fact, at work or with his mother at that time. But if, in an effort to reduce hooliganism, images from a closed-circuit television system are digitized, the same fan's face may be compared automatically and remotely with others known to be previous offenders. The question is then not one of personal privacy from prying eyes, however this may or may not be justified. It is rather an issue of what happens to the digitized data. Who then has access to the images and for what purposes? Can individuals control or limit the uses of the data derived from their behaviours?

Various proposals have been made in order to cope with such shifts, such as the policy consideration of 'informational privacy'. This helps to broaden the debate beyond the ubiquitous categories derived from spatial analogies (think of 'Internet sites' in cyber*space* for example), but it runs into some difficulties when body data enters the picture. But other definitions of privacy have also been suggested that relate neither to physical space or directly to digital data. These attempt to see electronic environments as 'public space'. Communications analyst Rohan Samarajiva proposes that privacy in this context is the 'capability to explicitly or implicitly negotiate boundary conditions of social relations'.[19]

Additionally, Samarajiva notes the social relational character of privacy, something also stressed by policy theorist Priscilla Regan. Regan claims that privacy should be thought of as serving not only 'individual interests, but also common, public, and collective purposes'.[20] At the same time, as Samarajiva's notion of privacy makes clear, claims about negotiating boundaries occur in technological contexts. Social relationships may depend on trust, but technological capacities in surveillance situations may strain that trust, for instance in consumer contexts. Conversely, as Philip Agre says from the perspective of communications studies, information infrastructures may also create 'the conditions for the construction of trust'.[21]

A further difficulty with the use of 'privacy' as a means of questioning surveillance is that, as noted above, the very concept is relative to period and place. Thus while the idea may have some shared resonance in European and North American societies – even there, considerable differences exist – privacy has far less rhetorical force in, say, East Asian societies. For example, the nearest word for privacy in Japan refers to an inner life that is shared with others in the same family, firm or club. This is indicative of some very different cultural approaches from the western world. Privacy is also relative to gender. This has implications for the domestic sphere, as noted above, but also to life chances as expressed in pre-employment screening, or to the differential targeting of women and men by commercial surveillance. On the other hand, it may in part be the equalizing effects of surveillance that exposes men to an uncomfortable degree of scrutiny – whether literal or digital – all too familiar to women, that has raised the 'privacy' stakes in an information age.[22]

The significance of these considerations is that while privacy is undoubtedly important as a mobilizing slogan, it does not necessarily get to the heart of the surveillance society challenge. Of course, it is possible to dismiss privacy altogether and claim that because few seem to care about it in practice it is not worth pursuing.[23] But assuming that the issues raised by surveillance can in some way be addressed in terms of privacy it is important to indicate how these can be generalized in ways that go beyond individualistic, ethnocentric and gender biased conceptions of 'public and private'. Categories that may answer to this need would include the practical idea of 'fair information practices' – important for any policy development in this field – but also some reference to broad notions of human dignity and social justice.

Such broad notions would perhaps privilege speech over space, for what really matters is our ability to disclose ourselves voluntarily to others within relations of trust. Even this would not seem directly to relate to matters such as street camera surveillance or drug testing in the workplace. Nor does it touch the question of surveillance as a means of maintaining social inequalities that is discussed later. But if the principle of voluntary disclosure in trusting relationships is extended from speech to embodied communication, then any kind of self-disclosure could in principle be included. The voluntary principle and the relations of trust – with individuals or institutions – would in turn presuppose some notion of informed consent, which is also present in fair information practices.

Given the role of new technologies in today's surveillance situations, however, the role of technology in the very constitution of public and private realms must also be addressed. Rethinking technology-society relations is instructive in this regard.

Recombining technology and society

Technology and society are bound together in a mutual process of co-construction. I referred earlier to ways in which surveillance societies are technology dependent and to the role of communication and information technologies in binding time-space in novel configurations. The previous section also addressed the issue of technology in the constitution of public and private, particularly – and by definition – in electronic environments. If ever it was correct to see technology merely as a threat to privacy, that time appears to be over. This is not least because much store is now put, in some circles, on 'privacy-enhancing technologies'. There is, in other words, no meaningful discussion of topics such as surveillance and privacy that does not refer to technology. Just to write the word 'technology' as a separate entity is misleading. As with the term 'time and space', that arguably should be reduced to 'time-space', so 'technology and society' would be better reduced to 'technosocial'. However ugly the term, 'technosocial' helps to point up these inextricable interactions and the implication of technology in social relations today.

A major problem with many contemporary accounts of new technologies is their implied determinism. Technological innovation is all too frequently seen as the prime mover, producing information societies and even cyber societies. However, this does not only afflict contemporary accounts. Numerous historical examples may be given of what James Carey calls the 'technological sublime' that looks to novel techniques, tools and processes – the telegraph, the telephone – to solve the problems of the day and to usher in a new kind of society.[24] But technological potential is never social destiny.

Such idolatries follow the ancient pattern of mystification and dependency-creation, not to mention a signal failure to produce the promised goods.[25] Even in the example just given, of privacy-enhancing technologies, one often hears hints of the technological fix mentality. Difficulties raised for data security in areas like electronic commerce are admitted, but alongside an expectation that new techniques will emerge for overcoming those too. At the same time, it must be acknowledged that some critics of technology dependence also fall into the determinist trap, this time demonizing the artefact for its allegedly baleful effects.[26]

It is easy to see how technology-based accounts of new social formations become popular. In the case of 'information society' it is true that new technologies pervade all aspects of life, that information dependency is engendered and that computers and telecoms offer ready-made tropes for understanding everything from social relationships to the workings of the brain. As Nigel Thrift notes, 'new machines become both the model for society and its most conspicuous sign'.[27] This may even apply in the case of surveillance, seen positively and apparently without irony as 'topsight' in the book *Mirror Worlds* by computer scientist David Gelernter. Gelernter argues that in the computer screen one views a mirror world of the real one. This enables the user to gain a whole picture of social and political situations, through systematic 'zooming in and poking around', 'like an explorer in a miniature sub'.[28] Surveillance society in a shoebox submarine.

Such technological determinism is misleading and unhelpful for a number of reasons. Apart from anything else it deflects attention from the real world of material bodies and active selves. The messy realities of city life, social divisions, economic inequalities and political conflicts may be regrettable but they are unavoidable. Many illustrations may be given of how technological determinism is simply wrong. For instance, much hype currently surrounds the idea of cyberspace, which for some, apparently, is a new kind of social reality, substituting for the world in which we live, move and have our material being. Global flows of data, and networks of persons in electronic relationships is seen as somehow transcending the city, leaving it behind. Yet it is more helpful to think of cyberspace as being superimposed on urban spaces, in that electronic networks and other forms of communication and transport are all intensified in the city.

The sociology of surveillance technologies does not call for a simple switch to social explanations, as if these could be made without reference to technology. Social determinisms, that reduce technological changes to social relations, are as inadequate as technological ones. Once in place, technological artefacts and systems effectively guide, constrain, enable and limit social activities. They may possess no capacity autonomously to produce 'impacts' but to deny the reality of their role within social relations is to turn a blind eye to one of the most pervasive features of social life today. This is, in fact, one of the strongest arguments that can be made about contemporary computer-based surveillance. Whatever it may mean for 'privacy' it undoubtedly has the effect of reinforcing social differences and divisions. An analogy with New York planner Robert Moses' very physical and visible low bridges and underpasses helps here. Moses created height restrictions that prevented buses carrying black and poor people from reaching certain quarters of the city.[29] I argue that new technology surveillance systems continue this invisibly today, affecting life chances through categorization and risk management.

Not all surveillance technologies are invisible, of course. Cameras can often be plainly seen on the street, and fingerprint or optical scanners require physical presence in order for them to work. That said, as Gary T. Marx points out, a trend within several 'new surveillance' technologies is towards their being both less perceptible and more powerful.[30] This is indeed so, but the invisibility to which I referred above applies either way. In each case, the real issue is not how imperceptible is the physical artefact but the invisibility of the underlying processes of systematic categorization, classification and social sorting that are technologically enabled.

This relates to a further point. Technological systems are both socially shaped and have social consequences, some of which go beyond the intentions inscribed in their shaping. Machines themselves may be minaturized or disguised and the silent and subtle process of surveillant sorting proceeds relentlessly. But both the visible and the invisible also operate in relation to human beings and organizations that design, install and operate such machines. This is the technosocial world alluded to above. The artefacts and systems are perceived and formed by social actors and social contexts, but they also serve to give shape to social relationships. This even includes, in the case of surveillance technologies, the power to 'perceive' those relationships in certain ways.

There is something contingent and open-ended about this, at least on the small scale.[31] James Rule and Peter Brantley, for example, found that closer scrutiny of work tasks in a New York printing company came about because a computerized system was established to check where customers' orders were in the plant. Once used for this purpose, however, such surveillance systems may continue to be exploited for worker supervision.[32] This process, which may be seen in numerous other contexts as well, is nicely captured in Clive Norris and Gary Armstrong's concept of 'expandable mutability'.[33] They use it to explore how surveillance cameras, installed for one purpose, end up with other tasks as well.

It is no accident, however, that similar technological systems find themselves employed across a range of different contexts. The data matching that creates lists of potentially wanted persons by merging data from more than one source is not limited to law enforcement. It is precisely such a technique that also allows marketing companies to target likely customers with advertising and inducements to purchase. What creates 'categorical suspicion' in one setting enables 'categorical seduction' in another. The technique spirals out of one setting and into the next, which may have quite different goals in view. At the same time, surveillant simulations, which attempt to tell in advance what behaviours will emerge or what future trends might be discerned, often may be traced back to similar sources in risk management. The desire to minimize threats and dangers, and to anticipate likely outcomes leads to the garnering and communication of knowledge useful to management control. Hence, surveillance.

This does not mean, though, that the same technological systems have exactly the same effects wherever they are established. The cultural context and the specific value goals each play their part. So-called 'privacy enhancing' technologies, after all, originate in the same technoscientific stable as technologies used to penetrate private spheres – encryption. On a broader scale, as I observed earlier, surveillance systems set up in different countries may have different effects according to local political practices or cultural and religious beliefs. As Agre observes in his critique of Gelernter's 'mirror worlds', 'computer representations differ from the reality of human representations in many ways, and the ability of computers to create and maintain representations of human activities presupposes a great deal of prior work'.[34] Not only do normative relations of representation differ in industrial and non-industrial life spheres, says Agre, but when the problems of identifiable personal data arose, database designers did not immediately or automatically try to decouple data records from human identity. Why not? Because powerful economic and political interests would like to keep open the possibilities of using for secondary purposes personal data ostensibly collected for only one purpose. Recognizing those larger contexts – the beliefs and ideologies by which organizations as well as ordinary people arrange their lives – is vital to understanding how surveillance technologies are developed and used, and how they might be modified and limited in different cultural environments.

Whether it is the development of street cameras for surveillance in the city, or the world wide web of personal data networks used in electronic commerce, or even the modes of genetic and biometric surveillance that use body parts and codes as identifiers and data, the technologies are inextricably bound up with networks[35] that include human actors and social organizations and structures. Each network has to be explored for its particular contribution to surveillance but each also has to be decoded as a whole. The codes by which they operate relate to a range of levels, from elevated conceptions of how humans are constituted through to currently fashionable modes of managing risk. Either way, they are far from neutral, and are thus vulnerable to ethical critique and political contestation.[36]

The problem of disappearing bodies is thus crucial to understanding surveillance societies. It shows how surveillance systems have arisen in an attempt to compensate for the disembodiment of many social relationships. And it reminds us that contemporary surveillance practices tend overwhelmingly to base themselves on abstractions rather than on embodied persons. The data image drawn from an assemblage of recorded behaviours is what counts. In a rapidly moving mobile world, our modes of social integration are increasingly abstract and surveillance practices try to keep up with our movements. They locate us, target us, and attempt to coordinate our activities.

The disappearing bodies theorem puts a new slant on privacy, too. In our nomadic world the society of strangers seeks privacy that actually gives rise to surveillance. Tokens of trust, such as personal identification numbers and barcoded cards, are demanded to demonstrate eligibility or reputation. Supposedly private spheres of the domestic or of the body are no defence against the surveillance that develops, not least because physical space is less and less in question. Electronic technologies raise fresh problems but recalling the significance of embodied persons and of justice suggests some new ways forward. Nonetheless, those new technologies never operate on their own, autonomously. They serve systems of imperceptible social classification and purposes that they come to embody. This is why they have to be understood as a new mode of social ordering. Why it is communication and information technologies that make the difference is explored in the next chapter.

Invisible frameworks

Twenty-first century surveillance societies depend on a complex network of communication and information technologies. The network itself cannot be seen but it supports all kinds of monitoring including video, satellite and biometric surveillance. As such, the network may be thought of as an information infrastructure. Wim Wenders' enigmatic film, *The End of Violence*, depicts the Los Angeles area as heavily dependent on such an information infrastructure. The shell of an astronomic observatory is used as a cover for a satellite surveillance operation where the plot is, as it were, watched and directed from the stars. While no such paranoid intentions lie behind this chapter, two motifs from the movie are relevant. One, the presence of a hidden infrastructure is well portrayed. Two, a leading character utters the immortal lines, 'With a system this big, the chances of abuse are high'.

Few who live in today's world can be unaware of the much touted impact of computers and telecommunications. Taken together, this area represents one of the fastest growing economic sectors in its own right, with huge implications for almost every other social, economic, political and cultural sphere. Government policies are geared to information technology visions and projects, from the early Japanese concept of an 'information society', or French attempts at the *'l'informatisation'* of society from the late 1970s,[1] to North American dreams of an 'information superhighway' in the 1980s,[2] Singapore's Intelligent Island aspirations of the 1990s, or Malaysia's 'Multi-media Super Corridor' project of the early twenty-first century. Two crucial items are often missing from such projects, however. One is a social account of where these new technologies came from and how they converged in the last part of the twentieth century.[3] The other is a sense of the broader social and personal implications – including the potential downsides – of the 'information age'.

With regard to the latter question, I fill out out further the case that information societies are by definition surveillance societies. It does not matter what is the current buzzword for societal arrangements that are dominantly dependent on information technologies – the term 'knowledge-based economies' is popular at the time of writing[4] – the fact remains that such societies inevitably pay more systematic and intensive attention to personal data than any that historically precede them. Ironically of course, those data are lifted out of the personal, face-to-face context. This is not in itself necessarily a 'downside' of technological diffusion. But the term surveillance society does have connotations that at least hint at possible negative consequences, in ways that unambiguously optimistic talk of 'information societies' and 'knowledge-based economies' does not. My point is rather that such societies are in part constituted by a surveillance dimension. This renders everyday life more transparent than ever before to a growing number of agencies whose design is to influence it.

Let me say a little about infrastructures. To be modern is to live within and by means of technological infrastructures, although it tends to be disruptions that draw our attention to them. Without a power failure that leaves us in the dark, or a series of potholes in the highway that rattles our cars, we take for granted that infrastructures are just there. Yet infrastructures are widely shared and humanly constructed resources on which we depend from day to day. They are, suggests Paul Edwards, 'a network of systems that collaboratively and synergistically produce a continuous flow of goods and services'.[5] Infrastructures are not just hardware, but also social organization, social knowledge, and so on. They are an invisible background supporting the natural, technological and social environments of modernity. They set limits within which we live – transport systems take us only to certain places, and tend to deplete non-renewable resources for example – and they promote some interests at the expense of others. As we have already seen, part of the New York road transport infrastructure excludes poor and black bus-riders from some desirable destinations. So infrastructures constrain and they enable aspects of social life, but without determining it.

Informational infrastructures in particular evidence and encourage a networking logic in which information is both raw material and product. The distributed nature of such networked systems amounts to what Paul Edwards calls 'virtual infrastructures'. Informational infrastructures alter more readily than some other infrastructures of industrial modernity and tend to allow for more feedback loops. At the same time, the military origins of computer-based information infrastructures have influenced the character of their civilian spin-offs. The holy grail of command and control systems that lies behind the fully automated battlefield may also be detected in other settings like urban policing systems and in commercial database marketing.

Such parallel development of information systems from one sphere to another is one important aspect of infrastructural enabling. Another, explored in this book, is the way that once in place, informational infrastructures provide a platform into which other kinds of technological systems may be plugged. Video and closed-circuit television systems on the one hand, and biometric and genetic methods on other other, depend on the informational infrastructure for their crucial surveillance power. Surveillance capacities of DNA records or television images are severely limited without the informational infrastructure. One further aspect of information infrastructures is the geographical range across which they can be used. Like airline infrastructures, informational infrastructures are truly global in scope, which means that surveillance systems may also globalize.

The big question addressed here is how and why information societies – a shorthand for societies fundamentally dependent on information infrastructures – are also surveillance societies, and how this relates to current debates about the global restructuring that has been occurring at an accelerated pace for the past 30 years. Part of the answer involves showing that although all information societies are also surveillance societies, their development varies according to local cultures, levels of technological development, political priorities and constitutional arrangements. In Germany for instance, one's image may not be used by others as it is in situations such as sports event policing in the UK or the USA. But surveillance societies are such in the sense that surveillance practices, so far as being limited to the nation state and to government, have come to pervade all societal sectors. Moreover, these practices are implicated in the changing role of the state, the economy and of culture.

To take the most important example, much discussion surrounds the altered, and according to some, diminishing power of the state. Part of the impetus behind this debate is that the state no longer needs to hold onto full powers of surveillance when social ordering is achieved by many other agencies that have their own highly effective surveillance practices. My argument that surveillance *societies* should be the focus of analysis is not meant to suggest that state power is in fact shrinking. What it does indicate is ways that surveillance is now a generalized social phenomenon in the sense that institutionalized monitoring is routinely practised by a range of agencies including, but also going well beyond, the state.

If information societies are surveillance societies, does this mean that they resemble high-tech police states? Is the coordination of time-space so tight that all private spaces are eliminated by a technological takeover? If not, what exactly is happening? I do not for a moment want to give the impression that surveillance societies are sinister theatres of cynical power but neither do I condone complacency. The concept of surveillance society designates less a fixed state than a social tendency, an underlying social trend of considerable significance. Thus I propose that what is happening is something akin to 'social orchestration' in which surveillance is an ongoing, interactive process. Major themes are discernible, power plays its part, and ordinary people usually collude with and sometimes capitulate to the system. But does this add up to control or coercion? It all depends.

Commonalities and variations

Surveillance societies have a lot in common but they also vary substantially according to national differences and economic sectors. The new technologies serve to intensify and to organize surveillance in new ways but they initiate nothing. Why are modern societies information societies? Because they depend, as Alexis de Tocqueville (1945) and others argued as early as the mid-nineteenth century, on unprecedented bureaucratic documentation and intervention. Modern government administration depends on the collection and recording of personal data. Equally, though, capitalist enterprises, the other key component of modernity, also monitor and supervise employees to an extent hitherto unknown, in order to enhance efficiency and profitability. Thus modernity means reliance on information and knowledge in generating and maintaining power. And because much of that information is personal, such focused attention to data on individuals spells surveillance.

Put this way, two things become clear. First, the magnification of surveillance capacities is simply one facet of modernity. It is part of the world that we have made in our attempts to bring social, economic and political arrangements into rational regimes of organization and control. Such regimes try to make up for the disappearing body. The invention of mass democracy and of increased productivity may be traced to deliberate attempts to make the world a better place, partly inspired by beliefs in providence, but predominantly under the sign of progress.[6]

Second, and following on from this, surveillance is not an intrinsically antisocial or repressive process. The focused attention on individual lives characteristic of modernity underpins eligibility to benefits of citizenship, such as the right to vote or to state support, and also may ensure that workers are appropriately remunerated, or rewarded with promotions and recognition of retirement at the appropriate time. The relevant data is on file, and may be produced to prove identity and to verify claims. The fact that surveillance practices are altering in the later stages of modernity, or that in certain circumstances they may be used in very negative ways, does not alter the case that surveillance is simply a fact of modern social life.

Why, then, did the term 'surveillance society' not appear until the 1980s? And why, when it was used, did it carry connotations of threat and warning? After all, the classic surveillance dystopia of George Orwell's *Nineteen Eighty Four* had been available and was well known from the early 1950s.[7] For several cold war decades the kind of police state that Orwell had depicted seemed to find its clearest exemplars in the Soviet Union and its European satellites and other state socialist pockets around the world. Two factors changed all this.

One was the demise of communism in the late 1980s, that left open the possibility that Orwell's work – as he himself had hinted – referred to other kinds of society as well. Perhaps non-communist societies could be surveillance societies? The other was the rapidly increasing use of computers for surveillance purposes, which started seriously in the 1960s, but which by the 1980s was thoroughly established in numerous sectors. The film version of *Nineteen Eighty Four* did not appear until 1984. Although I know of no study that demonstrates this, from about that time on the epithet 'Orwellian' was much more frequently applied to computer-assisted surveillance wherever it was found than to communist police states.

By the 1980s it had become clear that the technical basis for widespread and systematic political and economic restructuring was communication and information technologies. The Japanese Ministry of International Trade and Industry had vigorously promoted these new technologies as the route to an information society, and the French government pursued a similar line. Countries such as Canada, Germany and Sweden followed not far behind. The USA provided an international slogan that stuck – at least for a while – the 'information superhighway'. Several countries on the Pacific Rim also launched policies to create information infrastructures, and thus Singapore, Malaysia, Korea and Indonesia produced their own variants, with Hong Kong, as a Chinese node through the Pearl River Delta,[8] and South Africa as other cases in point. Computer-based technologies are indeed proving to be strategically decisive in the societal directions taken from the late twentieth century onwards. Even if the hyped information society slogans are taken with a pinch of salt, the reality of radically altered political economies and social relations remains.

The term 'surveillance society' emerged when enthusiasm for the new potentials of information technologies was reaching a peak. Sociologist Gary T. Marx first coined the term in 1985, to refer to what he argued was an Orwellian situation in which 'with computer technology, one of the final barriers to total social control is crumbling'.[9] While Marx had the USA primarily in mind, comparative historian David H. Flaherty was soon to suggest that 'Western industrial societies run the increasing risk of becoming – or may already be – surveillance societies, as one component of being information societies'.[10] Flaherty's focus was Germany, Sweden, France, Canada and the USA. While he acknowledged that some 'forms of surveillance are of course quite legitimate in a democratic society' he insisted that 'their cumulative impact on individual privacy is negative'. Like Marx, Flaherty saw new technologies as making a crucial difference to surveillance capacities. Yet his work and that of Colin Bennett[11] also pointed to ways in which surveillance practices vary from one national or regional context to another.

The fact of regional and national variation is an important point, for it indicates that although surveillance capacities may be built up by similar technological means, the effects of so doing are far from identical. The use of computer technologies in surveillance may rightly spark particular concerns about the risks to individuals in societies that are developing information infrastructures. But the surveillance societies in question differ considerably according to the level of technical dependence and, most importantly, by virtue of different cultures and policies in each situation.

Flaherty's own conclusion was that while pressures for the automation of personal data collection were 'almost irresistible' in all the countries he studied, at the time Sweden had more integration of public and private databases than any of his other examples.[12] But Flaherty's primary interest was in privacy and data protection rather than in the analysis of surveillance itself. Increasingly, similar technical means of supporting surveillance practices are used, but these are established in varying ways. In Germany and Israel, for example, carrying identity papers is taken for granted, whereas in Australia or the USA even proposals for national identity cards are resisted. In countries such as Thailand and Indonesia, government intrusions into personal life, by wiretaps for example, are much more commonplace than in Canada or New Zealand.

Surveillance diffused through society

Shifting the focus from the word 'surveillance' to the word 'society' highlights another dimension of contemporary life. The concept of surveillance *society* denotes a situation in which disembodied surveillance has become societally pervasive. The totalitarian fears of Orwellian control all relate predominantly to *state* surveillance, whereas the notion of surveillance society indicates that surveillance activities have long since spilled over the edges of government bureaucracies to flood every conceivable social conduit. While the state still accounts for much monitoring of everyday life, such government activities are just one of many areas within which surveillance data now flows. Another title from the 1980s, David Burnham's *The Rise of the Computer State*,[13] hinted faintly at this shift, but still concentrated on administrative surveillance. Surveillance is diffusing decisively into society at large, although it should be noted that this does not mean that the capacity to answer back has now exceeded the power of state surveillance upon its citizens.[14]

Government surveillance is still significant and its expansion may be prompted by many different kinds of challenges to national power. In the UK, the threat of Irish terrorism on the English mainland has much to do with the so-called 'ring of steel' that now embraces the City of London business district. This utilizes state-of-the-art video surveillance – some cameras can read words on a cigarette packet from 100 metres – along with complex computer systems for detecting any hint of terrorist activity. Any vehicle entering but not leaving the area within a given time triggers an alert and licence plates are checked against relevant databases.[15] In Japan, both organized crime – the *yazuka* racketeers and smugglers of illegal aliens – and terrorism – primarily the cult group *Aum Shinrikyo* who sarin-gassed the Tokyo subway in 1995 – have spurred government efforts to crack down, using expanded wiretapping, and the interception of fax, computer data and email transmissions.[16] Measures of this kind have aroused fierce opposition in both countries. Yet it appears that support for increased surveillance is stronger, especially when the threats to national security and well-being are so palpable and easily dramatized.

Nonetheless, the role of nation states is changing, and information infrastructures and surveillance practices are deeply implicated in these shifts. Vertical bureaucratic surveillance still exists but it tends to be less centralized as personal data circulates more and more between public and private (commercial) realms. The most important reason why surveillance data is circulating in this way relates to the role of insurance companies. The political economy of insurance has been a neglected area of analysis but it is crucial to understanding why surveillance straddles state administration and commercial sectors. As Susan Strange argues, insurance companies do not seek power over outcomes but they exercise it nonetheless.[17]

Insurers and risk managers exercise power with extensive consequences for the world market economy and for the allocation of values among social groups, national economies and others. They make contributions to the economic order independently of states, affecting life chances and fortunes on a broad scale. Market economies, as Strange stresses, multiply risks. The effect is that richer groups and institutions can choose to translate some elements of risk into an insurance cost: 'The poor, unable or unwilling, or both, to pay the premiums are left with the risk'.[18] Actuarial risks are statistically calculable, assuming the data are available. Surveillance comes in here as a means of discovering and manipulating those data.

When government policies increasingly assign liability for damage to persons, property or corporations, risk communication using surveillance data becomes more significant, as does the authority of insurers. But in addition to the calculations are some more arbitrary factors of guesswork and prejudice. Hence the well-known controversies over refusals of life insurance to homosexual men and less known cases of refusals of home insurance to persons in burglary prone streets. Insurance companies, depending upon their surveillance activities, make powerful decisions that affect people's life chances using incentives and disincentives that affect the choice and range of available options.[19]

The drive for effective risk management means that health services exist between government provision and for-profit companies, at least in a country such as Canada. The same drive pushes closer the connections between insurance and policing. Government regulated as well as private police forces increasingly respond to the needs and definitions of insurance companies, which dilutes state surveillance as such, but which simultaneously diffuses surveillance into other sectors. The near monopoly once held on bureaucratic surveillance power by agencies of the state is now considerably attenuated. But this does not for a moment mean that the volume of surveillance practices has diminished. Quite the contrary. Surveillance is merely bound up with the shrinkage of state power in relation to its proliferation in other spheres.

This then is the second sense in which 'surveillance society' has become an appropriate way of describing from one angle a significant feature of contemporary social life. Information societies are necessarily surveillance societies and they depend heavily on new technologies. But in addition, surveillance societies are such in the sense that surveillance is pervasive in every sector of societal life, courtesy of an integrated information infrastructure. Far from state surveillance being predominant, surveillance activities may now be found in work situations and consumer contexts as well, and this is examined in the next chapter. Moreover, surveillance data is networked between these different sectors, to create degrees of integration of surveillance systems undreamed of in the worst Orwellian nightmare, but with actual social effects that are far more ambiguous and complex. The best way to consider that ambiguity and complexity is to examine some key themes raised by the emergence of surveillance society.

Social orchestration

Surveillance societies are not totalitarian, even if they have the technical capacity to be such, and even if such a potential tendency cannot safely be discounted (as Gary T. Marx would stress). Surveillance societies are visible in all information societies, seen in terms of an intensified attention to personal data and a desire to influence everyday life. But they are not surveillance states, by and large. Surveillance is dispersed through all social sectors, which makes government surveillance activities appear as just one aspect of surveillance in general. But if earlier nation states aimed through rational surveillance to instil rational discipline and to create order, contemporary surveillance societies seem to be going beyond this stage. Order and control may still be significant motifs, but as surveillance slips into simulation mode, and as it develops distinct tendencies to interactivity, the terms 'order' and 'control' at least invite a less rigid and one-way conceptualization than they had in the heyday of modern bureaucratic domination.

Take Deleuze's (1992) notion of 'societies of control', for instance. He uses this term as a contrast with 'disciplinary society', focusing on the ways that computers track persons instead of barriers or walls enclosing and incarcerating them. The tracking relates to something else discussed earlier, the mobility that characterizes the present, itself representing a merger of speed, light and power. Nomadic bodies and digital personae are the subjects of contemporary computer-based surveillance, and are categories altogether more slippery and malleable than those utilized in previous surveillance regimes. Indeed, nomadic bodies, digital personae and relationships between them are themselves constituted by surveillance practices,[20] which is a further sense in which interactivity occurs. Note also that while bodies still occupy space, digital personae do not, but contemporary surveillance deals in both currencies at once, and interchangeably. The private may thus still refer to place as well as to virtual spaces.

These kinds of surveillance systems and practices are thus characterized by contingency and by a certain open-endedness. They could be thought of, I suggest elsewhere, as 'disorganized surveillance'.[21] The growing role of insurance companies, that demand more and more of surveillance practices to obtain data for risk communication, underscores this arbitrariness. Business practices, the intensity of competition between insurers and the prejudicial valuation of different social groups all contribute to the disorganized character of contemporary surveillance.

The process, seen variously here as seduction and influence as well as obligation to comply, using above all categorization and classification, may fruitfully be considered as 'social orchestration'. That is, some overall direction is sought (the conductor in the orchestra; the codes of the network) but the music is produced by active subjects in the orchestra pit who cooperate and collude with the conductor (in surveillance settings using credit cards or social insurance numbers, or passing under cameras and scanners). The music, to continue the analogy, is more likely to approximate jazz improvisation than the classical orderliness of Mozart, suggesting different levels of compliance in different settings. The judgement as to whether such surveillance society orchestration produces pleasing harmony or discordant cacophony depends, of course, on one's position as surveilled or surveillor as well as the other variables discussed earlier.

Leaky containers

In January 2000 a car chase with a difference took place on Ontario's Highway 401. When a stolen vehicle was reported the police checked with the manufacturer to discover what equipment was on board. On finding that it featured a global positioning satellite (GPS) navigation system, the task of tracing the vehicle became straightforward. Police observed the progress of the car on their screens and apprehended the thief by pulling up next to the missing vehicle in a Tim Horton's doughnut bar parking lot. The electronic car chase proved much less risky than ones involving high-speed action on the freeway.

Surveillance was once a process in which embodied persons were watched by others. In the development of modernity the systems that came to rely more on abstract personal data were also more specialized. They were government departments such as taxation offices or workplaces such as factories using so-called scientific management methods. What went on in one sector seldom affected another. The surveillance containers were pretty well sealed. The situation today is changing as those containers become more leaky. Surveillance practices and flows of data move much more freely between one sector and another. What happens in one area has implications for another.

This has in part to do with the growth of information infrastructures but this does not in itself explain the whole of the emerging process. Common infrastructural elements such as global positioning techniques may allow people in one sector to cooperate with people in another in surveillance situations. But the random occurrance of the electronic car chase shows the potential for what actually happens between other discrete sectors. So-called cross-system enforcement has been a feature of surveillance systems for some time and may be seen in fairly mundane settings. A student may not be permitted to graduate from university, for instance, until fees are fully paid to the residence where she or he lived. In this case one system which is academically founded is used by another which is commercially orientated in order to obtain compliance. But this is not the only way that surveillance containers show their increasing leakiness.

Surveillance societies exist wherever surveillance ceases merely to be a feature of discrete institutional relationships, and becomes routine and generalized across populations. The disappearing bodies of modernity disappear even faster with the advent of communication and information technologies, and this generates redoubled efforts to maintain the visibility of those rapidly vanishing persons. Information infrastructures, as they are established, permit fresh surveillance configurations. These not only enhance already existing systems; they also mutate into new patterns. But the patterns are not random. They relate on the one hand to the surveillance systems that were in place well before any thoughts of computerization, and on the other to a complex circumstance of deregulation and risk.

It should be stressed that the surveillance societies described here are not situations of totalitarian control, are not technologically determined, and do not come into being merely as top-down impositions. They evolve and mutate by means and directions that are at once technological, social-cultural, and political-economic. In most cases they are also subject to legal limits or constrained to some extent by fair information practices. While the technological aspects may be most obvious, especially at the small scale end of particular innovations such as remote cameras or wiretapping, the artefacts themselves exist in a political-economic and an infrastructural context. In Britain, for instance, fear of street crime acts as a powerful incentive for politicians to support the installation of closed-circuit television and video surveillance systems. But these systems are also promoted by the commercially orientated companies that produce them, as technical fix solutions to urban social problems.[1] At the same time, growing public awareness of proliferating surveillance practices means that at least some monitoring or data collection initiatives are resisted or modified during their implementation.[2]

This chapter is concerned with patterns of surveillance growth, or rather with the ways that the patterns become less and less easy to discern. The focus here is mainly on the large scale, political-economic and technological dimensions of these developments. The dynamic impulse behind modern surveillance can be traced to two major sources – the expansion of the nation state and of capitalist enterprise. Although these two may be seen to operate in conjunction with each other from time to time – in Victorian Britain the militia or troops were deployed to break strikes or to quell other forms of industrial unrest, for example – their surveillance operations were largely discrete and worked on different principles.[3]

The nation state looked outward to maintain external security, and inward to procure domestic peace. This yielded forms of intelligence gathering on foreign powers and on suspected enemies within, along with parallel systems of administration and policing. The use of paper-based filing systems, plus the relative autonomy of the bureaucratic organization, severely limited the extent to which surveillance could spill over the edges of those classic containers. The capitalist corporation, on the other hand, employed various modes of supervision and monitoring of workers in an effort to maximize or to streamline production. During the twentieth century, such corporations have steadily broadened their emphasis to include the gathering of consumer data through market research, and to glean information on the activities of competing companies.

All these systems were enhanced by computerization during the late twentieth century and all have expanded exponentially thereby. But other changes have also occurred in the wake of computerization, enabled by the existence of an ever-expanding information infrastructure. Not only has the sociological distinction between workplace monitoring and supervision become less salient, market research has exploded into a frenzied and multi-faceted search for opportunities in segmented markets, using advanced techiques of consumer surveillance. Not only does policing cross new boundaries, likening it for example to conventional intelligence gathering, but policing and intelligence services enter new, virtual territory as they attempt to bring order to the perceived anarchy of the Internet. I shall argue the combined influence of deregulation and risk management has done much to permit leaky containers to develop.

Policing by surveillance

The Police National Computer (PNC) in Britain provides a good case study of how within a specific political economic climate an information infrastructure has enabled not only a more efficient service, but has also opened the door to unanticipated uses and to a reorientation of policing itself. The system was first established in 1974 as a convenient way of holding the vast records of vehicles on the roads.[4] It gradually replaced a slow and cumbersome cardfile system, first with a massive mainframe, and more recently with smaller, faster units. Today, 45 million vehicle records are on the database, and the PNC handles 230,000 transactions per day, through 10,000 secure terminals connected to local police forces all over the country.

The greater computer power also enables the infrastructure to support different kinds of databases, revised local police operations and also new forms of networking. The national system works alongside the newer National Automated Fingerprint Identification System, which holds 4 million fingerprint image records. This in turn is already being upgraded through the use of 'Livescan' prints – a scanner system that sends prints directly to the identification database, which is replacing conventional inkpad methods. Another system, already referred to in Chapter 2, and in use since 1998 in the City of London's 'ring of steel' zone, is now being installed in the Docklands area of London. This is the Automatic Number-Plate Recognition system. It uses a neural net computer to recognize number-plates viewed by overhead cameras, checking them against lists of stolen or suspect vehicles. The original system was set up in response to a late 1980s Irish Republican Army

(IRA) bombing campaign in London, but there is no hint that the system will be dismantled as part of the peace process in Northern Ireland. Indeed, the police plan further networking, this time with the Driver and Vehicle Licensing Authority (DVLA) road tax and vehicle safety check records, and later with court systems, probation offices and other emergency services.[5]

Another aspect of the PNC in Britain concerns the unintended consequences of new methods of local policing which actually fed into the emerging high-tech system. The emphasis in the 1980s on community policing represented a return to more direct contact with local areas that would give policing a human face and encourage policing by consent. But the Audit Commission's report on detective efficiency in the early 1990s diverted attention to proactive policing that targeted the criminal rather than the crime. This signalled a greater use of human informers but also an intensification of the use of high-tech methods.[6]

The convergence of high-tech and 'human face' computing also involved a shift of attention from detection of crime to its anticipation and prevention. In Britain, the 'comparative case analysis' function allows officers to search a vast database of unsolved crimes for possible links. Success with this technique in high profile cases such as that of multiple rapist and murderer John Henry Bell lends support to the development of such systems. But these in turn depend upon the use by local beat officers of increasingly sophisticated mobile data terminals that allow them to enter information on crimes and on suspects, and to perform direct checks with the PNC. This encourages a turn towards greater data collection by police as yet more surveillance is required as a risk communication.[7]

Watching workers

A similar case may be made concerning surveillance in the sphere of the workplace. The flexible worker within restructuring capitalism is such just because he or she is expected to be geographically mobile, and willing to work variable hours. Under these conditions, older methods of keeping track of work become less salient, and new electronic methods become more and more appropriate. Work has become more individualized, and so have surveillance methods. Whereas in the nineteenth and early twentieth century it was putting all workers under one roof that facilitated easy surveillance, today's technologies relate more to the individual employee. As middle management has diminished, so more direct methods of observing all employees have been brought into play.

The growing development of information infrastructures along with specific devices and functions means that the monitoring of workers becomes increasingly easy. The availability and relative cheapness of surveillance tools – such as Mailcop, which alerts workers if their email use violates company policy – is part of the reason why workplace surveillance has become more commonplace. But it is also a question of disappearing bodies, as workers become more mobile and also as they become more and more dependent on new technologies for their worktime activities. Some email and Internet use has been shown to promote collaborative work, and to raise productivity, and is thus advantageous to firms. But these trends are in turn related to the quest for more flexible workers who are increasingly individualized[8] within the broader picture of restructuring capitalism.

Before an employee is even hired, she or he is likely to be checked, using special databases (including data mining techniques[9]) or genetic screening, to discover the likelihood of this or that person turning out to be a responsible and hard-working employee. In Britain, organizations will soon be able more easily to run background checks on potential employees using the centralized Criminal Records Bureau, a situation that has aroused little comment in the UK.[10] In this case especially, the simulation of future likely occurrences and conditions becomes relevant. Would-be workers are checked for propensities and inclinations, for early warning signs, rather than for what they have actually achieved, or what is their proven performance at work. Thus workers who may become pregnant or those susceptible to certain diseases may be disqualified from employment.

Tabs can be kept on workers in fixed locations, using, for example, surveillance cameras that may also be hooked up to the Internet, or active badges worn by employed personnel that locate them in a building or plant. The idea of 'webcams' is to give shareholders as well as managers the opportunity to see what is happening in the office or factory at any time of day or night. Active badges on the other hand inform their computers where workers are from moment to moment. The idea is to enhance convenience. Computers automatically bring to the screen the work of the person sitting in front of them, and calls are forwarded to the nearest phone to the worker.[11] Safety, or the reduction of superfluous hierarchical managerial layers, may be beneficial results of these surveillance devices, but they also illustrate the way in which surveillance steadily expands.

Employees on the move may also be tracked. Truckers' tachometers record their speeds, their routes and their breaks, and homeworkers may find that their email and Internet use is monitored. Non-work time may also become part of the surveillance picture as workers are tested for leisure time substance abuse or screened to determine the onset of pregnancy. Again, health and safety issues may be addressed by such means but they are also conduits for possibly questionable surveillance techniques.

While call centres are the epitome of intensively monitored electronic sweatshops, the methods used in them are far from unknown elsewhere. Indeed, detailed attention to daily tasks, courtesy of computer power, is an increasing feature of many jobs, especially in white-collar occupations. So while keystroke counting and call durations may be routinely scrutinized, posted and used as spurs to greater productivity in call centres, similar but not much more subtle methods have appeared as common responses to the economic restructuring of the 1990s. In 1997 the American Management Association started tracking the use of workplace monitoring, and found that within a year the number of firms monitoring their employees' telephone, email, voice-mail and computer use had risen from 37 per cent to 43 per cent.[12] Such micromanagement trends are paralleled elsewhere.

Some forms of workplace surveillance are direct and deliberate. The growing use of email for communication within and between workplaces has also spawned an industry of email control systems designed to check that the medium is used appropriately. Workers may be caught automatically using email for private communications, or surfing the Internet for non-work related activities. Some systems also show patterns of use that may be used to detect and curb labour union activity. Telephone uses may also be logged, again to discover cases of 'inappropriate use'. The growth of computer video technology is making the camera appear attractive as a surveillance tool in more and more workplaces. If employees work at home, using the computer, their activities can easily be tracked there too.

Other kinds of workplace surveillance arise as unintended consequences of other activities. Camera systems intalled for the purpose of preventing shoplifting in stores can become a general managerial tool, for instance. At the same time they may become more covert. In some British retail stores closed-circuit television cameras that were intended to keep an eye on light-fingered customers are also used to check on the internal threat of theft. But this is not all. The same cameras pick up other details of worker performance, such as compliance with till procedures or refund and exchange procedures, as well as emotional labour – how 'friendly' and 'helpful' staff appear.[13] This shows again how surveillance may spill out of one container and into another by virtue of extending a common technological system.

The advance of technological surveillance into the workplace has raised issues not so much about the control of workers by management, but about what areas of the workplace should be deemed private. Video cameras, keystroke counting, email and Internet monitoring are felt to have different effects on such privacy, and generate different kinds of response. The question has turned from an older labour union approach to the rights of employees. The Institute for Employment Rights in Britain, for instance, has argued that workplace surveillance is an alarming threat to worker privacy, and some precedents have been set in this regard. The former Assistant Chief Constable of Merseyside, UK, Alison Halford, was awarded damages by the European Court of Human Rights when her phone was bugged after she had complained of sexual discrimination.[14] The UK Institute for Employment Rights acknowledge that in addition to contributing to insecurity and stress, workplace surveillance may prevent workers from organizing collectively.[15]

Although some argue that it is 'technology' that is shifting the balance of power against the employee[16] the reality is more complex. Technologies are actively sought that will facilitate higher degrees of consumer management, for example, and these may have unanticipated consequences for workers. The most celebrated case is that of 'contact management' through salesforce automation. Contact management software sales amounted to US$2 billion in 1998, and are growing by 20 per cent per annum.[17] Contact management uses software that allows users to manage their contacts' names, addresses, birthdays and previous conversations and messages. Used primarily in sales and marketing, it now finds outlets in customer services and human resources. The software, developed to manage consumption, actually has a dual role, in that the user can also be monitored. Moment by moment sales volume tracking helps the senior management know not only how sales are faring, but also which salespersons are contributing most to their success. The same system, then, may have more than one surveillance function.

Covering consumers

The example of contact management also shows how companies began systematically to add consumer management to their strategies during the late twentieth century. The restructured capitalist market is increasingly demand led, as witness the popularity of 'just-in-time' management. The marketing aspect of this is that rather than producing for an uncertain market, companies now attempt to customize, to personalize, to cater for discrete niche markets to create the consumers they need. What was once a matter of mass production and mass merchandising is now increasingly individualized. The trend is towards one-to-one marketing and personalized techniques such as loyalty 'clubs', co-branded credit cards, named and narrow-cast mailshots and targeted advertising on invoices that are customized to the buying patterns of each consumer. This is consumer surveillance, which on the one hand is a new, technologically enhanced development of capitalist management, but which, on the other, has continuities with earlier twentieth-century market research and 'Sloanism',[18] and with the military technologies that spawned its consumer variants.[19]

The information infrastructure along with specific applications that take advantage of the declining cost and increasing power of computing capabilities have led to a massive growth in what is called 'transactionally generated' information. Customers, often unwittingly, leave a trail of electronic footprints, as each point-of-sale exchange is recorded. Some stores and systems only collect anonymous data in order to aid stock control, whereas others use a panoply of tools such as loyalty programmes and credit card purchases in which precise product details are connected with identified customers.

The advent of electronic commerce in the mid-1990s added yet another layer of consumer surveillance to those already employed. It used 'cookies' and similar devices to allow companies to follow trails of customer interests revealed in their 'mouse tracks'. Cookies are a means of storing data about what Internet sites have been visited on the computer user's hard drive. They permit companies to extract these data from personal computers in order to target their owners for advertising purposes. The travels of the metaphorical mouse, clicked on a succession of sites, are taken to indicate interest that may be exploited commercially. In 1999, a public controversy over the Pentium III chip showed how Intel and Microsoft use built-in unique identifers when personal computers log-on to the Internet. A growing number of electronic devices and software packages contain identifying numbers to help them interact with each other. This is a great boon to consumer surveillance which is designed to know in advance how production should be shaped to demand.

These technological capacities also allow greater 'personal' contact with customers through 'relationship marketing'. If workplace surveillance reflects a greater concentration on individual performance, then cognate softwares allow for increased individualization in consumer surveillance as well. As Mary Culnan and Robert Bies say, 'Instantaneous access to the customer's history by a customer service representative allows standardized, impersonal encounters with anyone who answers the 800-number to assume the appearance of a personal relationship'. But it is a co-constructed situation, also fuelled by the greater focus on consumer expectations. As Culnan and Bies continue, 'Because consumers increasingly demand value and service, the marketing strategies of successful firms are inextricably linked to the use of vast quantities of detailed customer data'.[20]

This last quotation also reminds us of some aspects of surveillance practices that should not be forgotten. Each expansion of surveillance occurs with a rationale that, like as not, will be accepted by those whose data or personal information will be handled by the system. Moreover, those covered by one system or another participate in their own surveillance. Most systems are triggered by the actions or behaviour of data subjects. Surveillance has two faces, and its benefits to at least some parties are almost always palpable. Some may not agree that the surveillance practice concerned is desirable or necessary and others may come to dissent when they realize the fuller implications of the system. But when it comes to participation, of course, the effectiveness of the system may well be limited by the non-cooperation of data subjects. Young people in the street learn to evade the gaze of street surveillance cameras, call centre workers use many devices to produce the effects of efficient work, and consumers may withold details from their warranty forms or their customer satisfaction records.

Deregulation and risk

What lies behind the blurring of boundaries? Of course, technical computing capacities are growing exponentially, and increasing standardization of systems allows for greater flows across boundaries. Telecommunications advances permit faster flows of increasingly detailed personal data across vast distances, making surveillance truly global in scope. There is something to Herminio Martins' thesis that the present world is more and more subject to the 'tyranny of the possible' in which new technologies are tried just because they are available.[21] But probably more significant is the extensive economic deregulation that has been occurring since the 1980s. This deregulating impulse has involved governments shifting the burden for which they were once responsible – commercial entities such as security firms take over work once performed by police services for example. Traditional economic sectors are broken down in the process, but so also are the conventional modern distinctions between public (state run) and private (commercially based) organizations.

The growth of private personal databases has been so successfully demonstrated over recent years that a number of jursidictions are working towards establishing privacy legislation to cover such systems. Quebec, which has pioneered this development, was offered evidence in the mid-1980s showing that the private sector held and exchanged more data on its citizens than did the public sector. The report, which disclosed the extent of privately operated personal databases, was called *L'Identité Piratée*, and it contributed to a climate of awareness and to the setting in place of legal limits of data exchange by the private sector by the early 1990s.[22] During the 1990s, however, the private sector development of personal databases grew at an even faster rate, fuelled especially by the marketing trends noted above. But it is not only that the private sector has grown faster than the public; personal data also flows between the sectors.

Increased flow between sectors happens for a number of reasons, several of which may be summarized under the deregulation rubric. Governments seeking to cut costs and reduce budget deficits may divest public database management functions to the private sector, as, for example, in the case of health information networks.[23] In another scenario, once public corporations may be privatized, placing personal data, collected by a government organization, in private commercial hands. Either way, the opportunities increase for data to flow more freely and for containers thus to become more leaky.

As I was writing this, a plan was revealed to combine forces between Kerry Packer's company, Publishing and Broadcasting Ltd and the giant US information provider, Axicom, to create a major database on Australians' personal details and spending habits.[24] Coming just weeks after Australia Post, a government business enterprise, had sent family lifestyle survey questionnaires to 5 million households, many questions were raised. Among them was a demand by a Labour Party information technology spokesperson, Kate Lundy, to know what had happened to the personal databases of Telstra, the privatized Australian telecommunications company. IBM, too, as a client of Axicom, and in partnership with Telstra, has an outsourcing contract for seven government agencies. It appeared at the time of writing that the Australian government could not guarantee that personal information collected by the government and now managed by private agencies was not being accessed by others.

What these examples show is the extent to which deregulation is contributing to the blurring of boundaries between sectors that handle personal data. The technological availability factor works with not only the desire of government and commercial corporations to increase their data handling scope and efficiency, but with the devolution of government data processing to private organizations. At the same time, some government functions, such as the provision of policing services, may also process data according to the needs of private corporations. The prime example here is the way that the dictates of private insurance companies have come increasingly to govern the style and methods of both public and private policing. Perceived risks to property and to public order are met with intensified communication of knowledge gleaned through policing, but the categories of risk are provided by the insurance companies.

In other cases, the blurred boundaries occur between policing and security services. In Germany, in the early 1990s, enhanced telephone surveillance practices permitted police to monitor calls without a special licence in suspicious cases, particularly where internal security was concerned. Ulrich Beck suggests that the aim was not merely to prosecute crime or to prevent danger, but to 'avoid even conceivable risks'.[25] Thus, he says, every citizen is treated as a risk factor. At the same time, though, such citizens will also see themselves as being at risk. Beck quotes Herbert Prantl's fear that 'people will think they're in a well-patrolled holiday resort, until they notice too late that it's a posh prison'.[26] In these ways, among others, personal data used for surveillance flows not only within but between traditional sectors.

Beck's analysis of the 'risk society' shows why surveillance has become more socially significant in the present. Ways of communicating risk depend on surveillance. Agencies that engage in surveillance use practices designed to find out what is going on. The net result is that surveillance moves steadily towards a more central position in the ordering of social life. Although risk is more obvious in realms such as policing, there is a sense in which the same kinds of outlook and practices also dominate more mundane areas of governance, and also the gleaning of commercial intelligence on consumer behaviour. The most obvious example of this is the surveillance processes that determines who is or is not a good credit risk. So, in certain respects, market research operates in ways analogous to policing, to determine in advance what sorts of behaviours are likely, and how best to promote strategies that will pre-empt risk. At all levels risk management has implications for electronically enhanced surveillance, leading to remote control, boundary blurring and a changing morality, skewed towards utilitarian probability.[27]

Surveillance as risk communication is thus the other side of the coin of the escalating power of insurance companies. As we noted earlier, there is little evidence that insurance companies seek such power over outcomes. Yet power is just what they wield. Their power is palpable in determining categories of risks and naming what is more and less insurable. They thus make eligibility or inclusion depend on calculating probabilities on a utilitarian basis rather than framing such decisions within a concept of need or of justice. Surveillance is signficant here because it is the means of determining risk and so, indirectly, of profoundly affecting life chances.

Risk works in at least two ways in the surveillance field. This, in turn, is explained by the fact that surveillance always has two faces. On the one hand, surveillance is seen as a means of minimizing and, if possible, of averting risk. To know in advance is to be forewarned, and to anticipate difficulties or dangers. But on the other hand, surveillance is seen by many as a cause of risk, of potential unwarranted government intrusion into private life or of commercial control of personal consumption. Like many other risks that have risen to the surface of public consciousness in the past 30 years, this one is often seen in terms of 'technology out of control'. As we have seen in this chapter, however, surveillance technologies, while they may have some momentum as it were 'of their own', also display a complex political economy. Deregulation may lead to risks being handled in new ways. At the same time it may also produce new perceived risks.

Surveillance societies exist today because of the need to make visible and coordinate the activities of disappearing bodies. Their extent is made possible by information infrastructures, which both support an increasing range of surveillance systems and permit the flow of personal data between sectors previously sealed from each other. The containers become leaky not only because of this but also due to deregulation and the increasing preoccupation with risk. This last factor also encourages the proliferation of categories and modes of classification that turn surveillance into a central means of social ordering. This electronic environment automates processes of selection, of inclusion and exclusion, thus turning it into an agency of social sorting. Ensuring that people receive the right benefits and others the appropriate advertising materials is one result. Reinforcing stereotypes, discrimination and social difference is the other. How this actually works out in daily life is described and discussed in the next three chapters.

○ PART TWO

The spread of surveillance

○──────────────────────────────────────

The rise of surveillance society may be traced to modernity's impetus to coordinate and control. The spread of surveillance society depends on new ways of expanding and developing earlier techniques which in some cases have new consequences. Surveillance exploits new sources of surveillance data and flows through new spaces. It is not necessarily experienced in new sites.

The issue of disappearing bodies becomes more acute as lives are lived increasingly in a world dominated by speed and mobility. A fast world is one in which more and more means are sought of providing tokens of trust to demonstrate eligibility and rights of participation. A constantly growing invisible framework – the information infrastructure – acts as a platform into which each new surveillance function may be plugged, but is also the means whereby data flow more freely between sectors that once were more discrete. The accelerating and proliferating flows reflect the increasing power of risk calculation and its attendant categories by which our behaviours are assessed.

Why do I stress that surveillance is not necessarily experienced in new sites? A major problem with many accounts of the so-called information society is that they can give the impression of some revolutionary social changes that transfer us into some imagined realm beyond concrete daily life in urban areas. This is especially true of those that take account of virtual and simulation technologies and hint that cyberspace is an entirely disembodied and immaterial state of affairs. In Chapter 4 I look at the city as a key site of surveillance. It is in urban areas that the experience of surveillance is most intense. So, far from cyberspace transcending the material world of conscious embodied persons, it is actually superimposed upon that world with some significant consequences. How cyberspatial and simulant surveillance works does indeed depend on abstractions, electronic impulses and discursive power. But its origins and its effects are far from mysterious and arcane. They reinforce and recalibrate rather familiar divisions based on factors like social class, race, ethnicity, gender and sexuality.

In Chapters 5 and 6, new sources of surveillance and new spaces for surveillance are explored. The body is the new source and the globe is the new space. Of course, neither is entirely new and neither places surveillance on a new plane. Their novelty has a lot to do with the information infrastructures now available to enable them to act for surveillance purposes. Strictly speaking it is not the skin-covered body as such, let alone embodied persons, that are used for surveillance sites. Rather, it is body parts such as retinas and fingerprints, and abstract body data, such as DNA traces, that are now enabled as surveillance sources. Equally, the idea of globalizing surveillance does not mean that some sinister world power is taking over. Rather, it hints at ways in which global and local forces interact for surveillance purposes such that disappearing bodies are made visible and risks are calculated over more extensive terrains. The impacts of these processes are mundane, local and experienced in everyday situations.

Surveillant sorting in the city

Most people today live in cities. Even for those who do not, the urban environment is never far away. Everyday life has become more and more urban in modern times and this has strong implications for surveillance. It is in the city that we experience surveillance in ways that are multi-faceted, multi-layered and moment by moment. In the world's affluent societies we take for granted the ubiquitous signs in stores and on streets warning of 'constant video surveillance'. Whether out on the freeway with its camera speed checks or indoors at the computer with its Internet privacy alerts there is no escape from one monitoring device or another.

Urban experience involves the regulation of daily life. Myriad checks are made to ensure that we are in the right place at the right time, travelling at the right speed or carrying the correct items. We are positioned, placed, directed and traced as we travel, buy, study, telephone, find entertainment and work. Sometimes as part of a social category, sometimes as individuals, surveillance sieves our activities in the city. This social sorting process, which depends on surveillance, is based increasingly on attempts to predict and to simulate behaviours: in other words, 'simulant sorting in the city'.

In this chapter a software game called SimCity is discussed as a means of thinking about surveillance in the city. SimCity enables users to design a city in residential, commercial and industrial zones. Users may also decide where tax revenue will be spent, where police stations, power plants and waste disposal sites will go, and watch as sims – the citizens – make their own mark on development. The real world of the city is thus simulated for entertainment and educational purposes. But what if SimCity were more than a toy, and if the real world was run this way? This is part of what I want to explore. How far has this toy has come to resemble the real world practices that affect the design and maintenance of the city? Is this social science fiction worth heeding?[1]

Today, without doubt, decisions about locating schools, stores, cinemas and sports arenas are based on just such simulations, and these simulations are based upon a massive growth of surveillance capacities in all sectors. Such surveillance, using computers, telecommuncations, video cameras, smartcards, barcodes, biometric methods, remote sensors and satellites provides the raw data. Those who get to play the game, one might say, use the data to manage the city. Through the vehicle of surveillance the real world comes to resemble SimCity.

Or does it? Are there really godlike operators who can control the city using a mouse and a keyboard? Such absolute power is scarcely visible in practice. The sheer mass of data would be impossible to handle. Even in SimCity one cannot keep track of everything. Players are forced to prioritize. The constant gathering, processing and interpreting of data destabilizes all notions of an all-knowing, all-seeing subject behind the scenes. Those who suggest the SimCity-type practices are taking over the real world are in danger, it seems, of being seduced by their own metaphors. While it may be true that urban planners are attracted to such simulation and modelling, their capacity actually to realize their dreams is surely limited. And what of those who attack the SimCity future as divisively dystopian, as portrayed in the film *Blade Runner*?[2] Have they, too, allowed themselves to believe the techno-hype about the efficacy of simulated cities?

A further question concerns the sim citizens of SimCity. Do they really have no say in how their city is run? In some accounts they appear as little more than cyphers, programmed cyborgs who do the bidding of the planners. But this hardly does justice to the situation. As we shall see in the later part of the chapter, while the SimCity metaphor provides some useful clues for thinking about simulant sorting in the city it remains, like all metaphors, limited.

Social control in the city

Making the city visible so that it can be a place of safety and of public order is nothing new. Roman buildings such as Hadrian's Pantheon were intended to create visual directives, such that, as Richard Sennett says, 'The geometry of Roman space disciplined bodily movement, and in this sense issued the command, look and obey'.[3] In Greek thought, too, the orderly city was a means of holding chaos at bay. For Plato and Aristotle the patterning and spatial arrangements of the city were a mirror image of what society should be.[4] Physical artefacts and techniques could help too. In seventeenth-century Paris, to reassure citizens that it was safe to go out, police lieutenant La Reynie appointed 'lighting inspectors'. By 1697, as he ended his career as chief of police, Paris had become a 'city of light' by virtue of the 6500 lanterns that he had installed.[5]

Ancient cities were also used to construct maps of hell in which the divisions of vice and virtue could clearly be displayed. As the process of urbanization began to pick up speed in the nineteenth century, the 'city of night' reappeared as a negative motif. There the 'dark satanic mills' were places to be feared and avoided. City conditions were often viewed as less than ideal, needing to be greened with gardens, or risen above by developing new senses of personal identity.[6] Also, in modern times spaces in cities frequently were designed to permit maximum visibility, to discourage deviance and to promote public safety. To see was to ensure social control, to plan for order.[7]

By the 1960s, various competing and sometimes complementary models of the city were available, each with its remedy for impersonality or criminality, or both. Jane Jacobs argued classically for cities as places of mutual recognition where neighbourliness and communal responsibility would provide whatever 'eyes on the street' were needed.[8] Citizens themselves could provide conditions for crime limitation. As Stanley Cohen observes, this vision does assume a certain cultural homogeneity,[9] but it is founded on an important principle of embodied personhood which is still worth seeking in a more electronic era. The other models, after all, exacerbate rather than ameliorate the segmentation and isolation of some experiences of city life. One of these is the urban fortress, now seen in electronic form in dystopias such as Mike Davis' *City of Quartz*, which focuses on Los Angeles.[10] The urban fortress is characterized by physical security based on technical isolation. Another is the idea of defensible space, which sets one area off against another in a struggle for competition for resources and privileges.[11]

It is important to note from the outset that surveillance may be seen here as productive power, and not merely in its more paranoid panoptic guise. Safety, security and social order are all seen by most people as positive accomplishments. Who would not wish to walk without fear on a street after dark? Who would not be relieved at the elimination of recklessly fast driving in urban areas? Who would not hope quickly to be alerted if fire broke out or a thief broke in? Many surveillance practices and devices are intended to improve city life in significant respects and are welcomed as such. The question is, what other effects accompany the positive face of surveillance, especially as it is automated and informatized? And, are the effects of surveillance positive for all or just for some? Simulant sorting works in several ways at once.

So, what of the start of the twenty-first century? How is the city made visible and order constructed today? Contemporary urban areas are rightly thought of as 'informational cities'.[12] The idea of maintaining visibility is present not only in a metaphorical sense of keeping digital tabs on populations but also in a literal sense of their being viewed by video surveillance. 'Smile!' instructs the rear side of all Tasmanian windshield licence stickers, 'surveillance cameras are everywhere'. Construction sites and central streets, shopping malls and department stores are all under constant surveillance scrutiny. At the same time, the information infrastructure allows those visual images to be checked, stored and compared with other kinds of personal data. Within the city, citizens may expect to be constantly 'illuminated' – made visible – by a multitude of means, not only from dawn till dusk but from dusk till dawn as well.

On a daily basis life in the city spells surveillance in constantly increasing contexts. From the road tolling system to the mobile phone call, the camera in the subway station to the barcoded office door key, the loyalty programme in the store to the Internet usage checks at work, surveillance webs are thick in the city. Yet the aim is not necessarily to catch a glimpse of every actual *event* – though that remains an important goal – so much as to anticipate actions, to plan for every event*uality*. The bustling co-presence of the town, with its square and its market-place, gives way to both more fleeting relationships and to the absence of persons in their particularity.

Those who are not available downtown need not imagine that their erstwhile 'private' spaces at home are sacrosanct. They are equally vulnerable to surveillance. The city is divided not only into overt lines of social demarcation in distinct spaces, but is also under regimes that maintain difference virtually, using computer capacities and statistics. As Paul Virilio says, 'In acquiring *closed-circuit optics*, statistical science . . . will probably see its power and power of conviction considerably enhanced, along with its discrimination capacities'.[13]

The means to this is the information infrastructure that enables the informational city to emerge. Cyberspace, far from being a merely immaterial domain, is a predominantly metropolitan phenomenon that develops out of the older cities. For example, with only 7 per cent of the American population, New York nonetheless originates 70 per cent of all outgoing international telephone calls. And with 17 per cent of the British population, London has 30 per cent of all mobile phone calls. The fact that data flows permit remote activities does not mean that all electronically mediated relationships are geographically stretched over huge distances. Cyberspaces are still concentrated around conventional urban areas.

At the same time, the informational city is planned such that its informational character is enhanced. Planners are using data gleaned from surveillance to gear the city to more streamlined communications and to benefit more from the invisible flows of data that now criss-cross it. Cyberspace as well as physical space now has to be factored into the planning process. Urban business zones are required for high-tech companies dealing in information just as heritage areas are required for tourism. As Stephen Graham points out, the Indian city of Bangalore is attractive for its highly skilled and cheap information technology professionals. And older industrial cities such as Manchester, Dublin and New York feature 'information districts' where cultural industries develop, based around ambient face-to-face interaction at street level *and* advanced global connectivity.[14]

Transnational corporations can seek out specific sites suited to their needs, from a growing array of potential urban areas. They scrutinize the areas concerned, choosing ones that offer the optimum range of high technology connections with the information infrastructure as well as opportunities for direct interaction wherever possible. Thus, says Graham, 'Cities – that is, extended urban regions rather than monocentric urban cores – are therefore the key anchor points in today's volatile, highly mobile and fragmented economy and society'.[15]

SimCity and urban realities

At least three possible ways of understanding 'SimCity' may be distinguished. First, the term refers to the software toy that has been available since 1989. In it, you start, from the ground up, to build a city, using bulldozers to clear land, installing power and utilities, placing streets and buildings in a pleasing and workable pattern, and allocating resources appropriately. Or else you use an already existing city started by someone else, or a version of a real city such as New York or Rome. Among other things, you can watch the crime rate grow, and locate police departments of the necessary size to deal with it. SimCity is used as a non-competitive game, although from the start its relevance to the real world was recognized.

Its maker, Will Wright, thought there might be a limited interest from urban planners, and by 1994 a Planning Commission handbook had been published to go with the game.[16] SimCity is a toy for trying out experimental urban designs, for visualizing a dream of an ideal city. Creating the perfect environment by virtual means is seen (at least by Wright) as continuing a tradition of 'starting from zero' that began with Walter Gropius and the Bauhaus commune after the First World War. The idea was to make something 'clean and pure'. It sounds Disneyesque, as does the handbook enthusing that the 'joy to be found in the program is tied up in the cosmetic surgery necessary to remove these blemishes from urban life'.[17] Much more negatively, Ted Friedman caustically suggests that SimCity 'rests on the empiricist, technophilic fantasy that the complex dynamics of city development can be abstracted, quantified, simulated, and micromanaged'.[18] For the gamer, says Friedman, the city 'exists in its own right, a substitute for nothing else – a quintessentially postmodern "simulation" in Baudrillard's sense, as "real" as any other representation and divorced from any need for a real world referent'.[19]

Second, SimCity may be thought of as a shorthand for the 'simulated city'. The idea that cities are influenced by Disneyland has become commonplace, especially in North America. The Disney Corporation has, after all, built its own city in Celebration, Florida, as well as influencing architecture and urban planning throughout the USA and elsewhere. Although covered shopping arcades such as Milan's Galleria Vittorio Emanuele have been around for over 100 years, the themed shopping mall with its many franchises is much more ubiquitous in North America.

The idea of 'theming' is central to Disneyization, along with three other features. One, the democratization of culture in which different styles and levels are mixed in a melange; two, merchandizing, in which the logo (like the Nike swoosh) becomes the selling point; and three, a strong focus on emotional labour, in which the cheerful worker is central to the action.[20] It is often suggested that the consumerist Disney vision is imposed on cities as a means of social control, for managing social diversity.[21] Here everything is marketed in a safe space created to stimulate desire. Social diversity is made less threatening and public space more secure.[22] But the connection of

Disneyization with surveillance is seldom made,[23] and yet this is the very mechanism that realizes the power of social control. Disneyland itself is safe and squeaky clean because it is patrolled by innocent looking extras who maintain constant surveillance. It is argued by some that this is also the aim of those who would manage cities today.

Third, then, we may see SimCity as a site of surveillance, based on simulation. Indeed, in the city surveillance is at its most intense and yet this is taken for granted, routine and often invisible. True, on a grand scale, surveillance is steadily being globalized and, on an intimate one, surveillance now infiltrates the human body as never before. But in the city surveillance is experienced constantly, from the first phone call of the morning, to the overhead camera in the street, to the retinal scan at the bank machine, to the tracking cookie[24] in the computer, to the barcode on the office key, to the automated highway toll, to the cellphone log, to the camera in the store, the station, and the bar, last thing at night.

Who wants all this personal data? It is required for management purposes, whether the manager is in the travel agency, the police station, the city hall, the supermarket, the hospital, the phone company, wherever. This knowledge is required particularly for calculating and managing risks. This is why such agencies want to know not only what you are doing and saying, but also – more significantly – what you are likely to do or say next. Their predictions are based on simulations that will enable anticipatory behaviour or pre-emptive action on their part.

Urban surveillance

Why is surveillance important for understanding the city today? Recall that surveillance has to do with focused attention to persons, and in particular with the gathering of personal data for specific purposes. The kind of agencies that collect and process personal data have been doing so for that past 200 years, to register voters, to record births, marriages and deaths, to enrol subscribers and to keep track of property transactions. Modernity is characterized among other things by the growth of surveillance. But the means of collecting data altered dramatically with the introduction of the computer, and allowed many others to get in on the act. Today, surveillance has been dispersed, decentred, disorganized, and is a feature of all organization in every city. Different agencies have different purposes in mind, and almost all would recoil in horror if they were associated with Big Brother. But whether their combined efforts add up to something that should still cause apprehension is a question worth exploring.

The value of the 'social orchestration' metaphor may be seen again here. Surveillance is not simply coercive and controlling. It is often a matter of influence, persuasion and seduction. We are all involved in our own surveillance as we leave the tracks and traces that are sensed and surveyed by different surveillance agencies. Our activities may well be 'orchestrated' in a sense, but at the same time our active participation is essential for the 'music' to be produced. We are indeed the bearers of our own surveillance, as Foucault noted, but our activities trigger surveillance mechanisms in different ways and with varying effects. The power of surveillance is strung out along a broad spectrum from tight, coercive control, through to loose and mild seduction; from obligation to influence. So the social orchestration produced by contemporary surveillance practices is, like music, both soft and hard, both gently wooing and compellingly direct.

Increasingly today's city is what Manuel Castells calls the 'informational city'.[25] He sees this as a historical transformation in which the new communication and information technologies are centrally implicated, while both informing and being informed by capitalist restructuring. In the city the older space of places is dominated more and more by 'spaces of flows'. The flows are enabled by electronic impulses and circuits and they are flows of capital, information, technology, images and symbols. In his epic trilogy on *The Information Age* Castells takes this further, showing more clearly how our experience of time and space is currently being modified by these processes. Indeed, according to Castells the new global city itself becomes a process as much as a place. While people still live in places, it is in the space of flows that function and power are organized.

Take for example the logic of industrial location. Production may be scattered over a range of different locations but this does not mean the process is unconnected or random. Far from it. Telecommunciations links enable constant contact between different aspects of production and also between the highly skilled knowledge workers in research and development, and the unskilled workers, elsewhere, who are still required for routine assembly and other tasks.[26] The work process is thus tightly integrated and coordinated, using flows of information rather than geographical proximity to hold things together. Similarly, the slowly growing practices of telecommuting, telebanking, teleshopping (and, for that matter, electronic commerce using the Internet), and distance learning also reduce dependence on old patterns of space and time. Flexibility, mobility and speed of communication make a huge difference to the way the city is organized.

But informational cities are also surveillance cities. Whatever the benefits of the new flexibility and mobility in the spaces of flows, those flows carry data and information about persons and processes so that their activities can be monitored and tracked. But this is not all. When speed has become so central, not only knowing what is happening in the present, but also anticipating what is about to happen also becomes crucial. Surveillance overtakes itself, as it were, to produce data on events and processes that have yet to occur in real time. Whereas once surveillance in the city meant the use of street lights and physical architecture to keep watch and to contain deviance, it now also means keeping electronic tabs, including camera images, on the population at large. It is not that older methods are simply superseded, but that new ones are superimposed. And the newer methods are designed to push surveillance beyond all its old limits.

There are some very mundane aspects to this, but ones that can easily go unnoticed – unlike the cameras that seem to breed on street posts. An example is public utilities, enhanced by connection with the information infrastructure. Residential power lines in some areas are checked by 'smart meters' that permit almost continuous digital sampling. As Rick Crawford shows, this allows watchers to 'develop a fine-grained profile of the occupant's electrical appliance usage'.[27] While electrical power monitoring has been used in the USA by drug enforcement agencies to root out illicit marijuana gardens that use high-power lights, the more lucrative purposes for smart meters would be market data-gathering.[28] Smart meters could help share the burden of power at key times, for instance during hot, humid weather, when air-conditioners are running on high. But equally, they alert their users to malfunctioning domestic appliances, or to the absence of certain kinds of domestic appliance, providing an opportunity for targeted advertising of new machines.[29]

The space of flows allows the new, information rich, global élites to create their own separate world and even to impose on a place their new secluded environments. They are global élites in the sense that they can also create similar symbolic areas throughout the world, in hotels, airports and transport and communication systems. In their home bases the élites inhabit little fortress zones, the gated communities that further insulate them from other, local people in the same 'city'. They may use various high technology surveillance tools for watching over their property or their children. They may also encourage the use of high technology protection against possible trouble from other sources. The Kew Psychiatric Hospital in Melbourne uses video surveillance to ensure there is no threat from patients to surrounding up-market apartments, for instance. Items such as residential smart meters enhance home security systems, which fact again shows how surveillance powers are distributed unevenly within any given population.

Behind all these moves lies fear. Fear of attack, of intrusion, of violence, prompts efforts to ward off danger, to insulate against risk. Architectural shelters that protect their inhabitants from hazards are nothing new. But their electronic and video enhancements are, and these are among the latest attempts to cope with intensified fear. According to Nan Ellin, in the late twentieth century fear generated divisive architectural policies that turned inward and backward rather than facing the actual social challenges of urban life. Fear may be met with turns to an idealized past, to a fantasy world – such as a themed mall – or to group cohesion and privatization, seen especially in gated dwellings.[30] Defensive spaces appear as the way forward, rather than what Ellin seeks: living places.

Surveillance practices are among the flows that enable the increasing division between the global and local in the urban environment. But not only division. The flows simultaneously connect and divide. They hook up the dispersed and the diasporic, uniting diverse groups in terms of shared identities and common interests. They may, for example, provide protection against racist attacks for beleaguered ethnic minorities in the city as well as, on occasion, also strengthening such racism.[31] The London Borough of Newham has installed a 'Mandrake' facial recognition system to locate known racial offenders on the street by comparing a camera image with those on a digitized database. Surveillance systems are a means of maintaining new relations of power and of resistance in the global–local city.

Surveillance flows have a direct effect on place. The new power in the space of flows requires that the city take a certain form. This is very concrete in specific buildings so that the city appears a certain way to outsiders and creates part of what Davis calls an 'ecology of fear'.[32] Davis sees market-driven urbanization as a transgression of environmental and social common sense. It produces avoidable tragedies from fires and floods to the video-recorded beating of Rodney King. Of course, city planning tries to exclude the very conflicts that it tends to generate. As Sharon Zukin says, the service sector society is a Disneyized dream where 'conflict [is] designed out and comfort designed in'.[33] Surveillance contributes to both features at once.

Take, for example, Victoria, the capital of British Columbia in Pacific-coast Canada. A recent clean air by-law banned smoking in all public buildings, from bars to homes for the elderly to the provincial parliament. At the same time video cameras were installed in some nightclubs and police renewed their commitment to enforcing a 'street camping' by-law.[34] This means that homeless young people, attracted by its affluence to Victoria, are routinely moved off the sidewalks. The reason is that Victoria is a tourist town with 'Olde English' charm, a Scottish castle and a replica of Anne Hathaway's cottage. The hyperreal city is remade for consumption by tourists. Its poverty can be swept off the streets, its violence contained by cameras and its impure atmosphere cleansed by no smoking signs. Certain symptomatic behaviour may even be deterred sucessfully although its causes remain untreated and unremarked.

You may correctly object, of course, that this represents an over-polarized view of the city. However, it is clear that many people in Victoria, and other large cities, support the vision of secure and sanitized public places. It is politically acceptable to do so. Global élites and desperate poverty do coexist in the city, but between them usually lies a large middle class. They may not aspire to the laptop, the satellite phone (or whatever is the current symbol of high-tech status), or the VIP-lounge culture of the élite, but they certainly wish to avoid the fate of non-consuming – or of choicelessness – that is the lot of the poor. Particularly persons in that fraction of the middle category, which David Ley calls the 'cultural new class', actively 'imagineer' new inner-city environments, where they are both producers and consumers.[35] Indeed, much witting and unwitting collusion with the 'SimCity' goes on, involving the majority of the population, enabled and encouraged precisely by the increasingly invisible mechanisms of surveillance.

Having painted a general picture of the real-time SimCity, let me make some of the connections clearer. Surveillance was once a limited affair that applied primarily to the activities of the state and of the workplace. Surveillance served bureaucratic organization in both cases.[36] Citizens and workers were the main categories in which people were placed and, as surveillance sectors, they were once relatively distinct. Partly due to restructuring and partly enabled by new technologies, however, these sectors are now much less distinct. They overlap and intersect with each other and have also been expanded by a huge increase in what might be called consumer surveillance. Moreover, mere bureaucratic power no longer seems to be the goal of surveillance. The same new technologies make possible new routines of modelling and profiling – in short, of simulation.[37] Surveillance may include control but it contributes to something much broader – simply producing knowledge useful for administering populations.[38]

The overlapping and intersecting nature of surveillance in the city today means that the different threads in the fabric are quite difficult to distentangle. What began with administrative tissues emanating from the state – social insurance, taxation files, medical records, census data, welfare claims, voting registers and so on – now has other layers added on top. These are frequently tied to commercial organizations, although they are also connected back to those of the state. The police, for example, gather data that relates to legal requirements, but these in turn may have to do with insurance, or with employment. Indeed, along with financial institutions, health and welfare services and motor vehicle agencies, insurance companies figure prominently in the groups to whom the police are accountable. As we shall see, this has much to do with the ways that policing has become part of risk management, for which surveillance knowledge is required. This is no longer knowledge of wrongdoing or of rule-breaking, so much as knowledge of who or what constitutes a risk. Rather like assessing the likelihood of traffic accidents, the chances of crime being committed are reduced to a risk calculus. This is actuarial justice, where one tries to work out in advance who will commit crime where, and if necessary deploy police power appropriately.

Under the camera

A striking example of the predictive powers claimed for new technologies may be seen in 'Cromatica', a subway security system that was first tested in London Underground train stations.[39] By connecting closed-circuit television cameras with an 'intelligent' computer system, the prototype monitors crowd flows and warns about dangerous congestion. It also alerts to cases of deviant behaviour such as people going where they are not authorized and it even spots potential suicides, or so it is claimed. The changing colours and intensities of pixels are continuously analysed to detect characteristic movements. Those contemplating suicide tend to wait on a platform, missing trains, before taking their final tragic steps.

Such systems have much to commend them for their potential to reduce risks and avert tragedies. But there are always questions to ask. The degree of 'intelligence' involved may turn out to be crucial, at least until technologies like Cromatica can correctly distinguish between events such as a controlled mugging and a casual meeting. And the risk classifications themselves are of course contestable. 'Abnormal' and 'bad' behaviours are not unequivocal categories. But beyond technical competence and social interpretation lie issues of unintended consequences and potentially sinister developments. Blanket coverage in areas with dense camera coverage permits remote tracking of persons as they move within range of one camera and out of another. The City of London, the core of the capital's banking and business enterprises, is one such potential hazard zone. The positive and productive power of a system like Cromatica could be eclipsed by unplanned – or, worse, planned – risky alternative uses.

Closed-circuit television and video surveillance in public urban spaces displays clearly the dovetailing of different surveillance sectors. The boundaries are blurred in this case too. To create safe, secure and attractive places for consumption, entertainment and tourism, many cities – especially in the UK – have turned to a camera system. Streets and public places are the responsibility of municipal governments and city councils and these bodies seek technical solutions to the surveillance quest. Because such systems require capital outlays beyond the means of many neighbourhoods, private capital is sought to back such schemes. In the UK, while central government funding contributes to some local television surveillance systems, it is also claimed that private capital is vital to much city centre surveillance.[40] In Glasgow, where 'City Watch' was switched on in 1994, tensions between the public and private interests were addressed if not resolved through the work of the Glasgow Development Agency, which claimed that visits to the city would increase if cameras were installed to deter crime and make the place safer.[41] But however initially important is the rhetoric of private capital support, it seems that the balance of expenditure is still tipped heavily towards taxpayers.

In order to disentangle some of the surveillance threads it is necessary to look at different sectors as if they were discrete. Daily life in the city involves life as a citizen, as a worker and as a consumer. Surveillance operates in as well as between all three sectors, and although each is increasingly geared to forms of risk management, they still retain relatively distinct purposes. Government departments oversee matters pertaining to taxation, regulation, social insurance and political participation. Indirectly, governments also provide policing services, once seen as law enforcement to maintain order, but today more accurately understood as contributing to the security efforts of different institutional areas.[42]

Corporations employ people whose records they hold and whose activities they scrutinize to ensure that productivity is maintained. Increasingly, corporations also attempt to coordinate consumption by keeping track of purchases and transactions so that they can manipulate the market-place for commodities. Remember, though, these are only analytic distinctions. Both city and corporation work together to create an infrastructure to foster consumption, and especially tourism. Technological potential makes some convergence possible. It is above all the database that allows for the sorting and classifying of persons that now occurs in all sectors – administrative, employment-related and commercial.

One of the most obvious signs of surveillance is the overhead 'electronic eye' of the closed-circuit television camera. Indeed, this is the most visible face of surveillance expansion today, even though miniaturization and secretion is also becoming more common. In city streets, above all in the UK, cameras have become a common sight. Indeed, Stephen Graham suggests that they will soon be a 'fifth utility' like water, gas, electricity and telephones.[43] The number of British cities and towns with such cameras grew rapidly in the 1990s, a dozen systems being added between August 1994 and March 1995.[44]

Also in the UK, vehicle registration-plate recognition cameras will soon cover the country in an integrated system, installed on all main roads, intersections, tunnels, seaports and airports. The cameras communicate in real time by microwave link and telephone line to the PNC in Hendon, London. At the same time, some roadside cameras are privately operated, for instance by the 'Traffic Master' company. More than 5000 units have been installed on freeways and other major highways as the backbone of a real-time traffic flow information service. Subscribers on Britain's car-clogged roads may be understandably grateful for information on flows and jams of traffic, available via on-board computers, phones and pagers. The system works by taking images of registration plates at regular intervals and creating an ongoing computer record of aggregate traffic flow.

Cameras have crept into buses, trains, taxis, phone booths and elevators. Where they have been installed, citizens seem to take them for granted. Indeed, my son just showed me a magazine garment advertisement whose caption is 'You are on video camera an average of ten times a day. Are you dressed for it?'. Cameras inspire the public display of performance, it seems.

To some, this last point speaks of the democratizing effects of the new technologies. If television shows use footage from home videos for comic purposes, and if 'crimestopper' shows re-enact scene-of-the-crime details for mass audiences, then surely cameras are tamed and domesticated by being a part of everyday life. Being filmed is taken for granted and the use of cameras by the many dilutes the power of those running large-scale systems. Such views should not be ignored or marginalized. As one writer observes, 'new spaces of visibility are being opened up' that have possibilities for resistance.[45] There are different kinds of visibility and different surveillance practices, related to different regimes of power. But it is naive to imagine that the placing of camcorders in the hands of 'bystanders in the street' can somehow be seen as more than a brief moment of subversive or resistant activity. Camcorders can do little to disturb the flattening effects of the official capital-intensive video gaze in urban spaces.

Cameras in public places address fear of crime, although this may vary from country to country. Jason Ditton's research on Glasgow suggests that cameras do not necessarily have a large impact on the fear of crime. Apparently, preparedness to use the city centre has not increased and feelings of safety are no greater than before cameras were installed. The only improvement, according to this particular study, is that fear of being a victim may decrease where cameras have been installed.[46]

What is true in Britain is not necessarily true in the USA. Concerns about 'privacy' seem largely to have been reduced due to the stress on safety that surveillance cameras supposedly grant. In Fairfax, Virginia, red light violations have been reduced through surveillance cameras at intersections. New York City Police say that in one housing project crime has dropped 44 per cent since cameras were installed. Controversies continue about the displacement effect, and the potential deterrent effect, but the rate of installation continues to rise despite residual objections.[47] What concerns some researchers in the field, however, is that such methods may be flawed in important respects. As well as doubts over displacement and deterrence, questions may be raised about civil liberties and the erosion of the democratic public sphere, about the advances in surveillance technologies to include facial recognition, about the technological fix approach that may displace more natural forms of surveillance in human interaction and about approaches that are limited to symptoms rather than causes of crime.[48]

Surveillance cameras also take care of people on the move – bodies in transit – in the city. For instance, children in British Columbia on school buses, or San Francisco commuters on public transport, can expect to have their rides monitored by cameras. Hooliganism, vandalism and graffittism are the key targets of 'Silent Witness', a miniaturized, versatile, sturdily built camera, developed from the original black box that monitors the movements of car fleets, trucks and public service vehicles.[49] In an attempt to minimize the dangers of robbery, assault or harrassment lawsuits to cab drivers, taxis in the USA, Canada, Australia, New Zealand, the UK and Mexico may be fitted with systems like 'Taxicam'.[50] Whether you walk, drive or ride in the city, the chances are that your journey is captured on celluloid tape.

The police themselves are using more and more high technology equipment in surveillance. In Canada, their patrol cars increasingly resemble mobile offices, with computers, voice radios, cellphones, video cameras, radar, remote microphones, fax machines, printers and vehicle locators.[51] Police make precinct and detachment profiles to give them an overview of the territories and populations for which they are responsible. They sometimes use computerized mapping systems produced by defence departments in the USA, or other countries. High resolution satellite images may now be bought in order to examine in detail areas of the city, down to a range of as little as 1 metre. Geographic Information Services images, once used for cold war purposes, are now widely for sale.[52] Crime 'hot spots' may be identified where domestic disputes take place or where youths may congregate, and geographic profiling techniques may be used to pinpoint the likely location of criminal residences.[53] But you do not have to be a criminal to be followed. Camera systems tend to inflate stereotypes, and operators often 'follow' suspects, even where the ground of suspicion is merely hairstyle, skin colour, clothing or age.

In Toronto, police hot spots are identified not only with high crime rates, but also with locations where 'annoying behaviour' has been observed. Quite how 'annoying behaviour' is constituted is not clear, although a clue is found in who might be annoyed. As the police services board chair, Norm Gardner, explained, 'These are tourist areas and even though there might not be a lot of crime, we want to reassure tourists in all areas of the city'.[54] Many of the hot spots pinpointed in 1999 were also relatively impoverished areas – ones, in other words, that surveillant simulation would also notice in its marketing modes.

Also in the Toronto area, the world's first fully automated toll road (as it was billed) opened in 1998. Highway 407 provides an alternative route through the busiest corridor in Canada, with tolls collected either via transponders in vehicles or by video cameras scanning registration plates. The technology is developed from that used for smart bombers during the Gulf War, identifying 'target' vehicles for tolls based on the distance driven and the time of day.[55] So, you use the highway, and are billed automatically. This is what you see. What motorists do not see is the way the data are then used to create real-time simulations of road traffic time-space movement across cities – extremely valuable to planners, especially in densely travelled urban corridors.

Profit-driven planning by corporations relies on such automated data gathering. Beyond this level, however, lies the opportunity for checking driving habits, seeking criminals, enforcing payment, and so on.[56] Recognizing this, the Ontario Information and Privacy Commission held discussions with the managers of Highway 407 that made it possible for drivers to choose to maintain their anonymity while still paying their tolls electronically. Surveillance that includes identifiable records may thus be avoided by those who trouble to take advantage of the opt-out. At the same time, the police, recognizing the value of such data for crime prevention or offender apprehension, will wish to use them if they can. In Britain, John Burrows, chief constable of Essex, has argued that police should have access to toll billing or traffic monitoring data for just such purposes.

But it is not only citizens walking in the street, or driving on the urban freeways, or potential lawbreakers in suspicious places who are under surveillance in the city. As we saw in Chapter 3, employees are also subject to increased monitoring. But because employment situations are somewhat different from other urban surveillance situations they are not discussed further here. Suffice it to say that in the workplace not only cameras, but also drug testing, polygraphs, keystroke monitoring and email surveillance may occur. This makes the workplace a peculiarly intensive surveillance site. Add to this the fact that accepting some surveillance is usually the price paid for keeping one's job, thus creating a different set of ground rules, and it becomes clear that workplace surveillance really belongs in its own category.

However, while companies continue to use surveillance technologies as tools to manage workers in the workplace, the last decades of the twentieth century also saw a massive expansion of efforts to use surveillance technologies to manage consumers. Indeed, this is where, arguably, the biggest growth has occurred, as capitalist organizations have weighted their activities more decisively towards consumption processes. Here we are back with a public domain, rather than in the more tightly rule-bound workplace. Much commercial surveillance has to do with shopping malls and consumer areas in cities, which are designed to attract and seduce consumers. Such areas may be placed under video surveillance in order to indicate that they are orderly and harmonized spending areas – little downtown Disneylands.[57] The very location of shopping areas may be influenced by simulation and modelling, to show developers the most suitable sites and zones.

As well as the central shopping areas in cities, consumer surveillance also takes place in other very significant ways. One of these is what Oscar Gandy calls the 'panoptic sort'.[58] By this Gandy refers to the ways in which companies use databases containing consumer information in order the more precisely to target advertising and the other allurements to consumption. North America and much of Europe are classified by zipcodes and postal areas into social categories, based on the simple but frequently correct assumption that 'birds of a feather flock together'. By combining geodemographic data with census information, and adding to it what is known about specific spending patterns (some of which may come from 'loyalty clubs' with their saver cards) companies know exactly where to send their mailings and to make their telephone sales calls. In the UK, some potential customers for Sainsbury's Internet-based home shopping service have complained that they are excluded by not living in an appropriate postcode zone.[59] Once again, by simulating the shopping preferences of neighbourhoods before the car has left the driveway or the phone has been lifted to place an order, consumer surveillance in the city plots and plans its campaigns with military precision.

Even if you are not a resident in the city you are vulnerable to surveillance. It is not just that you will be caught in the gaze of the ubiquitous cameras, but that agencies are ready to tap into information about you and to guide you to those places where you would most enjoy being relieved of your cash. Online city guides, for instance, available on the Web, use relational databases to allow visitors or residents to choose, say, a movie they want to see, and will then suggest a suitable nearby restaurant, based on previous selections. The serendipity of street strolling is gradually replaced, for online guide users, by a system that virtually indicates where people *should* go. It is run by 'collaborative filtering' that determines in advance what your personal tastes are likely to be, and informs you as to how your simulated desires may be fulfilled.[60] Of course, holders of certain credit cards may also expect certain privileges; they go straight to the front of the line. Visitors to the Eternal City during the millennium year 2000 could use a 'pilgrim's card' with a memory chip that enabled holders to book visits to the Vatican, and that led them to restaurants and hotels. The card included data on identity, reserved hotels, medical data and travel plans.[61]

The other is surveillance via electronic commerce. In the very short time that has elapsed since the Internet took off as a site for electronic commerce, huge strides have been made. The personal computer has become a place where sale pitches are made and from which personal data is sent. The hard drive of the computer is now a repository for 'cookies', records of which sites have been visited and what choices are made as users surf the net. When a site is revisited, the record is updated, and the user is vulnerable to increased marketing pitches, personalized to the individual. Once again, it is a simulated user, the sum of Internet transactions, who is in focus, but this makes no difference to the effect. Choices are channelled and desires directed by cookies and their related agents.[62] However, it is important to note that cyberspace is essentially an urban phenomenon. Electronic commerce, despite the global promise, tends to be used fairly locally. Virtual spaces are often tied to real places, which they represent and articulate. In many ways new media capacities are used as another layer of communications within, not beyond, cities.[63]

SimCity and the real world

Are real cities coming to resemble SimCity and if so, in what ways? Surveillance is the means whereby knowledge of populations and individuals is obtained in order to minimize risks of many kinds. People provide the data, sometimes knowingly, sometimes unwittingly, as they go about their daily lives in the city. Increasingly, surveillance data are used for simulating, modelling and anticipating situations that have not yet arisen, and decisions are made on the basis of such information. Much planning, policing and marketing is based on such simulations. Moreover, agencies and organizations involved in planning often try to coordinate their activities. In Britain, for instance, town centre management initiatives and safer city programmes bring together those responsible for city centres and urban spaces.[64] Risk management is fed by surveillance.[65]

Surveillance is generated by the need for tokens of trustworthiness in increasingly private and privatized societies. The police officer does not know that I have taken a driver's test, so I have to show my licence. The store owner cannot tell by looking at me that I have money in the bank, so I have to produce a credit card. Mobile and flexible lifestyles are individualized, and are ones in which more relationships are fleeting, transitory and inconsequential. While privacy may be seen by some as the need caused by greater surveillance, privacy is actually part of the problem. And the more people are categorized and classified by surveillance systems, the more they are sorted and split up into segments of the population, with whom they have some traits in common. Surveillance often appears to be interested only in those fragmented interests, not in the whole person, let alone the whole community or city. At the same time, the intentions of some surveillance programmes and devices are positive. Safety, security and convenience are sought through surveillance systems, which is why – when we are aware of them – we collude with them so readily.

It comes as no surprise, then, that inequality is basic to such surveillance cities. Some can afford to pay for minimized risks by insuring themselves against them. Others are more likely to be vulnerable to risk just because they do not have the means to pay. Thus, in answering the question about SimCity and the real world, the social science fiction literature tends towards a dystopian 'yes'. The real world does increasingly resemble SimCity. In the worst case, *Blade Runner* type situations of urban decay and social exclusion privilege the powerful rich and marginalize the poor, relatively immobile and choiceless. Violence and vicious cycles of deprivation are bred, only to be met by more punitive and panoptic measures.

The city is divided by simulated surveillance mechanisms into zones, with electronic and armoured barriers between them. The Disneyfied city centre shopping malls become no-go areas for those classified as not belonging, by virtue of their credit ratings or their ethnic background. As Roger Burrows puts it, 'Buildings themselves become increasingly sentient as computerized systems of recognition include the new rich and exclude the new poor. The new apartheid becomes very much a technological matter as the homeless and poor are channelled away from the air conditioned virtual environments of the geat middle mass of the population'.[66]

If surveillance does not actually create inequalities in the city, it certainly tends to reinforce or accentuate them. The city in which mobility is high, where strangers encounter each other, can be a place of stimulation, of excitement and of the cross-fertilization of customs, styles, ideas and practices. But it is also a place of potential danger. Meeting others who are not the same as you may be a great source of mutually enriching conversation, but it may equally be a situation that inspires fear generated by the perceived threat of 'otherness'. The capacity to cope with difference[67] is challenged in the city, all the more so in the multicultural metropolitan areas of today's global cities than in those about which Georg Simmel classically wrote in the early twentieth century.[68] The society of strangers, accentuated in the city, was for Simmel a situation in which relationships could both flourish and fragment.

As I suggested above, both the purveyors of the SimCity vision of urban planning, with its great faith in technoscience, *and* the prophets of doom who see only dystopian disaster looming in the simulated surveillance city, seem sometimes to have lost touch with the real world. It may be, of course, that a participatory version of SimCity, that is online to all citizens, may be one way of deflecting the worst case scenarios. The 'Iperbole' system in Bologna is just such an experiment, although it seems that, as with a number of such initiatives, several problems have yet to be overcome in realizing the potential for involvement of citizens in virtual planning.[69] It may also be the case that the full effects of social divisions that are exacerbated by the simulated digital mapping of the city to reveal prime consumer locations and police hot spots, to preserve the past in heritage parks or to extend consumption in yet more malls, will have to produce more dire social consequences before action is taken to prevent their recurrence – by which time it may be too late.

The worsening of social divisions, paradoxically through surveillance for risk management, is one negative outcome of SimCity as surveillant simulation. It is one that calls for a renewed sense of what social justice in the city might comprise. But the difficulty here is that such ideas are increasingly hard to come by. Because surveillance is a mode of social orchestration that operates, not according to some shared standards of morality and justice, but according to merely utilitarian norms, it tends to bypass the language of justice.[70] It contributes to the removal of life situations from moral scrutiny. It works by means of sorting mechanisms that are just that – mechanisms. Like bureaucracies, they tend to exclude personal responsibility, feeling, emotion or moral judgement. Yet they work all too effectively, despite their self-referential character. They create digital personae, complementary computer selves that may not be recognized by, yet profoundly affect the life chances of, their human namesakes. And as the sorting mechanisms of surveillant simulation continue to be used to manage risks, those human namesakes are more and more at the mercy of a myriad of agencies that, they must fondly assume, have their interests at heart.

More and more, then, we all live in SimCity – urban spaces that are simulated to appear real, but are not; and urban spaces where surveillance is simulated so that it is *all too real*. Feedback loops ensure that knowledge of what we do in the simulated spaces is reappropriated – sometimes before we act – to anticipate our actions, channel our desires and constrain our deviance. SimCity in the real world is a digitized means of social orchestration. All too often it is visually impaired when it comes to justice and insensitive to human-scale needs and responses. It may turn out that it serves to dull such responses.

Things do not have to be this way. Jane Jacobs, the rightly celebrated analyst and critic of the city, observed that peaceful relations in the city are best maintained by people themselves, managing their differences through an 'intricate, almost unconscious network of voluntary controls and standards'.[71] What sort of security do cameras and the other apparatuses of urban electronic grids provide? What else can they provide? As Jeremy Seabrook says, 'Security, if it arises from anywhere, must arise from the tenderness and vigilance of people committed to the daily protection of one another'.[72] SimCity or electronic amnesia? The real world of embodied persons remains to be retrieved in the city.

Body parts and probes

As Palestinian workers whose jobs are in Israel cross the border from the Gaza Strip each day, they are required to run their hands over a scanner and present a matching smartcard. The unique handprint determines the eligibility of certain Palestinians to work in Israel and is also used to check that they return to the Gaza Strip after work. The decision to use biometrics, or body measurement, was made by Israeli officials in March 1999 and it is symptomatic of a trend towards its more general use.[1] On its own a handprint would be a slow and cumbersome way of carrying out such checks. But yoked with an image database, biometrics becomes a significant surveillance tool.

Beyond biometrics, another form of body surveillance is also gaining ground rapidly, based on genetics. In health care, policing and the workplace, DNA data is increasingly sought. As a weapon in the struggle with disease, for example, it is believed to hold tremendous powers of prediction and prevention. But the same techniques may also be used with less positive outcomes. The 1997 film *GATTACA* depicts a state of genetic apartheid that distinguishes between the 'Valids' who are permitted to enjoy all educational and professional opportunities and the 'Invalids' who form a sort of biological underclass. Continual genetic surveillance of employees' hair, skin, blood and urine at the GATTACA corporation ensures that the social sorting is effective and, in principle, unchallengeable. A surprising degree of conformity to the system is portrayed in the film. How far this is mere fiction is part of what I want to explore here.

In these two ways, along with others such as drug and alcohol testing, what I call body surveillance is rapidly becoming a key component of surveillance societies. A Russian proverb says that humans may be thought of as 'body, soul and passport' and a few years ago I suggested this be updated to 'body, soul and credit card'.[2] The point I was then making is that documenting individual identity underwent a shift in the twentieth century, from predominantly print-based information required by the state to the proliferation of electronically-stored data required by commercial businesses. In this chapter, however, we shall consider what might be thought of as a return to the 'body and soul' definition, although the latter has little or no significant role.

How does this fit with the 'disappearing bodies' theory? Surely the argument thus far depends on the increasing invisibility of bodies, not their presence? The answer to this preliminary puzzle is that embodied persons are no more in view in body surveillance than they are in the world of digital surveillance. Abstract data pertaining to or derived from bodies is all that is sought for biometric- or DNA-based surveillance. Consciousness, souls, sociality, or whatever else may be thought to make up human beings are actually absent from the requirements of surveillance as understood here. The body is simply a source of data even though it is thought to reveal much about the individual.[3]

Body surveillance does not represent a contraction of demands for identification. It is the co-opting of the body itself as a means of identification and of predicting behaviour or conditions. As far as identification is concerned, some subtle shifts have taken place. From checking identities by what one has, such as a passport, and by what one knows, such as a personal identification number, a fresh factor has emerged: checking by what one *is* – body parts.[4] Those intricate lines that form a fingerprint, the geometry of hands, thumbs or fingers, and the patterns of cones and rods on the retina are the commonest candidates for body surveillance. To these may be added voice modulations, images of the face and genetic clues that may be gleaned from body fluids. Such identification relies on electronic databases and still relates in part to the state, but its implications take us well beyond the world of passports and credit cards.

In the last part of the twentieth century the body became, once again, a source as well as a site of surveillance. I say, 'once again' because there is nothing intrinsically new about the body being used in this way. Bodies have always been in view, one way or another. Over 100 years ago, criminal anthropometry claimed that body shapes, especially the head, could spontaneously reveal the unlawful proclivities of the person. Today, the development of new biometric technologies means that the body itself can be directly scrutinized and interrogated as a provider of surveillance data. Information for identification may now be extracted from the body that can override the person's own claims to a particular identity. The body has now been reappropriated on a new plane of systematization for the abstract data it contains.

Data originating in the body is used for the same kinds of purpose as more conventional modes of surveillance, to sort and classify, to determine eligibility, to qualify and to disqualify, to include and to exclude. The body need no longer merely be watched to track its behaviour or its whereabouts. Surveillance now goes under the skin to monitor, check and test in order to identify and to classify. The subtle shift is one of technological sophistication in body surveillance and its broadened use from potentially criminal to general populations of citizens and consumers. In an effort to ensure more accurate and foolproof identification, attention turns to body data. But not only this. Body data may also have predictive power, especially when DNA is added to the equation.

The body from site to source

From the birth of modernity, the body achieved new prominence as a site of surveillance. Bodies could be rationally ordered through classification in order to socialize them within the emerging new nation state. Bodies tended to be distrusted as sensual and irrational, and thus in need of taming, of disciplinary shaping to new purposes.[5] By associating a name or, later, a number with the body, each person could be distinguished from the next. Thus, if for example a name appears on a voters' list and if an embodied person shows up to record a vote, the citizen can be recorded as having voted, after which that person may not vote again. Similarly, citizens of modern nation states are required to carry all manner of personal identifiers that ensure their smooth passage through benefits offices or customs and immigration departments. Papers and cards are part of the essential personal paraphernalia of modern life.[6]

In these cases, however, the means of identification is external to the body. Indeed, the volatile and unpredictable body is put in its place by the cognitive focus on the name or the number. This situation still obtained during the period of large scale bureaucratic computerization from the 1960s onwards. Although at some point it might be necessary to ask persons to identify themselves verbally, the trend set in train with computerization was towards the automated cross-checking of identity. Trustworthy third party sources could be enlisted to ensure that the individuated person was indeed eligible for benefits or qualified to drive a car. Thus a web of first, documentary, and then digital identification systems could locate and distinguish individuals when required. It was often almost incidental that a body was also associated with the person whose identity was being checked. The number and name were what really mattered.

But computerization was to bring other issues in its train, especially as communication and information technologies made possible the almost instantaneous transfer of documents and financial, medical or other sensitive information. The ease with which these can be intercepted by third parties has generated what the US Public Interest Research Group calls 'identity theft', said to be the 'fastest growing crime in the nation'.[7] It occurs in various ways, including at automated bank machines, through email that uses others' addresses, by sending false messages on the Internet or by breaking into computer systems to gain access to personal data. Various forms of encryption that provide digital signatures or pseudonyms have proliferated as means of combatting such 'identity theft'. As I mentioned earlier they are often referred to collectively as 'privacy enchancing technologies'.

The quest for accurancy and precision continues, however, and now other new technologies are enlisted as adjuncts to the computer. Prominent among these are techniques known generically as 'biometrics' because they refer to measuring or monitoring parts of the body. In 1998, for instance, the Nation-wide Building Society in the UK tested iris-scanning equipment at some of their automated bank machines.[8] The concentrated wealth of features in the iris makes it an ideal candidate for automated identification. But the human fingerprint also remains popular as a means of identification, especially since the capacity of digitized print images has grown greater, and costs have fallen. Its uses range from a traffic control system in the Shaanxi Province of central China, where smartcards holding drivers' records are verified by stored fingerprints,[9] to a 'BioMouse' that uses fingerprints as passwords into laptops or computer systems.[10] Hand scanners serve similar purposes, for examples allowing only authorized users to work out in the University of Montreal's athletic complex.[11]

Several significant issues are raised by this. It is important to chart the back-ground to body surveillance in various kinds of documentary and digital iden-tification. A social historical account serves to show how the new biometric technologies are given their chance. Although enabled by computerization, body surveillance represents a merging of techniques not previously thought of as 'information' technologies. Despite their relative novelty, however, these new techniques are appearing in all surveillance sectors. They are seen in government administration and in policing, but also in healthcare, the workplace and consumer spheres. In each sector, moreover, it is important to examine the implications of body surveillance for reconfigured relations of time and space, for the boundaries between the public and the private, and for the interactions between technology and society. In a world of identity politics and risk management, surveillance is turning decisively to the body as a 'document' for identification, and as a source of data for prediction.

Identity, identification and modernity

Recognizing a person's separate identity depends on three things: a body, a memory, and rights and responsibilities. Erving Goffman, in his classic work on *The Presentation of Self in Everyday Life*,[12] stressed the importance of the face and the body for recognition and everyday encounters. A person is an ineluctably social being; individuals are 'embodied social agents'.[13] We re-quire the recognition of others to be identified as individuals.

But the body does not suffice on its own. We must also give an account of ourselves that confirms our identity, and must also be committed to that story.[14] This authorizes our past as truly ours. Beyond this, a person's iden-tity is also bound up with social expectation; agents are responsible for their actions. A growing emphasis of the modern world, paralleling the focus on responsibility, has been to attribute rights to individuals to which they or others may appeal in law.

In early modernity, as Nicholas Abercrombie and others point out, the long drawn-out discovery of the individual had contradictory consequences: 'As individuals become more separate and different, they are more recognizably unique. In turn, uniqueness and identity are closely connected and the identification of individuals makes their control that much easier'.[15] How did this happen? The coming of modernity meant that individuals were granted an increasing range of rights, starting with civil rights before the law, and moving to the political rights of citizens and social rights to welfare. But to obtain these rights, bureaucratic structures required careful scrutiny of the grounds of entitlement according to consistent rules. So people had to be registered, and their personal details filed, which of course paradoxically facilitated their increased surveillance. Freedom from one set of constraints – those of feudal societies – provided opportunities for new forms of surveillance and control.

By the last quarter of the twentieth century extensive systems of mass surveillance had been established throughout all liberal capitalist societies, each of which depended on the documentary identification of individuals. In the late 1970s, for example, James Rule and others examined the uses of six of the most widely-held personal documents in the USA: birth certificates, driver's licences, social security cards, passports, bank books and credit cards.[16] These documents provided vital links between the individuals holding them and the organizations issuing them. Just how document-dependent individuals become is dramatized when something goes wrong. We all know how awkward and inconvenient it is when such a document is lost or destroyed. From the organizational viewpoint, certainty is enhanced, when dealing with large numbers of otherwise anonymous individuals. Which motorist can renew a licence, and which is wanted for violations? Which welfare claimant is a genuine case, and which is double-dipping? Which consumer can purchase this appliance, and which is liable for outstanding debt? The documents will tell.

Rule and his associates noted a trend occurring in the 1970s: the move from self-identification to direct checking. Birth certificates, the production of which is a routine requirement for other documents, are easily obtained by fraudulent means. Yet they still retain some aura of credibility despite their lack of solid warrant. Where credibility is felt to be lacking, however, organizations could increasingly resort to direct checking. Rule found that independent outside sources such as credit bureaux would be used for credit card applications, police records and driver registries for driver's licences, or immigration databases to check passport presentation at borders. Rule concluded that 'The perfection of direct checking within and among organizations is the wave of the future in mass surveillance',[17] and so it turned out. Increased computerization made direct checking easier and more efficient, even though individual agents are often still warned at some stage that they should not provide false information.

Today, surveillance influences populations in all technologically advanced societies, although the strength of influence differs according to social factors. The black single mother in the American inner city will find her life much more closely and punitively scrutinized than her counterpart who is an affluent divorcee in the suburbs. 'Dataveillance' is now a taken for granted aspect of modern life as new configurations of computing with telecommunications capacities have become available.[18] Cross-checking is made simpler through dispersed and networked computer systems. With a range of personal data systems, remote from each other but connected electronically, and a consistent mode of identification, dataveillance can flourish, 'feeding on itself', as Rule would say.

However, dataveillance did not proliferate just because new technologies became available. As Colin Bennett notes, these practices were 'especially eagerly embraced by governments with neo-conservative agendas'.[19] Arguably it was just such choices, emerging from the new political economy of the 1990s, that lay behind the development of the technologies, including their much hyped 'convergence'.[20] The shorthand 'information age' sums up neatly some key characteristics of contemporary societies but it is the implication of new technologies within the current restructuring of capitalism that gives that age its unique dynamic.[21] That same restructuring also demands greater attention to detail as competition and awareness of risk grows. Such details include knowledge of production processes and of consumption which is gleaned through surveillance.

A key aspect of this restructuring is risk management, a mode of operation that finds echoes in several surveillance sectors. Police are just one of several agencies that collect and classify personal data on behalf of other institutions in order to minimize risk.[22] But while the knowledge sought may in a sense be personal, it is really only individual, and relates to risk at that. That is, the knowledge is inevitably abstracted from the flesh and blood person who relates to others.[23] In order more exactly to determine the nature and extent of risk, more and more precise knowledge is sought. To decide questions of eligibility, or even of guilt, the risk profile becomes crucially important. And to work properly, for most purposes it must also be attached to an accurate identity.

It is thus risk management practices within restructuring capitalist societies that generate the quest for more foolproof, and fraudproof, methods of establishing identity. This is how the body is 'brought back in'. Once it was merely the existence of unique bodies that was part of the rationale for individuation, and for stabilizing difference. But now, for example through fingerprinting, other signs of bodily distinctiveness are appealed to. Direct checking from the 1970s owards became a matter of verification by a third-party organization. This was done digitally by methods such as data matching once dataveillance regimes were electronically established in the 1980s.

From the 1990s, however, it became clear that direct checking would take on yet another meaning: access to tissues, fluids, images and patterns available from the body itself. Just as direct checking across agencies avoided confrontation with the embodied agent, so direct checking of data produced from within bodies also requires no access to the speech or the memory of the person. It is, once again, abstracted from the person.

Body surveillance technologies

To gain entry to a secure or sensitive place one conventionally has to use a password to prove identity and eligibility. Some coded message, memorized by the intending entrant, is repeated at the threshold before entry is permitted. From the late twentieth century, magnetic stripes and barcoded cards were been commonly used for such purposes, whether to enter the laboratory, the prison or the bank vault. The emergence of body surveillance technologies, however, dispenses with cryptic words and numeric codes held in human or machine memories. Some part of the physical body (eye, hand, finger, face, voice) is presented to the verification machine. Another level of coding, beyond words and numbers, and relying neither on memory or on the need to produce a card, turns the body into a password.[24] Apart from the ways in which this may (re)constitute the body as a text, it is a reminder of how access and inclusion, and the distribution of entitlements or powers, may now depend on the display of some body feature.

The machine that confirms identities is usually some form of computerized scanner, which checks the biological feature against the digital file that contains exactly the same characteristics. Thus inmates in Cook County, Illinois, submit to retinal scanning every time they go from jail to court and back. Welfare recipients in Connecticut and Pennsylvania have their identities matched to their records by finger imaging. Frequent travellers from Montana to Canada may use an automated voice verification system run by the US Immigration and Naturalization Service to cross the border. According to Davis, in 1997 there were already over 10,000 locations in the USA, from bank vaults to blood banks, where one had to present a body part to go through a door or gain access to a file.[25] Although commercial sources exaggerate the significance of each new product, biometric measures are not merely science fiction. Enough evidence exists to indicate that these modes of identification are becoming increasingly important.

The use of body parts or processes for identification and surveillance purposes is not new. Fingerprinting has been carried out routinely for many decades, as has the use of polygraphs or 'lie detectors' which were first used in the USA in the 1930s. As Steven Nock argues, such techniques come in a long tradition of 'ordeals' that are meted out to establish or maintain reputations.[26] However, these body surveillance technologies are very limited in scope. And they are not always acceptable, for instance in a court of law.[27] They are used, typically, in cases where suspicion about activities or doubt about identity already exists. They relate to a concept of justice that relies on testimony and evidence to determine individual guilt, not one that routinely places whole populations under 'categorical suspicion'.[28] Body surveillance is consistent with the emergence of a behavioural approach that cares more about the prevention of certain behaviours than their causes, or the social conditions that may help give rise to them.[29]

A consistent feature of contemporary body surveillance technologies is their computer dependence. In the USA, for example, the FBI (Federal Bureau of

Investigation) began in 1990 to convert its 40 million fingerprint cards and crime history records into digitized records as a part of its ongoing computerization programme.[30] As computer power grows, so more applications, previously beyond the reach of automation, become possible. It makes sense from the point of view of surveillance studies to consider certain biotechnologies as information technologies.[31] This is partly because computerization provides a common digital language for generating, storing, retrieving, processing and transmitting data from different technological fields, especially in this case from biotechnology. But more profoundly, when it comes to genetic information the connections are even closer. Decoding, manipulation and reprogramming are central to genetic sciences.

The Human Genome Project, to take the most significant example, is committed to nothing less than the creation of a vast genetic database that determines the location and chemical sequence of all genes. It is an international and collaborative gene-mapping scheme of major scope accompanied by extravagant promises. Its proponents claim that early this century medical science will receive a massive boost in its capacities to predict, prevent and treat genetic diseases. Because the project's huge surveillance implications relate to both positive medical potential and undesirable social control, most research in the area has a built-in ethical research component.

Some so-called 'genomics' companies see their task as using genetic information to increase the production of certain drugs. Others, however, such as Incyte Pharmaceuticals in Palo Alto, California, or Celera, in Rockville Maryland, sell only data that others use to identify potential drug targets (persons, in other words), depending for their predictions on massive computer power. Along with other agencies that have become more concerned with anticipation and pre-emption, enabled by new surveillance technologies, the emergent health care paradigm moves steadily from 'detect and treat' to 'predict and prevent', with specific therapies aimed at the causes of disease.[32]

Through mapping human genes, detailed information may be obtained about biologically determined features of individuals.[33] The biosurveillance made possible by this relates to the likely course of individuals' physical and psychological development. Such scientific foreknowledge of potential life courses is thus of great interest especially to employers and insurance companies. They wish to use such data as a means of discrimination between candidates or clients, based on genetic testing and screening. As we shall see, the combination of rising employer health insurance costs and the increasing reliability of genetic testing is likely to encourage the development of such biosurveillance on a large scale. Once again the body becomes the password. With a genetic code, entry or exclusion may have very serious social as well as personal consequences.

What sort of social consequences? When genetic tests are run in organizational settings, the contexts themselves may produce further inequalities. Some research in the USA concludes that attitudes to genetic testing vary by social class, among other things. Working-class people, for instance, are more likely to conform to organizational policies requiring genetic tests than are their middle-class counterparts.[34] Similarly, when genetic testing becomes part of public policy, it may have negative as well as positive consequences for certain groups. In Canada, where interest in genetic testing may be found in health care, in the justice system and in employment situations, First Nations groups may end up being at risk in both senses. It is well known that such groups are often considered least healthy, are subject to higher incarceration rates than other groups, and are most dependent on social assistance. While the discovery of a genetic link between First Nations people and a specific type of diabetes promises more rapid and appropriate treatment,[35] the dangers of genetic determinism or genetic apartheid for such groups are also palpable.

The drive for perfect knowledge, which includes information about future developments and not merely about past histories, is fostered by risk management discourses, which are in turn the stuff of which insurance companies are made. Restructuring capitalism, and the technological facilitation of fusion between different kinds of information, permits surveillance to move beyond paper files and digitized documents and to infiltrate the body itself. The body, in turn, is treated like a text. It becomes a pass*word*, providing a document for decoding. But texts are best understood in contexts. To illustrate this one may examine body surveillance as it appears across the whole range of surveillance sectors.

Body surveillance in different sectors

Body surveillance may be found in all social sectors. Two things should be noted about this. The first is that the very notion of sectors sounds rather watertight when in fact they are increasingly porous. Deregulation and networking mean that surveillance data leaks with greater ease from one sector to another, making them less discrete. Nonetheless, the sectors may still be considered as existing at different points along a spectrum from more to less coercive power. Categorical suspicion may classify subjects at the sharp end of, say, policing, while categorical seduction is more likely to operate at the other, corporate, end.

The second point is that by examining the ways in which biometrics are actually used in each sector, some dangers of technological determinism may be avoided. The tendency of studies that focus on the technological is to accept the hype produced by designers and manufacturers, which exaggerates both the use and the usefulness of novel techniques. The fact that some companies are testing biometrics that use body odour today[36] does not mean that we shall be passing through smell scanners tomorrow. A survey of the current surveillance uses of biometrics shows that the humble fingerprint – now digitally scanned and stored – is still the technique of choice, although in the workplace genetic screening and testing is gaining ground.

During 1997, the Canadian province of Ontario started to follow the lead of states south of the border in easing the way for increased government use

of biometric technologies. The Social Assistance Reform Act[37] allows muni-
cipalities and the province to identify welfare recipients using biometric data.
The aim was to ensure that applicants are only registered once, that when
they claim, their identity can be authenticated, and also to permit applicants,
recipients, spouses and adult dependants to gain access to their records.[38] It
was estimated at the time that metropolitan Toronto could save $4.5 million
a year in reduced welfare caseloads, and a further $2.7 million in reduced
cheque processing and other administration.[39] Of course, a neo-conservative
agenda is also visible here; one that desires to demonstrate that it has no time
for the feckless or the fraudulent. The provincial premier, Mike Harris, expressed his hope that schemes would be established to consolidate health cards,
driver's licences and other goverment identification on one card, based on
finger-scanning technology.

Rather like supermarket checkouts, such scanners have glass plates on which
the finger is placed. A high resolution optical image is caught by a camera
and is then converted into a template containing a mathematical equation.
For user verification or identification the system takes a live scan of the
fingerprint, comparing it with the stored template. As long as the finger scan
is encrypted in different ways for different uses – say, drivers' records and
health records – then the same scan may be used for different purposes without the danger of records being shared between agencies.

Such reassurances do not always satisfy those closest to welfare recipients
who argue that fingerprinting of any sort is too reminiscent of the way that
criminals are treated. A further concern is that if biometric methods become
universally popular then the only way of ensuring that biometric identification
is carried at all times will be to install the chip that bears its codes under the
skin of the individual.[40] Because of the already proven use of fingerprinting
for law enforcement, and because of the high cost and potential inaccuracies
still experienced with some other methods (such as retinal scans or face
recognition), fingerprinting is likely to be seen as one of the best biometric
options available.

It cannot be denied that many if not most biosurveillance methods develop
from the policing and security sectors. This is why when government administration or commercial organizations such as MasterCard proposed the use of
fingerprint scanning they have to deal with the question of stigma. The FBI
spent $640 million on 'Afis' (automated fingerprint identification system),
which was completed in 1999 with 43 million records.[41] But some countries
are quicker to adopt biometrics than others, and some techniques catch on in
one country but not another. Higher levels of concern about security, and
greater fear of crime, may help to account for the faster take-up rate of digitized fingerprinting in the USA than, say, in Canada.[42] Equally, the more
intensive use of video surveillance via closed-circuit television in the UK may
explain why face recognition technologies are being developed more rapidly
there than in some other countries.

So, while banks such as Citicorp may test face recognition technologies[43]
their development is more likely to take place in law enforcement contexts.

Britain is a world leader in this field, as photographic technologies have been added to the more familiar convergence between computing and telecommunications. The British Home Office, Police Foundation and chain store Marks and Spencer's have each funded research to produce reliable automatic visual recognition of suspects.[44] Limited systems are already in use, such as the 'Football Intelligence System' in Greater Manchester. Information and photographic records of suspects and offenders associated with soccer violence is collated such that pictures of 'likely suspects' can be drawn from the database. The National Criminal Intelligence Service database used photophones to transmit digitized photographs of suspected hooligans to participating football grounds in the 1996 European championship. Similar systems are being developed for use at Sydney International Airport in Australia.[45]

Other techniques that cross the border from policing and law enforcement to the economic private sector include genetic testing. The use of DNA samples from suspected rapists and murderers is well know, and has led to a number of convictions and re-trials. Evidence of criminal activity of involvement may be obtained from DNA samples in plucked hair, blood and saliva that match each unique individual. The American CODIS (Combined DNA Index System), is a national DNA identification system. Fifteen or more states are now using collected samples to add to the CODIS databank. In Canada and the UK, too, such samples may be collected without consent, as DNA profiling becomes routine.[46] Whatever might be said about the diminution of due process, or the failure to invoke rights not to self-incriminate (the right to silence) in such cases, the fact remains that DNA testing by police is relatively uncontroversial. The same may not be said for genetic tests and screens in the workplace.

Employers, wishing to minimize risk, use a variety of body surveillance techniques in the workplace. These include random testing for drugs and alcohol, especially in North American workplaces,[47] as well as genetic screening and monitoring. They may use genetic screening to determine susceptibility to disease – such as breast, ovarian, colon, thyroid, eye, kidney and skin cancers, or Huntington's disease – among employees, or to check levels of damage from exposure to hazardous materials at work. But genetic discrimination could result on the basis of such tests. At the same time, fear of such discrimination could discourage some people from undergoing tests from which they might benefit. This points up once more the all too frequently forgotten fact that surveillance has two faces. The same genetic test may be the means of personal benefit, say, enabling the person to seek treatment for a medical condition before it is too advanced, and of personal discrimination, blocking the path to promotion or retention.

The desire to control the workforce is far from new, of course, just as concerns with aspects of the body and its condition are not new either. But during the twentieth century technical and bureaucratic types of control have become less effective, which is one reason for the turn towards 'personal control'. An additional reason is the perceived failure of socializing institutions such as family and school. What is new is to see the workplace as the locus for social control over personality and health, via pre-hire screening, drug testing, polygraph testing, stress management, wellness programmes, AIDS testing and programmes for alcoholism, weight reduction and gambling addiction.[48] This is the background to the use of DNA evidence in workplace body tests, and also represents a blurring of the boundary between state sponsored and private forms of social control. In many cases, such as urinalysis for drug testing, part of the purpose is indeed to produce the 'perfect worker', but another part is to make a symbolic moral gesture to the public, as to where true standards are to be found.[49]

Controversy breaks out when genetic testing starts to be used as a condition of employment, and it is against such discrimination that legal protection has been sought in the USA and elsewhere. In the late 1990s Lawrence Berkeley National Laboratory in California was successfully sued by seven employees who learned that blood and urine obtained during pre-employment medical examinations had been tested for syphilis, sickle cell anemia (black applicants), and pregnancy (female applicants). The appeals court ruled that such tests required the consent of the employee, unless they have a direct bearing on one's ability to do the job.[50] Further controversy surrounds the accuracy of genetic testing. After all, genes alone do not determine an individual's future health. Diet, exercise, psychosocial factors and economic class may affect an individual's health almost as much as genetics.[51]

If in the workplace the capitalist corporation intensifies its body surveillance in an attempt to perfect the worker, in the market-place the consumer is increasingly subject to biometrics, a process that is stimulated particularly by the projected growth of electronic commerce. While the potential for electronic commerce has been clear for some time, the relative lack of security – especially of identification – has proved a major deterrent for some. But not only burgeoning electronic commerce is behind the quest for biometric identifiers. Risk management in general lies behind many attempts to ensure biometrically that identification of clients and customers is as accurate and as efficient as possible.

While fingerprint-based biometrics are, understandably, still prevalent in government administration and in policing, the situation is much more volatile in the private sector. Here, fingerprint biometrics are not unknown – MasterCard is moving to such a system to combat credit card fraud[52] – but other methods are more widespread. While genetic profiling and screening is perhaps the fastest growing (and the most controversial) form of body surveillance in the workplace, in its present state of development it is unlikely to become popular in the market-place.

In the commercial, consumer sector a range of biometrics is vying for pre-eminence, and none is yet a clear winner. Indeed, competition will probably ensure that this situation will continue for some time, at least until some standards have been established. The first commercial biometric, a hand scanner used in a Wall Street firm to monitor employee attendance, was introduced in 1974,[53] but it was only in the 1990s that the techniques improved and the prices fell sufficiently to make them commercially viable. Lotus employees pass through a hand scanner to pick up their children from day care, and Coca-Cola uses hand scanners to ensure that only identified employees punch their time cards.[54]

The most widely used commercial biometric is the handkey[55] which is in use for frequent travellers in the New York and Toronto airports at immigration desks, and was the means of controlling the access of 65,000 athletes and their teams to the Olympic Village in Atlanta in 1996. Despite some negative responses, biometrics based on fingerprints are also in use commercially, including the so-called BioMouse, used for securing access to computers. Single fingers, or all fingers and thumbs, can be scanned in, scrambled, reduced and stored, ready for use each time the authorized person wishes to use the machine. Systems such as this are likely to prove popular because they can also be used for remote log-in, ID card validation, electronic signature and financial transaction authorization.[56]

The eye is another key body part suitable for biometrics. Retinal scans are the most accurate identifiers, but because of their expense and their slightly awkward use they tend to be favoured mainly by governments. The CIA (Central Intelligence Agency), for instance, uses retinal scanners along with voiceprints in its top security computer vault in Langley, Virginia. The person has to lean over and place his or her face on a bar close to the machine which passes a red light beam across the eye. Iris scans, on the other hand, are favoured for automated bank machines partly because they dispense with positioning devices and beams. As the customer approaches, video cameras zoom in to identify the form as a person, and then fix the person's coordinates. From a metre away an eye image is taken to be matched – in two or three seconds – with the digitally encoded iris image on file.[57] OKI Electric Industry, Japan, and NCR Knowledge Lab in London, UK are among those testing iris scanning devices.

Movement, action and risk

The body has become not only a site of surveillance but a source of surveillance data. The practice of locating, tracking and controlling bodies is as old as history, although it was routinized and intensified by the disiplines of modernity. The idea of checking identities by reference to unique features – above all, faces – is equally ancient, although only in modern times have distinguishing characteristics such as fingerprints become important for verifying identity. Beyond identification, as we have seen, surveillance seeks data from bodies themselves. This may be genetic or it may relate to tests for drug and alcohol abuse. Today, different aspects of body surveillance are becoming increasingly significant at the same time, which suggests that they may be related. Looking at movement, action and risk shows how.

First, modern societies are marked by mobility, which means that bodies are on the move. Today's transportation enables people to travel, by transit systems across the city, and by airline systems around the world. People travel for work and for pleasure, in the tourist delights of the rich and in the tragic displacements of refugees. Mobility means different things to people in different social groups. Travel is experienced differently by the urban commuter in their air-conditioned car on the freeway than the low-wage earner who waits in the rain for a crowded bus to get to work. Such mobility also means that we tend to interact more and more with strangers, people with whom we have no real relationship, who do not know who we are or if they can trust us. So symbols of the stable self, such as driver's licences, credit cards, passports or identity papers, have to be presented to prove ourselves. The society of strangers requires tokens of trust.[58]

As Simmel (1971) observed, a delicate dialectic is set up between remoteness and intimacy within the society of strangers and this is accentuated in contemporary conditions. Each token of trust now connects with others in a web of identification and credential surveillance systems. Such systems serve to keep tabs on those moving bodies and to ensure that only authorized bodies enter certain rooms, cross certain borders, claim certain benefits or travel on certain highways or airlines. They are a means of social control, social orchestration and social influence. But actual moving bodies are not the only things to be caught in the electronic eye. An increasing proportion of significant interaction today is bodyless, mediated above all by electronic means. This is how the two kinds of body surveillance come to be connected.

The more other means of mediating social relationships appear, the more the signs of surveillance appear with them as well. What worked to coordinate and control bodies in conventional time and space can be transposed into the virtual world of 'cyberspace'. This newer sphere of transactions, and thus of flows of information and power, is now a further site of surveillance. As Paul Virilio says, here 'people can't be separated by physical obstacles or by temporal distances. With the interfacing of computer terminals and videomonitors, distinctions of *here* and *there* no longer mean anything'.[59] But it is precisely in those channels that carry the flows of information that precision is increasingly required. They are too porous for cyberspace to be secure, hence the quest of privacy enchancing technologies and of body surveillance to keep identities intact.

Second, consider the category of action. By this, I refer back to my introductory comments on personal identity as being a matter of recogizing a unique body, of gaining access to memory and of according responsibilities and rights to the person. Body surveillance reduces identity questions to what can be found in the text of the body itself. It bypasses the acting subjects, who may wish to explain themselves, or to put things in a longer historical context, by appealing only to the speechless 'truth' that DNA samples or handscans can provide. It is data from the object of the body rather than speech from the acting subject that is to be relied on in the last analysis. Good reasons for using body surveillance may be produced, showing that criminals may more easily be apprehended or that fraud may be reduced in commerce. But body surveillance should also be viewed as part of wider social trends.

Ontario's information and privacy commissioner, Ann Cavoukian, advocates biometric encryption for secure identification, for instance in health information networks. She points to the paradox that biometrics is a sinister surveillance threat if it is identifiable, but when encrypted becomes a 'protector of privacy'.[60] Thus the interests of both individuals and organizations are served. Individuals can keep their privacy through the anonymity of encryption and organizations can be assured of the authenticity of the individuals they conduct business with. Few would wish to quarrel with this argument as it stands. It does not mean, however, that organizations are any less distrustful of the individuals they deal with, or that such individuals are any less concerned to guard their privacy. It is, after all, because of the quest for privacy within the society of strangers that tokens of trust are required in the first place.

The choice to take surveillance through the threshold of the skin and inside the physical body may raise privacy questions. Are our truly private parts now within the body rather than on its surface? But it also has to be seen in the context of a new behaviourism that treats the body as an authoritative text. In the quest for more and knowledge to combat risk, body surveillance appears as a worthy source. It promises to offer not only detail of what has happened in the past – how many times previously this person has entered this building or has made that transaction – but also of what will happen in the future. Risk discourses are especially concerned with knowledge of the future. As Ulrich Beck says, the 'centre of risk consciousness lies not in the present but *in the future*'.[61] Thus body surveillance, above all that which uses DNA, appears as the natural next wave. This is not merely the perfect match, sought so assiduously by those obsessed with identification, but the dynamic match, that holds histories and simulated futures for comparison and checking.

The result is that body surveillance takes its place as part of a more general transformation of the ways social activities and human agency are understood. In the workplace, it is no longer merely one's qualifications, aptitude for the job or personal bearing at interview that counts. A 53-year-old man being interviewed for a job with an insurance company revealed that he had hemochromatosis but was asymptomatic. At the second interview he was told he might be hired, but with no insurance plan. He agreed to this but at the third interview was told that he could not be hired because of his genetic condition.[62] One's potential future health condition is now grounds for job discrimination, segregation and classification. In policing, too, the future is in focus. As Ericson shows, 'Risk communication systems turn the moral discourse of deviance into a utilitarian morality of probability calculus . . . Gutted of moral wrongdoing, deviance is treated as a normal accident . . . a contingency for which there are risk technologies to spread the loss and to prevent recurrence'.[63] Body surveillance, bound up with identities and identification provided by police, signals another moment in the shift towards actuarial justice.

Risk and security may appear to be highly important to social well-being. This is especially so in societies that tend to minimize the signficance of the past, and are prepared to rely on imagined futures (simulations) to guide practices and policy in the present. If the primary documentary identification is the human body itself, then this is bound to sit uneasily with views of identity that go beyond what can be learned from a bodily ordeal or the test of tissue and fluid. Autobiography and the social web of identities are diminished if not discounted in such body surveillance identification regimes. Beyond this, too, one must ask what is the likely next stage. And one may ask this, not as another exercise in social science fiction, but as a way of following current techno-logics. If it becomes common to have to present a chip – in a smartcard – bearing a biometric identifier, then the requirement to carry this chip at all times will become strong. The only way to guarantee this would be, as Roger Clarke says, to 'mount it in the carrier' – that is, 'to instal it in the person's body'.[64]

Such a scenario, third, raises further questions. These are not just questions of moving bodies and bodyless transactions, coordinated in time and space, or of the paradoxes of the private and of human action, when identification is reduced to direct access to the body. The further questions concern relations between technology and society in general. Surveillance attempts constantly to upgrade the knowledge it obtains for risk management, in the belief that the more advanced the technoscience instrument, the more accurate the knowledge. In the case of body surveillance and identification, precision is the aim. But what do the 'advances' entail? On the one hand, a new mode of justice emerges to keep in step with the focus on the future and on risk. On the other, the possibility is mooted of body modification in the interests of infallible identification. Are these the price that must be paid for 'advance'?

One obvious question concerns the reliability of the new body surveillance technologies. As noted above, the most reliable identifiers are also the most expensive. Digital fingerprinting, which builds on older technologies, tends to be used for administration purposes, particularly welfare. But fingerprinting can exclude otherwise eligible persons who may have skin diseases. A case in point is Kenneth Payne, a Los Angeles man who qualified as a teacher in his forties. He cannot obtain employment because he suffers from atopic dermatitis, which makes his skin blister and peel, thus spoiling his fingerprint. For security reasons California requires all teachers to pass a fingerprint test. No print, no job.[65] The much more accurate retinal scan is restricted due to its price. Understandably, people also feel protective of their eyes and are concerned about light beams passing across them. Voiceprints and facial scanning have yet to find widespread use, and there are questions about accuracy. Faces may change considerably at different times of the day, and voices may alter when someone has a cold.[66]

Similarly with the use of DNA, accuracy is not guaranteed by any means. Moreover, employers may use genetic information in different ways, depending on the situation. When testing applicants for jobs, it may be assumed that the genetic predisposition alone is enough to disqualify someone, despite what is known about other factors, such as environment, which will affect an individual's susceptibility to disease. If, on the other hand, screening for the effects of toxic materials is in question, employers have been known to bring the 'other factors' into play: 'They tend to give the benefit of the doubt to the chemicals . . .' and to 'hold the outside environment or people's life-style choices responsible for worker disease'.[67] And as with biometrics, it must be acknowledged that the body itself may be incapable of yielding the secrets for which it is infiltrated. None of us has perfect genes.

In the area of drug testing, too, certainty is a rather forlorn wish. The world of sport is awash with controversies regarding illicit drug use. Idols such as Ben Johnson have toppled and crashed following positive drug tests. The International Olympic Committee wields considerable power here, affecting not only top league players but, through a trickle-down effect, local and amateur players as well. But are the tests trustworthy? In the cases of Linford Christie, Diane Modahl and Petra Corda, positive testing was followed by their being found not guilty, which raises sharp questions for the integrity and reliability of the relevant tests. Similar issues are raised, of course, about drug testing in the workplace.[68] But reliability of tests is not the only risk factor.

Huge potential dangers are also raised of biometric data circulating between databases and being traded between companies. Similar challenges arise in the realm of genetic data. These hazards lie behind the pressure for encryption and for one-to-one (smartcard) matching systems. When identification is required, the biometric reader would simply match the particular body part with the data on the card.[69] The person holding the card would retain control, or at least that is the theory. It is particularly when the next step, chip implants, are proposed that other surveillance spectres raise their heads. Civil libertarians baulk at this and in so doing find themselves in the unfamiliar company of religious fundamentalists. In 1995, for instance, American televangelist Pat Robertson hosted a segment of his show called 'Biometrics: chipping away your rights'. He declared that 'The Bible says that the time is going to come that you cannot buy or sell except with a mark placed on your hand or on your forehead'.[70] The so-called mark of the beast appears to have arrived with biometrics and genetic IDs.

It is interesting that the chip implant has such negative and repressive connotations among civil libertarians and fundamentalists. This is the other side of the coin from arguments for technological enhancement of the body – the creation of cyborgs – as a route to freedom.[71] In some feminist writing, for instance, the cyborg features as a liberator that allows for playful transgressions of old boundaries and the political potential to revise categories such as gender.[72] For Sadie Plant, the body may be transcended technologically so that it may be represented more flexibly.[73] Virtual emancipation.

Such flexible representation stands in rather stark contrast with the desire directly to tap into the body to obtain information untainted by the subject. This latter cyborg, it seems, is stripped of consciousness and the capacity to answer for itself, all in the paradoxical interests of accurate identification and precise prediction. In order to work, the old disciplinary technologies that attempted to direct the body still relied on ideas such as reflexivity, self-consciousness and even conscience. Newer regimes of risk, surveillance and security require less and less that the subject be – literally – response-able. If what was said earlier is correct, though, such attempts to extract speechless testimony from the body are on a collision course with self-attesting embodied personhood.

To connect the biblical book of Revelation directly with biometrics is a typically literalistic ploy of fundamentalism. It tends to produce cynically dismissive responses, which could, ironically, fuel the very complacency that the more apocalyptic doomwatchers wish to combat. A non-literalist reading of the same text, however, is salutary. This ancient book that warns of things to come and promises hope for the faithful is surprisingly appropriate in its assessments of power and knowledge. The beast whose mark is inscribed in the bodies of would-be buyers and sellers is a 'beast from the earth',[74] the symbol of a kind of false faith or an ideology.[75] Fundamentalists connect too fast the literal biometric or barcode with the mark of the beast. But the mark is just that, a signifier. The first-century writer of the apocalypse could never have dreamed of barcodes! But the thing signified – the embedded ideology or false faith – is the real danger.

By this interpretation neither the technology nor the social entity need be identified precisely. But the relevance of the idea of the beast's mark to any kind of identifiers, including biometrics, becomes both more plain and more plausible. Simulated surveillance, that attempts to bring imagined futures to bear on the practices of the present, depends upon a dream of perfect knowledge.[76] This dream has the ideological power to breathe life into the polycentric webs of the contemporary network society. The mystical mark confirms those in the thrall of the system. But the dream is a deceit, no less than was Jeremy Bentham's when he first projected the panopticon as secular omniscience.[77]

Deceits are dangerous. When they affect areas such as body surveillance they are also very powerful and socially far-reaching. They drive the quest for biometric, genetic and other body data on the assumption that more precise prediction is both possible and desirable in all cases. But risk management also changes the rules. It skews justice actuarially and subtly switches morality for probabilities. It is implicated in fresh efforts to classify and to contain certain groups, as witness the examples given here. Persons on welfare, asylum seekers and refugees, these and similar groups of relatively disadvantaged persons are the first recipients of biometric and DNA measures. It is thus hardly surprising that the stigmas of criminality or poverty are a source of anxiety when similar methods are proposed for bank machines and credit cards.

In the steady shift from identification papers to body surveillance, reliance on data images rather than persons with distinctive biographies is further strengthened. Risk management, obsessed with accurate information, now sends its surveillance probes under the skin. New technologies are rapidly being developed, harnessed and – importantly – recombined, to pursue these ends. Whether or not implants become a widespread reality,[78] the resulting involuntary cyborg will be increasingly dependent on technologically encoded body data for access and eligibility to the mundane functions of everyday life. Genetic testing, as it becomes more widespread, will also check for eligibility and access to resources. It adds to the panoply of social sorting devices.

Given the realities, urgent questions are raised about the means, both political, educational and, perhaps, even technological, of limiting the potential damage that such deepened dependence on the data image could cause. Data from the body is back into the surveillance scenario in ways far more systematic and pervasive than the old practices of phrenology that predicted behaviours from cranial structures. Those who imagine the 'bumps on the head' school of social classification is rendered harmless by historical distance – a quaint if questionable mistake – should familiarize themselves with its twenty-first century computer-assisted counterparts.

Global data flows

Global data flows may sound mundane or melodramatic depending on whether you are a stockbroker or a moviegoer. But the idea that data referring to our personal lives might circulate beyond our own country or that our ordinary email or phone messages might be intercepted is not something that occurs to us routinely. Yet to buy an airline ticket is to trigger a global data flow of personal details. And personal messages of many kinds are subject to interception by a massive electronic intelligence network that spans the globe. Even birthday greetings are subject to scrutiny.[1]

Details in those data flows are used to categorize and to target individuals. Although it is unlikely that the airline ticketing data will be used to check on the racial origins or medical condition of passengers, it may affect their life chances by placing them in a particular consumer group for marketing purposes. And although most messages sent by ordinary people are of no interest to international intelligence services, members of Amnesty International, Greenpeace or Christian Aid, or people who include sensitive words in their messages might want to be more circumspect.[2]

The monitoring of everyday life that characterizes surveillance societies produces data flows of all kinds that may travel a very long way. The point of that monitoring is to categorize and to classify words and activities in a computer-enabled sorting process. Like other kinds of surveillance, those involving global data flows are related increasingly to risk management and to the restucturing of economies and politics in informational societies. The global dimension offers wider spaces within which surveillance data may flow and thus a wider scope for its socially-ordering consequences.

The routine surveillance that characterized the twentieth century was generally limited to specific sites. The human body was watched in fixed environments like jails and factories, designed literally to keep those bodies in place. Personal details were recorded on paper files for government bureaucracies, for use within the territory of the nation state. But in the later part of the century, capitalist restructuring, encouraged by government policy, led to new relationships between the economy, the state, society and culture. One crucial aspect of this was the development of an unprecedented global inter-dependence, enabled by new technologies. Surveillance went global. From international efforts to curb drug trafficking to the promotion of electronic commerce, global surveillance grows constantly. At the same time, subtly enabled by computer technologies, surveillance also changes in character.

Where once surveillance came in containers – first the walled city, later the capitalist workplace, then the nation state – globalization represents one way in which surveillance now crosses borders promiscuously. (It also crosses the border of the body, penetrating beneath the skin, thus displaying sim-ultaneously macroscopic and microscopic growth.) At first the technical augmenting of surveillance simply allowed different kinds of agency, not-ably government and commercial ones, to exchange personal data. But globalization opened the door to further interchange, not just between dif-ferent sectors, but between different countries and international agencies. Surveillance data quickened its flow, finding its previous containers increas-ingly porous. As in other areas, globalization means a focus on 'flows'. Just as there are today flows of financial information – popularly perceived through the 24-hour operation of worldwide stock markets – so there are flows of surveillance.

Computer-enhanced surveillance created a more fine-meshed net than could paper documentary methods within discrete organizations. In globalizing situations surveillance is stretched, such that more and more can be done at a distance.[3] It represents a kind of remote control that is intrinsic to glob-alization. As global flows of technology, information, people, images and symbols rise in volume, so surveillance is employed to track and monitor these movements.

Surveillance now not only keeps track of *past* movements, it tries to anti-cipate *future* flows. Governments use new methods to automate the policing of borders, constantly crossed by tourists, businesspersons and migrants. Employers watch their workers in distant branch plant locations at the same time. Marketing companies follow their customers to exploit every opportun-ity for sales. Surveillance strategies are reinforced for globalizing situations. Surveillance methods and practices flow from one place to another as multi-national corporations scatter their sites across the world. Global markets are tracked using the Internet.

Globalization is a markedly uneven process. The concept of globalization sounds general, universal, and, of course, somewhat intangible. Although it does in a sense happen everywhere at once, globalization has neither the same causes, or courses, or consequences when looked at in different contexts. Globalization actually accents social and economic difference, at the same time as bringing about some superficial similarities, such as the arrival every-where of Big Macs and Coca-Cola. The globalizing world is one in which power is being radically redistributed, tipping it in favour of those with most direct access to the wealth of transnational corporations, and to what Castells calls the 'switches' within the network. The result is that the rich are getting richer and the poor, if they are not actually getting poorer, are getting richer at a far slower rate than the rich.[4] Not only this, new surveillance techniques also discriminate between other kinds of wanted and unwanted persons, often based on race and ethnicity as well as economic standing.[5] Computing and telecommunication power are crucial to the very concept of globalization. The accelerating speed of communications conquers space but the new technologies are also vitally implicated in asymmetrical globalization. Surveillance technologies, in this realm as in others, tend to reinforce difference.

In order to understand contemporary global surveillance, several different dimensions of the phenomenon must be explored. First, as the meanings of globalization are manifold, some clarity is called for. In particular it should be noted that a more global world is not a less local world. Processes of globalization and localization are inherently interconnected. It is also important to understand what is new about globalization today and how this affects surveillance. In particular we shall see that global surveillance is not the product of some centralized would-be world government. Global surveillance exists in the new spaces of flows, in channels and in networks. Power is vital to such surveillance but it is decentralized and shifting power, not a planetary panopticon.

This may be seen, second, in the different ways that surveillance power flows in different parts of the world. In some ways surveillance in Europe, North America and the Pacific Rim converges and consolidates itself, but in others it diverges and diffuses. Moreover, surveillance globalizes in different ways in different sectors. Security concerns spawn post-cold war surveillance, and this, along with fear of crime, contributes to high-tech border policing. The increasingly flexible worker calls forth new surveillance regimes in employment situations. And the world wide web becomes one of the fastest growing means of marketing commodities, using surveillance.

Last, these different modes and experiences of surveillance engender varied responses that are themselves globalized. 'Privacy International' for instance, disseminates knowledge about surveillance and coordinates resistance to it in many different countries by means of the same medium, the Internet.

Globalization and surveillance

'Doing things at a distance' is, as Anthony Giddens says, a key to understanding the contemporary world. This phrase certainly helps us grasp global surveillance. The deal once clinched in verbal agreement and a handshake may now be arranged remotely, even automatically, as happens constantly in the world's stock exchanges, for instance.[6] Checking on the progress of the company in which investment has been made, or, more particularly, on what the workers in that company are up to may also be done remotely. Equally, companies may wish to track more accurately the doings of their customers and that too may be done at a distance. Geographic information systems come to their aid, for central to these are various forms of remote surveillance and multi-scale mapping.[7] Put geographic systems with a GPS and add the appropriate remote sensing equipment and the results are striking. As Michael Curry says, 'one has created a system of great power, and of great utility for the storage and analysis of information and for extended surveillance on individuals and groups'.[8] New technology enables, though it does not initiate, new global practices.

This takes us well beyond the merely 'worldwide' economic and political systems which have been evident for a very long time. Part of the meaning of modernity is that capitalism and industrialism have expanded to a level that encompasses the world either directly or indirectly. Globalization is first and foremost an economic process. Thus, as Castells neatly puts it, the economy has the unprecedented 'capacity to work as a unit in real time on a planetary scale'.[9] Capital flows become global and detach themselves from the workings of specific economies. Labour does not flow in the same sense but does become a global resource. Firms may locate anywhere in the world that they can find appropriate labour at the right price and this sometimes produces new surveillance effects. Firms may also recruit skilled labour from everywhere and labour will enter any market when pushed by war or poverty or pulled by new hopes for their children.[10] This last flow is often restricted by immigration controls which again have surveillance implications.

A good illustration of globalizing economic practices that have strong surveillance implications is airline ticketing. This is especially so since the development of major groups of airlines that run interlinked frequent flyer clubs. If one flies with Canadian Airlines and is a member of the 'One World' programme, one is welcomed as a 'Sapphire' customer when flying with the Australian Qantas. On Canadian Airlines flights, however, the greeting for persons holding exactly the same cards is to 'Gold' club members. Why? Because the frequent flyer personal data is routed automatically with the passenger, wherever they go. The data remain the same even if the local greeting changes.

Airlines have to handle sensitive information on passengers, medical conditions, dietary needs (that may indicate religious affiliation), on dignitaries, deportees, unaccompanied minors or potentially awkward political affiliations.[11] Passenger name records become part of the departure control system and these records are purged after arrival but kept for a number of years for management analysis. But the frequent flyer data, though it is in many cases subject to the European Union Convention on Data Protection, is much more widely used for marketing purposes. As Colin Bennett says, 'international airlines have considerable power over individuals through the personal information that they collect, process and disseminate during the now routine process of undertaking international airline travel'.[12]

I noted earlier that globalization is first and foremost an economic process. But this is not to deny for a moment that it has other aspects. It is just that the capitalist system is the single most significant global force. But as Leslie Sklair argues, there are three levels of 'transnational practices': economic, political and what he calls 'cultural-ideological'.[13] To look at 'transnational practices' is to go beyond the merely 'international' practices that exist within state-centred analyses. Transnational corporations are the primary economic actors, the transnational capitalist class the locus of transnational political practices and consumerism is at the core of transnational cultural-ideological practices. Nation states are still the spatial reference points of the global system (so they are not somehow 'superseded' in surveillance or any other terms) and they are still militarily significant. But as a reference point the capitalist system offers much more than either the nation states or transnational corporations.

Sklair's admirable analysis of the global system points up the way in which dominant forces in each sphere try to monopolize key resources for which there is great competition. Transnational corporations try to control capital and material resources, the transnational capitalist classes strive to control global power, and the transnational agents and institutions of the culture-ideology of consumerism attempt to control the realm of ideas.[14] He argues that the triumphs of capitalism in the 1990s – especially in its tilt towards consumerism – were no illusion. The global system is indeed almost completely in the thrall of capitalist corporations, classes and culture. But more can be said about the *ways* in which capitalist control is assured, and particularly about those that involve surveillance. For while it is true, for example, that the mass media help to create new lifestyles[15] of consumer culture, new technologies are also deployed in the more direct targeting of customers in the wealthier parts of the world. While no one, however poor or marginalized, can escape the media images of the consumerist 'good life', those with the capacity to consume are more intensively monitored to ensure that they will not fail to continue to do so, at ever spiralling levels of spending.[16]

A similar question might be raised about Zygmunt Bauman's critique of globalization. He objects to the use of the 'panopticon' metaphor for understanding most current surveillance. Specifically he rejects Mark Poster's notion of a 'superpanopticon' that 'hooks our bodies into the networks, the databases, the information highways',[17] insisting instead that whereas the panopticon was meant to instil discipline, databases merely confirm credibility. Consumer creditworthiness in particular may be verified by databases. Bauman then puts his weight behind Thomas Mathieson's idea of the 'synopticon'[18] of mass media, in which the many watch the few – on television – where the few are the global consumerist élites, especially as seen in the showbusiness way of life.

The problem here is that Bauman misses the classificatory or social sorting power of today's panopticon, which is precisely aimed at global, or at least highly mobile, consumers. He is right, of course, to note that the shadow of the old panoptic methods may still be seen among the immobilized and the excluded, especially those who are incarcerated. Even there, the idea that the panopticon might be a 'house of correction', that inmates might be reformed, has now been dropped in favour of mere exclusion.[19] But social sorting processes based on abstract aggregate and individual data make surveillance automatic across all socioeconomic strata. This is an aspect of panopticism even though it is far removed from any prison.

Either way, the question of consumerism – alongside workplace and administrative power – is crucial both to capitalism and to contemporary surveillance. If Sklair is right, consumerism is the ideology that offers the indispensable rationale for continued capitalist accumulation within the global system. Without it the system fails. If, in addition, it is correct to see surveillance as a major means of maintaining and raising levels of consumption, this also has implications for attempting to regulate or to resist surveillance. Interestingly enough, it was during the 1990s that newly transnational attempts to raise awareness about negative aspects of everyday surveillance arose.

One other aspect of globalization must be mentioned at this point. Globalization is not another word for 'westernization'. Global flows occur in several directions simultaneously. 'Glocalization' is Roland Robertson's preferred term for describing the interlinked character of the global and the local. In this perspective there may well be some homogenizing effects of some global culture – Disneyization,[20] let's say – but local contexts will always shape those effects in specific ways.[21] This is because different nation states had different origins. In Europe they were relatively autonomous. In the New World native peoples were decimated to make way for modernity. African countries had modernity imposed by colonialism. And east Asian economies modernized in relation to external threat.[22] In addition, different kinds of national project and cultural background are evident in different countries. The global influence of the West may still be highly visible. But Japan and other Pacific rim countries have had global status for several decades now and flows may as easily have their origins as their destinations in them.

Modern surveillance started life in European nation states. In North America, many European-style surveillance practices were taken over within their governments. But in North America, workplace (and later consumer) surveillance were also perfected, often based on new technologies, to be exported back to Europe in some early global flows. On the Pacific Rim, however, entry into the global system also meant that largely home-grown surveillance practices, such as those relating to Japanese 'just-in-time' management and 'total quality control'[23] appeared within the global system. These became transnational practices as they were adopted elsewhere. Pacific Rim countries may also exhibit surveillance practices that set them apart from other countries, based for instance on less pronounced levels of individualism. The importance of national goals to life in say, Singapore or Japan, has no equivalents in other parts of the world, and can permit much higher levels of intrusive surveillance than would be countenanced in surveillance-conscious regions such as Scandinavia.

Take 'Japanization'. The so-called Japanese miracle that transformed that country into a leading industrial and then high-technology economy was not confined to Japan. It was exported through Japanese direct investment in other countries, and emulated by countries who saw Japan as a model. In the former case, what were thought to be Japanese methods, especially in automobile manufacture, found their way into other parts of the world as offshore branch plants were set up, and agreements were reached between Japanese and foreign companies. In the latter, companies such as Ford tried to copy the Japanese by introducing tighter labour discipline, increased output and enhanced worker flexibility in European Ford plants.[24]

Although the term 'Japanization' appeared in the mid 1980s[25] the slogan did not become popular until the publication in 1990 of *The Machine that Changed the World*.[26] Many took Japanization to be a new paradigm, both analytically and in terms of a need to rewrite management and labour strategies. Governments as well as firms saw Japanization as a means of restructuring that would make labour more flexible and productive. Japanese competition and overseas investment has become significant within the restructuring of European and American manufacturing, and new production and employment practices have been disseminated within competitor countries. These now include the USA, Canada, Mexico, Brazil, Britain, Germany, Italy and Sweden.[27] The success of these methods was dependent, says Peter Turnbull, on 'a social organization for the production process intended to make workers feel obliged to contribute to the economic performance of the enterprise and to identify with its competitive success'.[28] Where it occurs, Japanization contributes to global flows of surveillance methods.

Surveillance is a very significant aspect of transnational practices within the global system although it is not always recognized as such. Its scope may be illustrated by case studies of surveillance practices in different sectors. Although entirely state-centred ways of understanding the global system simply miss the point, the state has not lost its salience for surveillance. National security is still a telling argument for surveillance. This can be illustrated from globalized communications intelligence, from the changing character of border controls and from globalized policing.

Economic rationales lie not far behind these issues. They come into the foreground in two key contexts: workplace and consumer surveillance. Workplace surveillance in globalized settings means that transnational employers can keep track of production in sites scattered worldwide and also that methods flow from one setting to another with increased ease. Consumer surveillance, especially that involving electronic commerce, drives data persistently across borders, even though much electronic commerce is in fact local. In all these cases global and local surveillance interact in ways that can be analysed though not disentangled.

Global security: Comint

'Comint' is shorthand for communications intelligence. Only in the late twentieth century did the immense power of this secretive international network come to light. In 1996 an astonishing piece of research – worthy of intelligence services themselves – was published under the title *Secret Power*.[29] Its author, New Zealander Nicky Hager, shows how not even the then prime minister, David Lange, knew what was going on in his own backyard. The latter made speeches to the effect that New Zealand was glad to have an independent intelligence service when in fact the American National Security Agency (NSA) called the shots and even appointed the director of the New Zealand operation. Hager also demonstrates that despite the rhetoric of friendly relations with neighbours in the Pacific region, the UKUSA (UK–USA agreement) system in New Zealand systematically favours the rich and powerful. It was absolutely no help in, for example, warning of the French attack on the Greenpeace ship *Rainbow Warrior* in New Zealand in 1985 or preventing the anti-democratic coup in Fiji in 1987.[30]

What springs to mind most readily when the term 'global surveillance' is used? It would be surprising if some form of transnational interception of messages were not thought to be the acme of such a system. Comint engaged in just this kind of surveillance for most of the twentieth century although its character began to alter during the 1960s. What started as a means of intercepting military messages and diplomatic communications has for the past half century been more geared to the collection of economic intelligence and information about scientific and technical developments. In 1992 NSA director William Studeman commented that the 'demands for increased global access are growing' and that one of two key growth areas is business use.[31] Comint may also target narcotics trafficking, money laundering, terrorism and organized crime. It is used to obtain sensitive information concerning individuals, as well as on governments, trade and international organizations.

Comint represents the effort to gain access to, intercept and process every important modern form of communication, in every significant sphere, and in many countries. Such an ambitious task is supported by the activitives of the UKUSA alliance of English-speaking nations, and above all the American NSA. It is estimated that each year 15–20 billion Euros are spent globally on Comint, especially by the USA and the UK, but also by the 'second parties' – Australia, Canada and New Zealand – plus 30 other nations including Russia. Signals intelligence (Sigint), of which Comint is a part, includes among its investors and users China and most Middle-Eastern and Asian nations, particularly India, Israel and Pakistan.

In the post-cold war period Comint interception has taken on the traits of normal business firms. It has to balance budgets and ensure that customer requirements are met. It works through several stages. These include gaining access and collecting data – a task that is becoming increasingly difficult – processing data, which includes classifying and in some cases summarizing messages; and the analysis, evaluation, translation and interpretation of raw data into finished intelligence. It is agreed that in most cases persons and companies from countries included in the UKUSA agreement will not remain identifiable.

Comint intercepts international communications that pass through international leased carriers which are national or private post, telephone and telegraph companies. They traditionally used high-frequency radio but now include systems based on microwave radio relay, sub-sea cables and communications satellites. Since 1990, most communications have been digital, and Comint also collects Internet data. As Duncan Campbell notes, 'Because most of the world's Internet capacity lies within the United States or connects to the United States, many communications in "cyberspace" will pass through intermediate sites within the United States. Communications from Europe to and from Asia, Oceania, Africa or South America normally travel via the United States'.[32] The NSA uses 'bots' (rather like regular Internet search engines) and 'sniffer software' to collect Internet data of interest.[33]

Since the 1970s a system known as ECHELON has automated Comint processing at several sites. It made possible the continued examination of messages whose volume had become too great for manual classification. 'Watch lists' that compile names that are of 'reportable intelligence interest' are now automated using a key component called a 'dictionary'. These dictionaries store extensive databases on specified targets, including names, addresses, telephone numbers and other selection criteria. Such dictionaries have been found, for example, to intercept every telex message that passes through London every day; thousands of personal, business and diplomatic communications. ECHELON computers also sift through fax and modem data, as well as topics of communication, and, since 1995, voiceprints. Pager messages, cellular mobile radio and new satellite communications are also vulnerable to such interception.

Among other things, ECHELON collects economically sensitive information. It is not used directly by companies, who have no right of access to such information, but individual government ministries do set its tasks. These range from estimating future commodity prices to determining other nations' positions in trade negotiations, monitoring international arms trading and tracking sensitive technology. In the UK, the GCHQ (General Communications Headquarters) is obliged to intercept foreign communications 'in the interests of the economic well-being of the United Kingdom'.[34] This may include company plans, telexes, faxes and transcribed telephone calls. American companies in particular are known to have benefited from Comint information, such as when Boeing and McDonnell-Douglas beat Airbus Industrie in a bid for Saudi airline business. In addition, confidential details of Japanese vehicle emission standards have been discovered, as has knowledge of French participation in 1993 GATT (General Agreement on Tariffs and Trade) discussions, and of the Asian-Pacific Economic Conference in 1997.

Various changes are in the air, however. The shift to using fibre optics means that physical access to cables is necessary for interception. Commercially available equipment now rivals that of Comint. And both civil and commercial cryptography is making interception more and more difficult. In the early 1990s the NSA was behind the proposed 'Clipper Chip' system of cryptography that would leave ultimate access in their hands. When this failed due to popular protest the NSA attempted to require non-government agencies to keep copies of all users' keys, again so that they could maintain a right of access to private and commercial communications. European objections to this system of 'key recovery' led to years of negotiation, and at the time of writing the situation remains unresolved. The NSA even persuaded major electronics companies such as Lotus, Microsoft and Netscape to reduce the security of email and Internet systems used outside the USA so that they could still break codes and gain access to messages. However, private crypto- graphy has been growing apace and it is likely that at least some aspects of Comint and the activities of the NSA will be restricted by this growth.

The case of Comint illustrates well Sklair's three levels of transnational practices – economic, political and cultural-ideological – as it is implicated in all three. Economic intelligence-gathering for the consumer society is clearly a significant aspect of ECHELON, perhaps as important as the military was in cold war times.[35] But ordinary, everyday communications may also be intercepted, which again shows how the largest scale of global economic and international operations is articulated with the mundane minutiae of local life through the medium of surveillance.

Global security: controlling borders

The 'police archipelago' is how Didier Bigo describes today's transnational police computer networks, particularly in Europe. Police systems, that until the mid-twentieth century tended to be mainly within cities, have stretched the range of their operations to include states and provinces, national territ- ories and now, international contexts. Borders are crossed both physically and electronically. But the networks not only keep track of what goes on between as well as within countries, they increasingly comprise formerly distinct agencies. Customs, immigration, visa departments, consulates, pri- vate transport companies and private surveillance organizations as well as national police forces all share data within these networks. This creates new categories of relationship between such agencies and those they keep track of: wanted and disappeared persons, those refused entry permits, deportees, refugees, migrant workers, and so the list goes on.[36]

Probably the most obvious case of heightened awareness of border controls relates to international drug trafficking. Local violations nearly always take place in the context of transnational arrangements for procuring, transport- ing and selling the substances. But more subtle forms of illegal activity cross borders silently and invisibly in cyberspace. Electronic fund transfers that may involve fraud or money laundering call forth new forms of surveillance – not to mention new standards of policing policy – in the attempt to reduce crime across borders.[37] But apart from clearly criminal dimensions of border crossings, numerous new everyday occurrences create new questions for the monitoring of borders. These include trans-border commuting to work and increased international tourism that now leaves no country untouched.

One of the most striking developments of the past few decades has been the widespread appearance of a global criminal economy. Manuel Castells lists some of the actors as follows: the Sicilian *Cosa Nostra*, the American mafia, Colombian and Mexican cartels, Nigerian criminal networks, Japanese *Yakuza*, Chinese Triads, Russian *Mafiyas*, Turkish heroin traffickers, and Jamaican *Posses*.[38] He regards the international networks of their activities as being an essential part of the new global economy. They deal for the most part in weapons, nuclear materials, illegal immigrants, women and children (for prostitution), body parts and money laundering. The flexible networks of criminality find numerous ways of bypassing controls, hence the huge increase in attempts to mount operations that are also based in networks to combat global crime. Trying to curb such activities may curtail civil liberties. When certain immigrant groups come to be associated with, say, drug trafficking or prostitution, xenophobic reactions against those groups may result. In some cases this leads to an 'ethnicizing' of practical criteria of surveillance.[39]

It is in the face of such conspicuous global networking of criminal activities that increasingly global networks of policing and surveillance have been established. The very idea of transnational policing is relatively new. Previously, police dealt with mainly internal security, and armed forces mainly external. In Europe especially, police are becoming more transnational, with 'Europol' being the specific network that corresponds to the fully international 'Interpol'. They rely to a considerable extent on the European Intelligence System and the Schengen Information System, the high technology networks which serve to coordinate their activities. What has yet to be determined is how far the new systems are as successful in protecting the personal data they use as they are in procuring the data in the first place.[40] This is not just a question of how to 'protect privacy' beyond national jurisdictions. The Schengen agreement, for example, focuses transnational police work on 'unwanted and undesirable' individuals and groups – both international criminals and unwelcome aliens.[41]

Sorting persons and groups into categories, such as un/desirable or un/wanted is an area that attracts new technology applications. The transnational police information systems are ideally suited to such uses. Although many such methods originated in the USA, they are now being exported, particularly to Europe. Innovations in undercover methods especially, first developed in North America, now appear in European contexts. The earlier uncertainties and caution in the USA about undercover methods became increasingly weaker during the late twentieth century, as fear of crime rose as a reason for adopting them.[42] Such methods tend to depend heavily upon communications and information technologies. As Gary T. Marx argues, this helps to create convergence and thus greater homogeneity between different jurisdictions.[43] The apparent sameness has to do with shifts towards crime prevention, rational strategies of categorical suspicion, an interest in problem solving and system intelligence, a greater reliance on citizens and an extension of law and policy to once-ignored and unregulated tactics. This technological normalizing of what was once 'high policing' creates potential problems, especially in countries like France that have been known to use undercover tactics for political as well as criminal ends.

Biometrics is an increasingly popular tool in the policing of borders. In 1997 the European Union opened the way for the development of a centralized database of digitized fingerprints of all asylum seekers from political persecution in member countries, called Eurodac. The laudable aim is to compensate for the lack of papers held by such persons and to ensure that they are not simply sent on from country to country. But it could also have other unforeseen effects. For one thing, as Irma van der Ploeg observes, identity is established rather than merely verified by such a system.[44] Thus, she suggests, if the taint of illegality hangs over a particular migrant's identity, then the stigma will be present for all future official transactions in which he or she may wish to engage.

Although in most countries many citizens consider that some migration controls are appropriate, there are both ideological and economic pressures to open borders. On the one hand, many internationalists argue that open borders make sense if the world is to avoid war and injustice. It is also hard to deny fairly open policies in countries such as Canada, the USA and Australia, that were built on relatively free entry. Is America not the land of opportunity? In Israel too, the admission of Jews from anywhere is crucial to the Zionist idea that the state is a haven for all.[45] Beyond these reasons, however, is the economic self-interest of countries who might wish to open their borders to sources of cheaper labour or as a means of harmonizing relations in a free trade area. Ideological reasons for a more general opening of borders tend to stumble on actual inequalities and injustices, on the existence of repressive regimes and on the huge disparities between levels of education, health care and income that are evident in different countries.

An argument for easing border controls heard more frequently from the 1990s onwards has been the globalization of the market. Indeed, some argue that in a global village, migration becomes inevitable and uncontrollable. As new technologies make passing information about jobs and housing easier, and as costs of transportation decline, so the search for cheaper forms of labour will increasingly be met by migrant groups from other countries. Caribbean and Mexican labour comes to the USA, Turks, Yugoslavs and Greeks come to Germany, and North Africans find employment in France, Italy and Spain. The flow of such persons is growing steadily in all the contexts just mentioned, and in Europe at least the rate of flow of illegal migrants far outstrips that of registered ones.[46] Although this represents a small proportion of the total global labour force – only 1.5 per cent of which (or 80 million persons) worked outside their country of origin in 1993, half of whom were in sub-Saharan Africa or the Middle East[47] – it is not insignificant.

What increases and decreases the volume of migrant labour flows, however, is not demand for labour so much as tightness of restrictions. Between 1988 and 1994 the German migrant labour population grew by almost half, while in the UK, with stricter limits, there was hardly any expansion. The globalization of labour did not oblige Japan to have a guest-worker programme when many other countries, especially in western Europe, did, and nor did it stop Japan from having tighter controls on illegal immigration and asylum seekers.[48] Germany requires all citizens and aliens to register when they re-locate, keeps a central aliens register on all resident foreigners, and requires all residents to carry national identification documents when applying for jobs.

The USA, on the other hand, has a larger illegal alien problem than Germany, and also would have a politically hard time introducing a national ID card. Nearly 4000 border patrol agents are employed, along with much equipment (including computer systems), particularly along the Mexican-American border, but even this deployment does not deter 200,000–300,000 undocumented aliens entering the USA each year. As Thomas Espenshade concludes, '. . . undocumented immigration at roughly present levels is a price that Americans pay to maintain an open society'.[49]

The globalization of police surveillance, focused on border controls, follows the growth of both the formal and the criminal global economy. Each is predicated on a general economic restructuring, and is enabled by the diffusion of new technologies. While the use of the latter does encourage a particular approach, and facilitates particular kinds of surveillance, the tech-nologies themselves determine nothing. Social and cultural factors in specific contexts guide the development and use of surveillance technologies and the networking they support. The globalization of police surveillance, using similar technologies on different continents, may introduce some homo-geneity to the networks in question. At the same time, heterogeneity and diversification is also visible in the various jurisdictional cultures where the new networking appears. Similar technologies may have different outcomes at Europol's La Haye and its American counterpart at El Paso Intelligence Center. They may also interact in different ways with other agencies such as customs and immigration.

The key changes, as Bigo rightly observes, are that police operate through networking, and that they do so increasingly at a distance.[50] This is a drive towards remote control. They operate both downstream, within a given coun-try, and upstream, through collaboration with the country of origin of the migrant or the criminal. Thus direct relationships diminish, to be replaced by practices where one seeks to determine before the fact the populations susceptible to infractions. Targeted categories are checked, through intensi-fied surveillance, via computerized statistical analysis. The attempt is made to anticipate the rate and volume of flows of persons in different categories rather than merely to follow individuals after they have violated some law.

Bigo also points out that these new surveillance practices are at once less disciplinary and less static than before. It is a far cry from the panopticon, and much closer to virtual reality technologies. In the process of 'morphing', a virtual assembly of many data fragments takes place to construct all the positions of individuals in the midst of the flows. From the initial image of the immigrant or the suburban youth to the final one – terrorist, trafficker – the stages of transformation are virtually reconstituted. As Bigo says, these devices do 'less to dissect the body than to channel the flows'.[51] But their social effects are nonetheless powerful because the preconstructed categories

concern minorities, and especially ethnicity. They serve to reinforce classificatory – and stereotypical – thought, which assigns persons to certain groups
and locations, thus adding validity to a particular kind of knowledge.

It is this classificatory power which lies behind the new techniques, even
though the new technologies facilitate and reinforce that power. Bigo argues
that Gary T. Marx's arguments about the 'new surveillance' could mistakenly give the impression that the 'effects' are 'caused' by technological forces.
For one thing, police in several countries, including the UK, Denmark, France
and Italy, have expressed reservations about abandoning personal contacts
for technological ones. But more importantly, insists Bigo, the new surveillance is about identifying, categorizing, standardizing, ordering and controlling minorities. The underlying trend is towards proactive anticipation rather
than reactive firefighting.[52]

The world wide web of surveillance

Identifying, categorizing, standardizing, ordering and controlling also sum-
marizes the aims of marketers who now more than ever 'think global'. If global
flows of intelligence data are increasingly concerned with economic competition, it is also the case that economic competition encourages flows of
workers and raises issues of border security. And if global data flows relating
to the workplace are flows of management techniques for obtaining worker
compliance and commitment, then the global flows in the consumer sphere
relate to parallel techniques for guiding consumption, based upon actual
transaction data.

Interestingly, while new productive regimes depend at least in part upon
human relations for their success, attempts to manage consumption also rely
on more 'personal' knowledge of customers. Manufacturers and retailers wish
to establish service-type relationships with their customers, collecting, storing
and manipulating information about them in order to influence their behaviours.[53] Database marketing acts as a discriminatory technology,[54] taking
aspects of Taylorism[55] out of production and into the marketplace. In this
case, consumers are graded and guided, based on personal data taken both
from public sources and from direct recording of customer behaviour.

Database marketing is now heavily involved in what I call the 'world wide
web of surveillance'.[56] The term is a metaphorical one, encompassing any
forms of surveillance that occur in cyberspace, or in computer-mediated communications. All uses of the Internet, the world wide web and email systems
are traceable and this capacity is rapidly being exploited as these media are
commercialized. Netscape knows each time that a browser of theirs is in use.
When in 1996 a new Netscape 'communicator suite' was being launched, a
Danish software firm discovered that operators could read anything on the
hard drive of a computer logged onto a website. By means like this companies are able to profile Internet users, either through user registration data or,
more frequently, without the knowledge or the consent of net surfers.

This is achieved by websites that send automatic messages back to their owners about remote users who have logged onto their pages. This can reveal data about users' machines, log-on habits, specific purchases and thus their perceived needs, based on site visits. Some transactional information is passively recorded, such that the webmaster can determine what files, pictures or images are of interest to the user, how long was spent with each, and which sites were visited before and after the one in question. The data processing company Internet Profiles (I/PRO) indicate just how well and by whom a site is used. I/PRO's clients include Yahoo!, Compuserve, Netscape and others.[57] So-called Cookies (client-side persistent information) give extensive tracking capacity to companies, eager to exploit the valuable segmented data on discrete individuals. Cookies allow websites to store information about visited sites on the user's hard drive, then they read the drive each time a site is visited to discover if the user has been there before. The advantage to the customer, it is said, is that customized advertising, tailored to individual needs, may be targeted only at those for whom it is truly appropriate. The advantage to the company is that the market can be known in an individualized manner.

Much is made of the potential for 'intelligent agents' to short circuit the tedious process of deploying Internet search engines to find useable data. Not without irony, the 'agents' that now use increasingly sophisticated tracking and mapping techniques are called 'spiders'. There is as yet little evidence of their use in consumer tracking and profiling, but the potential is obvious. 'Data mining' is a technique increasingly widely used on the Internet, and is used by the Chicago Tribune Company, for instance, to analyse the behaviour of consumers as they move from site to site. Only large scale corporations can afford to use techniques such as data mining. So while numerous companies – such as 'Snoop Collection' from the 'Background Investigation Division' in Chico, California – will offer for a fee to find out about specific individuals, large corporations routinely mount such searches to find detailed consumer information.

GeoCities is a major web portal with nearly 20 million visitors a month. In 1998 it sold to outside marketers information solicited during its registration process, despite explicit online assurances that it would not do so. GeoCities was charged by the FTC (Federal Telecommunications Commission) with 'misrepresenting the purpose for which it was collecting personal identifying information from children and adults'.[58] But such appropriation of personal data is increasingly common on the Internet. It often takes the form of new categorical sifting. 'Clickstream' monitoring, for instance, tracks web surfers on a page-by-page basis. Combined with 'collaborative filtering', which makes educated guesses about personal likes and dislikes by comparing one profile with others in the database, powerful new marketing tools are created.

Computer companies are also involved in the quest for high value personal data. Early in 1999 plans were made by Intel to launch the Pentium III chip, which in its initial version had a unique ID (processor serial number or PSN) that could be read by a web server. The machine could then be associated with any other available identifiable information, including that from clickstreams and collaborative filters. A cleverly conceived boycott was launched by Jason Catlett at junkbusters.com, which in under a month claimed that 38 per cent of Chief Executive Officers in the USA opposed the Intel PSN.[59] The effect, had the PSN been released in its original form, would have been to allow the records of many different companies to be merged to provide an extensive activity profile, without the knowledge or consent of the user. In the event, Intel stood down and disabled the identification feature. But it is still not clear whether or not customers will be obliged to reactivate it as a condition of doing business with any given company.

Consumer surveillance using the Internet is a fast-growing phenomenon in the richer parts of the world. The more an individual wishes to participate fully in the consumer society, and especially in electronic commerce, the more she or he will be subject to deeply intrusive surveillance. Where the mass media no longer have the direct impact that it is assumed they have in poorer parts of the world, intensified methods are sought to reinforce the cultural-ideological practices that are crucial to the maintenance of the capitalist system. The synopticon may still work in some regions, but those in the wealthy world no longer trust it alone.

Globalized surveillance

Globalized surveillance is an intrinsic aspect of the general economic restructuring of capitalism on a worldwide scale that is commonly referred to as globalization. Transnational surveillance practices may be found in every significant social, economic and political sector, although their consequences vary from region to region and from sector to sector. Thus we find police networking transnationally, using advanced information systems to trace, track and channel flows of lawbreakers and migrants, and marketing companies competing to obtain personal customer data, also using advanced information technologies to trace, track and channel flows of consumption. We also see how systems developed for one purpose, such as military intelligence, may be retooled for another, such as transnational economic and technological intelligence, and how methods developed in one part of the world – such as Japanese management or undercover police investigations – are exported to another in constantly shifting flows of techniques as well as actual data.

Transnational surveillance practices are themselves changing rapidly, especially as they are enabled by new technologies. This means that globalized surveillance is not necessarily the same as that which emerged in any one discrete national situation. The leading trend, in most sectors, is towards classificatory, pre-emptive surveillance, that tries to simulate and anticipate likely behaviours. But those classifications themselves represent a form of power, not least because they tend to distinguish between categories of persons to whom different treatments will be meted out. Criminal, ethnic and consumer groups are all subject to such sorting and selecting devices which, however virtual they appear as data constructs, have concrete consequences for life chances in the real world.

The partial exception to this trend is the kinds of workplace surveillance discussed here under the rubric of Japanization. As we note elsewhere,[60] however, this sector is far from immune to the effects of discriminatory surveillance technologies, based on biometrics as well as on more conventional performance and behavioural data. On the other hand, knowledge-based risk management is key to understanding the contemporary operations of human resource departments in transnational corporations. Some aspects of so-called Japanization involve closer attention for example to the non-work lifestyles of employees – which again extends the scope of surveillance – but in all cases the ultimate aim is to procure greater commitment to the company, greater productivity from the worker, and thus greater profits for the system.

Surveillance data flows freely in global spaces. In many instances, the aim is to improve security and reduce risk. Especially in high profile contexts such as drug trafficking and international terrorism, surveillance provides welcome reassurance both for national governments and for ordinary people in everyday life. Or at least it did until the terrorist attacks on the World Trade Center and the Pentagon on 11 September 2001. Since that time, surveillance relating to security has been stepped up radically and, despite the relatively low-tech nature of the attacks, high-tech preemptive fixes still predominate (*Sociological Research Online*, Vol. 6, No. 3, 2001, http://www.socresonline.org.uk/6/3/lyon.html). But the larger question is, whose security and which risks? As I have argued, globalization is primarily an economic phenomenon in the sense that the interests served are above all those of transnational capitalism.[61]

This global economic order both demands mobile, flexible workers who are willing (or obliged) to cross borders for employment, and seeks intelligence on what competing companies and countries are up to. And it is the main driving force behind the risk calculations that provide those essential categories for the automated social sorting that surveillance enables. Any and all groups from poor migrant workers to rich Internet surfers are subject to such sorting. If the ongoing significance of local everyday life relationships is to be preserved in a world dominated by the global market, the power and influence of those with access to the switching mechanisms of global surveillance networks require analysis, critique and challenge.

PART THREE

Surveillance scenarios

At the end of the nineteenth century, a citizen of London, New York or Tokyo thought of daily life in mainly local terms. Face-to-face contacts still predominated, even though the telegraph and the telephone system were already making a difference to the better off. You would have been aware of the need to register a marriage, the birth of a baby or a death. And it would not have escaped your attention that the developing police forces kept records or that your employer supervised your work. But everyday life was lived largely outside the routine scrutiny of organizations and agencies.

What a contrast with the lives of ordinary people at the start of the twenty-first century! Today, everyday life is constantly monitored. The plastic cards in our wallets contain barcodes, magnetic stripes or computer chips that connect us with a vast skein of agencies with which we have no face-to-face relationships at all. Our personal data circulates within and between machines, along fibre-optic cables, and via satellite, in ways that we can scarcely conceive. We are watched on the downtown street by ubiquitous cameras, and our employers want urine and blood samples to find out about drug use or to detect genetic disease. Even our supposedly 'personal' computers betray our Internet surfing activities to marketers who also wish to enter selling 'relationships' with us.

We have explored some of what this means by examining the shift away from face-to-face relationships and embodied communications, the mushrooming growth of information infrastructures, and the flows of personal data within surveillance networks. We have also seen how the city is still the place where surveillance is most intensively felt, how the body itself is now interrogated for surveillance data, and how surveillance data flows are globalizing.

This section explores the meaning of surveillance society in three further dimensions. In Chapter 7 I look critically at the main resources available for interpreting surveillance sociologically. I suggest that several strands of modern and postmodern theory make useful contributions to our understanding but that we also need to seek new theoretical directions if the complexities of contemporary surveillance are properly to be grasped. While non-sociological or policy-orientated readers understandably may wish to skip or skim this chapter, it does contain some clues as to how the rest of the book's argument holds together.

In Chapter 8 I turn from the interpretive to the political questions. Although I have stressed that surveillance has two faces, and that it should never be thought of simply as malign or sinister, I have observed that surveillance does display some characteristics which should rightly give us pause. Resistance is appropriate in some contexts and I survey the ways that this occurs as well as – importantly – why it often fails. In Chapter 9, finally, I broaden the question to enquire about what sort of social world is in the making when surveillance processes are so prominent, and yet so poorly perceived. How is the shift to the postmodern implicated in surveillance? Is the surveillance society an inevitable outcome of technological innovation and 'progress'? Or do resources exist to challenge, channel and change the modes of development that touch our lives so pervasively and profoundly in the twenty-first century?

New directions in theory

In the 1994 film *The Net*, Sandra Bullock finds herself without an identity. That is, she has been stripped of all her electronic coordinates, an ordinary person in extraordinary circumstances of loss. She desperately seeks the means of piecing together again the symbols of self and the tokens of trust without which she is bereft and agonizingly anonymous. Wim Wenders' 1991 picture, *Until the End of the World*, tells a different story. William Hurt, carrying a top-secret device, is on the run from industrial bounty-hunters. The breathtaking global chase is both physical and electronic and slows only in the Australian outback, where the film ends. This movie explores ways in which, despite the array of communication and information technologies that supposedly connect us, self-understanding and real human contact are elusive.[1]

The tension between the two films says something about surveillance. We rely on surveillance technologies to hold things together and to provide the acceptable currencies of identity and eligibility. Yet the same technologies fail to provide a satisfactory account of our lives let alone to infuse our relationships with a sense of meaningful interaction. And as we have seen, surveillance technologies may also be used to channel our lives in directions we do not desire or to thwart us from proper participation in aspects of social life. In theorizing surveillance, an understanding of new technologies can easily be out of touch with the crucial dimension of lived experience. Given the structural disappearance of bodies, with which surveillance tries to cope, what are the prospects for a return to embodied personhood as a mode of critique within a sociology of surveillance?

At the start of the twenty-first century it is clear that communication and information technologies have become central to understanding social change. Computer dependence has become a feature of both global connections and of everyday life. Indeed, globalization and daily living in the contemporary world are in part constituted by our relation with computers. No country wishes to miss out on the establishment of an information infrastructure. Few citizens or consumers wish to be excluded from the network of information flows, at least as far as having access to telephones, televisions and the Internet is concerned. But the obverse of the information society is the surveillance society. The world of electronic connectivity works both ways. It brings the global village to our doorstep. And at the same time it extracts personal data from us that are then processed, manipulated, traded and used to influence us and to affect our life chances.

Explaining how and why this happens has become a matter of controversy. The sociology of communication and information technologies started, naturally enough, by demonstrating how computerization enhances and sometimes alters social processes such as bureaucratic organization.[2] As the nation state and capitalistic enterprises were the first to engage the new technologies, questions arose of how balances of power might be disturbed, or social control might become less restrained.

Anthony Giddens warned of the increasing potentials for totalitarian government, and Gary T. Marx cautioned that 'new surveillance' technologies used in American policing may portend the coming 'maximum surveillance society'.[3] In these kinds of account, the classic concerns of sociological analysis reappear. We participate, wittingly or otherwise, in the production of social forces that may one day overwhelm us. The dream of greater control could boomerang back to demobilize us as sovereign subjects. This kind of account resonates with an equally classic narrative – the revenge of the modern machine.

But what if the computer is more than a modern machine? What if the computer is implicated in the social and cultural transformation of modernity itself?[4] And what if it thus requires novel modes of analysis appropriate to this putative transformation? This would alter the picture somewhat. Placed next to the social sifting and sorting power of today's surveillance practices and the rapid rise of risk management as a rationale for surveillance, the questions posed have a fresh mein. Does this mean that older models, such as the panopticon, require revising or rejecting? Either way, what constructive new directions for theory are needed to make sense of surveillance today?

Such questions have prompted a number of interesting and important studies showing how databases may be thought of as discourse[5] or how surveillance has slipped into simulation mode.[6] These take their cues from the work of Michel Foucault and Jean Baudrillard rather than from more classical sociological sources. They claim to show, moreover, how those older approaches are no longer adequate. For example, the rational autonomous individual, central to Max Weber's sociology of bureaucratic organization, may be viewed not so much as an 'anthropological invariant'[7] as a construct. Now, argues Mark Poster, computer databases may construct 'subjects' or, rather 'objects', whose identities are dispersed. As such they may still be subject to domination but in a new modality. Bentham's panopticon gives way to the electronic superpanopticon.

The concept of the panopticon actually straddles these different stories. The idea of an all-seeing eye, enhanced electronically, is common to both sorts of account.[8] But it is put to quite different uses. On the one hand it relates to its modern utilitarian Benthamite frame, where the prison architecture becomes an automated machine. On the other, in a more postmodern mood, the panopticon is a form of discourse whose repertoire is realized in simulation. The question is, are these two approaches incommensurate, as participants in the debate themselves maintain, or do they provide complementary accounts that together yield a fuller picture of the phenomena in question?

This is a question of some moment, for both analytical and political reasons. It raises, first, an issue of sociological concern: what theory is adequate to the present information-saturated social environment? The insights and limitations of each kind of theory may be explored with respect to a specific set of circumstances, the digitization of surveillance. But, second, much hangs on this question politically. Developing appropriate responses, particularly those involving regulation or resistance, depends crucially on understanding what kind of power is exercised in surveillance societies today.

Computers and modern surveillance

Four strands of surveillance theory may be distinguished, each profoundly connected with classic conceptions of modernity. In the next section, I examine some postmodern strands. Surveillance may be understood in relation to the nation state, to bureaucracy, to what might be termed technological logic (or 'technologic' for short) and to political economy. In each case, the accent is on the increasingly routine, systematic and focused attention paid by organizations to individual's lives – hence, 'surveillance'[9] – as part of an overarching processs. And in each case it is noted that computerization was introduced from the 1960s to enhance and expand the surveillance function.

As we shall see, however, there are limitations to these accounts, which I anticipate briefly here. The computer appeared as an adjunct, a feature added as it were from the outside. The result is that technology often tends to be viewed as external to social relations, and only internal to the discrete social sectors within which it is 'applied'. Realizing the potential for a sub-field that might be called 'surveillance studies', in which commonalities would be recognized between practices in different sectors, was to depend both on the proliferation of computerized surveillance and on the rise to prominence of Michel Foucault's studies of power-knowledge.[10]

The four strands may be characterized briefly as follows. The nation state orientation focuses on political imperatives that require surveillance, within geopolitical and military struggles. It leans, theoretically, on the work of Mosca, Pareto, Sorel and Michels, and points up the internal control achieved in a given country, even though the incentive to perfect the system is struggle between states. Christopher Dandeker rightly argues that the military origins of modern surveillance have been understated.[11] Externally, military power becomes increasingly bureaucratized in modern times, and this is paralleled by the bureaucratization of policing internally. For Dandeker, the corollary of external military organization is a pacified internal situation[12] and both require a steady augmentation of surveillance. Professional and bureaucratic military power can only exist dependent on a taxation system within capitalist economies.

The extremes of nation state surveillance are clearly visible in pre-1989 eastern European societies with their notoriously intrusive and fearful secret police services, such as the KGB (USSR), Stasi (East Germany) and so on. But George Orwell, and his novel *Nineteen Eighty Four*, provided the most lasting and vivid metaphors for state surveillance. Big Brother's supposedly benign face looming down from the telescreen on the hapless Winston Smith; the bureaucratic 'doublespeak' from the Ministry of Truth. Though they could be read as commentaries on communism, they were actually warnings about the surveillance potentialities of any modern nation state. Big Brother could appear in a capitalist context. Giddens' sociological cautions about modern nation states and totalitarianism are bred in the same theoretical stable.

The second strand of surveillance theory is closely related to the first, although its key theorist is Max Weber. Its best literary exponent, however, would not be Orwell so much as Franz Kafka. The latter's novels of political control, such as *The Trial*,[13] depict the terrifying fear instilled by uncertainty. Who wants this information, what do they already know, is it correct, and what will be done with what I divulge? These novels express the experiences of those dominated by bureaucracy rather than Weber's colder description of the machinery of bureaucratic organization itself.

Weber's (equally chilling, in the end) iron cage portrays surveillance as a product not of struggle between states or of rapacious class interests, but of rationalization. Irrationalities may successfully be eliminated by bureaucratic means, producing rationally calculable administrative action. The surveillance function lies primarily in the files, those dismal dossiers that store information on each individual, the knowledge of which produces and reproduces power. For Weber, bureaucratic surveillance is a means of procuring efficiency, especially in the large scale and unwieldy tasks that confront any expanding modern nation state.

It was such Weberian approaches that inspired some classic accounts of computerization in bureaucratic contexts, notably James Rule's pioneering study of *Private Lives, Public Surveillance*.[14] Rule highlighted the ways in which the shift from paper to computer files occurs but he also showed that some features of government surveillance reappear in commercial contexts. Writing in the late 1960s, his work embraced not only the computerization of bureaucratic processes in the realm of the state but also those visible in the rapidly growing operations of credit card companies. Rule tried to assess against an ideal typical total surveillance situation how large scale bureaucratic institutions encroach steadily into new domains. A Weberian stance may also be detected in David Burnham's cautionary study, *The Rise of the Computer State*,[15] a book even more concerned about the centralizing of state power through the use of computer databases. In this book however, the motif of technologic, the third strand of modern surveillance studies, is writ large.

Although for a number of reasons Jacques Ellul's contribution to sociology has seldom been seen as mainstream,[16] it is in his work in particular that insights into the technologic of modernity appear. In contrast with many others who use 'technology' to refer both to artefacts and to processes, Ellul worked with the broader concept of *la technique*. It is *la technique* that integrates the machine into society, that constructs the social world that the machine needs. *La technique* is above all an orientation to means rather than to ends, that seeks relentlessly for the one best way to operate, and in so doing steadily seems to erode human agency. It tends to be self-augmenting, irreversible, all-embracing and progresses geometrically. One of Ellul's telling examples is policing. As it is technically augmented, policing requires increasingly that all citizens be supervised, in the interests of apprehending more efficiently those who behave criminally. The perfection of unobtrusive police technique puts all under discreet surveillance.[17]

Many sociological studies of policing in the late twentieth century start with a deferential nod towards Ellul. Gary T. Marx's well-known investigation into American undercover practices is one case in point; Richard Ericson and Kevin Haggerty's *Policing the Risk Society* is another.[18] Some of Ellul's explicit ideas also survive in the hands of others in the surveillance studies field. Langdon Winner's use of 'function creep', for example, suggests that once in place a surveillance technique such as a digitized identification number will tend to expand to cover other purposes.[19] And Oscar Gandy sees the extension of personal record-keeping systems and precision marketing in terms of Ellul's 'self-completing system' even though he warns against 'assigning it intelligence and needs or some kind of integrative reality'.[20]

Although Ellul's own work represents more of an orientation than a triumph of detailed empirical demonstration of the power of *la technique*, it is clear that as least as far as the technicization of policing is concerned his fears were more than justified. Today's high-tech methods have turned officers into information brokers, operating not only according to legal warrant, but also to the codes of insurance companies.[21] Given the rise of database marketing with its consumer group classification and social sorting strategies, one wonders what he would have made of electronic commerce.

One difficulty with the Ellulian approach, some argue, lies in its apparent determinism, and the relative lack of attention paid to the politics of resistance or what Giddens calls the dialectic of control.[22] I say 'apparent' determinism, though, because Ellul maintained throughout his work a stong sense of the ambiguity of technology. His is not, in my view, an essentialist account that can only find negative expressions of technology, although one might be forgiven for coming to this conclusion from some of his work.[23] It would also be somewhat surprising if someone celebrated for his underground resistance work during the Second World War were not also committed to questioning technology politically.

Political economy, the fourth strand in modern surveillance theory, places new technologies firmly in arenas of conflicting interests – thus, in principle at least, stressing more the contestability of surveillance. In practice, even some political economy approaches lay such heavy weight on the might of capitalist corporations and the global capitalist system that the impulse to extend surveillance appears almost as invincible as in some Ellulian accounts. Surveillance is here seen as a strategic means for the reproduction of one class and its interests over another. It is especially prevalent in capitalist product-ive relations, where in the early industrial period placing workers under one factory roof facilitated their central coordination and control by making them more visible to owners and managers.

Various writers, notably Harry Braverman,[24] undertook Marxian surveil-lance studies that were to stimulate a long-lasting debate on the nature of workplace power.[25] But by the 1970s and 1980s this was being successfully expanded to include the political economy of capitalism in its increasingly consumer phase. Frank Webster and Kevin Robins, for instance, analyse not only the surveillance aspects of Taylorism in workplaces, but also of social Taylorism or 'Sloanism' applied in consumer contexts, in the attempt to manage consumption through the collection and processing of data on con-sumer behaviour.[26] They see an electronic panopticon at work.

Another major study of the political economy of personal information is Gandy's *The Panoptic Sort*,[27] which draws extensively on Weberian approaches – the rationalization of marketing – and also uses Foucault's description of the panopticon as its leading metaphor and analytical tool. Gandy's approach is instructive. He sees consumer surveillance operating on panoptic prin-ciples, whereby personal data is used to sort populations into consuming types. Electronic technologies are harnessed to assign varying economic values to different groups, and thus to computerize the production of inequality. This 'discriminatory technology . . . discards at the same time as it skims off the high-quality targets of opportunity'.[28]

These four strands of surveillance theory make considerable strides in help-ing to explain why surveillance is so important to modernity. More particu-larly, they show how computerization magnifies certain surveillance functions as well as making possible their extension into other spheres. From the polit-ical imperatives of nation state power comes a reminder of the long term historical forces behind surveillance, although this perspective offers little that would prepare us for the growth of economic as well as military com-petition between states. The association of surveillance with bureaucracy also has deep roots in modernity, with the ongoing and relentless pursuit of rationalization. The quest of prediction and calculability redoubles with the onset of computerization. However, unless this perspective is linked with others it tends towards one-dimensionality, and to seeing technological devel-opment as an essentially rationalizing process.[29]

While determinism is even more likely to be linked with increased surveillance as a product of technologic, this third position nonetheless has some
solid virtues. In particular, this strand stresses a cultural vision, the dream of
perfect knowledge, to be realized by technological means, of which surveillance is a prime instance. Uncoupled from any other goals apart from the
bureaucratic end of efficiency, it is easy to see how surveillance could be
thought of as self-justifying as well as self-augmenting. The determined drive
to perfect technologically-aided perception expresses a deep desire in contemporary culture. It has psychological and also religious dimensions, which
is also part of the Ellulian argument.

It is almost uncanny to see how each new technology is never sufficient. As
a colleague observed to me, commenting on closed-circuit television surveillance as an example: 'as soon as you have one camera, you want to see around
the next corner . . . then you want to see in the dark as well, so you add
infrared cameras. Then you want to see more detail so you add more powerful zoom lenses. And then you think, if only I could hear what they are
saying as well, so you add powerful directional microphones to your
cameras . . .'[30] Ellul insists that this techno-cultural imperative has religious
roots in a misplaced western faith in human capacities to solve social problems without reference to transcendent criteria. In the end, a candid acknow-
ledgement of human finitude, frailty and dependence is the Ellulian antidote
to such modernist hubris.

It comes as no surprise that political economy approaches often cast
sceptical eyes on such ideas as technologic. They emphasize as ever the
role of the state and the economy in shaping surveillance practices and
processes. To my mind this complements rather than contradicts the technologic position. This final approach offers the timely reminder that any technological encounter – not least those involving surveillance – will display
subject positions that are either dominant or subordinate. How far this
perspective admits of bureaucratic imperatives or of the role of conscious
agents in surveillance situations depends on which theorists are in question.
Webster and Robins, and Gandy, mentioned above, allow for both in their
work.

The modern strands of surveillance theory discussed here show how computerization enhances and extends familiar processes, often producing some
fresh fears about centralized control, or the violability of personal life. But
they often tend to view technology as a separate category from social life,
that impinges upon that life, albeit in more invasive or even more carceral
ways. One might be forgiven for asking if this kind of approach is adequate
to the conditions that obtain at the start of the twenty-first century. Technology has become the very medium of everyday life – one has only to be in-
truded upon by cellphone conversations or observe bank machine transactions
on any street corner to see this – such that an increasingly dominant proportion
of social relations are in part constituted by technology. It is these kinds of
insight that have spurred efforts to reconsider surveillance in terms of a
superpanopticon and of simulation.

Superpanopticon and hypersurveillance

It is ironic that Foucault, who had almost nothing to say about computers, should inspire some radically new approaches to digitized surveillance. Collectively, they might be thought of as postmodern perspectives. The source of the Foucaldian irony is not hard to trace, however. Foucault popularized the idea of the panopticon as the epitome of social control in modern times. What had once featured merely as an innovative and influential approach to prison architecture, produced by an eccentric social reformer, was reinvented by Foucault as a paradigmatic examplar of modern discipline.

Jeremy Bentham's late eighteenth-century design for a panopticon prison relied on an elaborate apparatus of blinds on the inspection tower windows to prevent inmates seeing their observer, back lighting to illuminate prisoners and a semicircular arrangement of classified cells so that the category as well as any action of prisoners was immediately apparent. The idea was to automate the disciplinary system, to induce self-monitoring in prisoners, and to render real-life inspectors all but redundant. It has not escaped the attention of a number of commentators that electronic technologies permit the perfection of such a panopticon, but now through software architectures.

Although it was Foucault's insightful analyses that stimulated the association of the panopticon and electronic surveillance, it was, ironically, a fairly unFoucaldian version of the panopticon that first appeared.[31] The panopticon, it seemed, could be fitted into existing analyses of discipline and social control without the baggage of discourse. It was left to Mark Poster to pick up on the distinctively discursive elements of Foucault's analysis, which he does with his reminder that 'databases are configurations of language'.[32] Thus Poster deliberately deflects attention from what he argues are the action-orientated surveillance theories deriving from Marx and Weber. For Poster, the recognition that databases deal in symbols and representations opens them to poststructural analysis.[33] This undoubtedly places theory in a more postmodern frame.

Poster elaborates on discourse in order to make the connections with databases. Subjects, first, are configured as such, or are given cultural significance, through language. In modern contexts, where individual consciousness is privileged, this means that subjects tend to be fixed within binary opposites such as freedom/determinism. In everyday life, subjects are constantly reconstituted through interpellation or 'hailing'. Thus we unreflectively accept our designation in particular subject positions (student, employee, cabdriver, chairperson) as part of our daily interactions. Such interpellation – still at the level of language – is never complete or final. It is ever open to challenge, reconfiguration, resistance, even where identities appear to be fixed. The cultural construction of the subject by such means indicates how 'discourse was configured as a form of power and power was understood as operating in part through language'.[34]

As Poster observes, Foucault does not follow through with a theory of discursive power, so much as its demonstration through his famous histories of punishment and of sexuality. Discourse reveals its power by positioning 'the subject in relation to structures of domination in such a way that those structures may *then* act upon him or her'.[35] The panopticon's power does not reside simply in the (supposedly) ever-observant guard. Rather, it is manifest in the way that the whole discourse and practice of the system bears down, constituting the subject as criminal and normalizing him or her into rehabilitation, or as Bentham conceived it, moral reform.[36] For Poster, computer databases bring panoptic principles out of the jail and into mainstream society to operate as a 'superpanopticon', reconfiguring once more the constitution of the subject.[37]

The database extends writing, according to Poster, removing it further from any one 'author' than conventional, non-electronic writing does. The database also adds both a new mobility (it is transferable in space) and durability (it is preservable in time) to writing. The database 'text' is no one's and everyone's. And yet it is owned by some institution – a library, a corporation, a hospital – and thus amplifies that institution's power. People know this and from time to time admit their fears to a pollster or even refuse to divulge requested information – for instance, on a membership or warranty form. But at the same time, and apparently impervious to moments of resistance, power is extended effortlessly. This is in part because subjects constantly participate in their own surveillance by making cellphone calls, automated bank transactions, Internet bookings and so on. Thus, concludes Poster, 'Individuals are plugged into circuits of their own panoptic control, making a mockery of theories of social action, like Weber's, that privilege consciousness as the basis of self-interpretation, and liberals generally, who locate meaning in the intimate, subjective recesses behind the shield of the skin'.[38]

The personal database connects identifying symbols such as government social insurance numbers with discrete records of benefits claimed or tax paid. In the case of corporations, records of purchases and other transactions are made, such that a picture can be created of legal compliance or of buying habits. These, Poster suggests, count as instances of Foucault's 'grids of specification'. The subject is multiplied and decentered in the database, acted on by remote computers each time a record is automatically verified or checked against another, without ever referring to the individual concerned. The database as language performs certain actions. Computers become 'machines for producing retrievable identities'.[39] Electronic interpellation thus takes writing into another realm, hinting at how the subject is reconstituted. At the same time it reveals the potential for domination inherent in the databases as well as possibilities for its modification within the overall process.

The panopticon produces subjects with desires to improve their inner lives. In contrast the superpanopticon constitutes objects, individuals with dispersed identities, who may remain unaware of how those identities are construed by the computer. We are once again back with disappearing bodies. Modern surveillance has everything to do with individuation,[40] distinguishing carefully between one identifiable individual subject and the next. But postmodern surveillance takes this further, into the multiplication of identities, split off from and yet reconnectable with the individuals whose data constitutes them. The identities thus constituted are simulated, as a variety of what Baudrillard calls 'hyperreality'. Individuals have new forms of presence. As Poster says, these are subject positions that define them for all those agencies and individuals who have access to the database.[41] But what are the origins and consequences of such simulation? For one answer to this we must turn to a second strand of theory.

William Bogard uses Baudrillard rather than Foucault as his theoretical springboard into the simulated world of surveillance. For Bogard, it is simulation that represents the crucial omission from contemporary modern accounts of surveillance. Again, electronic technologies are the key. Virtual replace actual processes and electronic signs and images of objects and events replace their real counterparts.[42] What began in military fields with wargaming techniques or stealth weapons has spread via areas like ecological environment simulations, or corporate simulations of their markets, to surveillance. In contrast with Foucault, much of Baudrillard's work is precisely predicated on the development and proliferation of communication and information technologies.

For Baudrillard, simulation is the 'reproduction of the real' by means of codes and models, 'in the same way that computerized images are a function of their program'.[43] Simulation tries to achieve a reality effect while simultaneously concealing the absence of the real. The real becomes redundant as a referential ground for the image – hence, hyperreality. The hyperreal, then, is the code (the 'technologies of signalization') that precedes the 'real' and brings it into being. In Baudrillard's 'telematic societies' – information societies to others – simulation is the 'reigning scheme'.[44] This how the code comes to prominence as the mode of domination and control.

In Baudrillard's scheme, images once represented the real, as, he suggests, in the Christian communion, where the bread is the 'body of Christ'. Then, false appearances developed, to be attacked by Karl Marx as the illusions and fetishes of a capitalist order. The information age ushers in a third stage, in which modern modes of representation break down, as the image is shown to conceal an absent presence – there is no real. Baudrillard presses on to consider a fourth moment, where social relations themselves are hyperrealized. This, he controversially claims, spells the 'end of the social', which is Bogard's entry point for considering surveillance.

In Bogard's account, 'hypersurveillant' control both intensifies surveillance and attempts to take it to its absolute limit. The speed of computing allows surveillance to overtake itself, as it were, and to operate in advance of itself. It turns into a technology of pre-exposure and pre-recording, prior to the occurrence of the behaviour or the event in real time. The Cromatica system that predicts suicide attempts on underground train stations provides a good example.[45] For Bogard, the panopticon is not only digitized, so that it can be understood as a form of discourse; it is seen thus as a strategy of exposure and recording, conveys it into a paradoxical realm where surveillance looks *on* the screen, rather than behind it. As in Poster's work, an impatience with modern accounts pervades this text. Bogard, too, aspires to go 'beyond Marx and Weber'.[46]

Speed is central. The idea behind surveillant simulation is to win the race to see first, to foresee. Paul Virilio dubs this principle 'dromology'.[47] It works as control by deflecting the attention to appearances, by generating uncertainty. Such appearances already occur in the physical panopticon and their intention is to create uncertainty.[48] But the panopticon generates uncertainty about what the observer might be able to see now, rather than about what might be 'seen' of what has not yet happened. The computer profile, which organizes multiple sources of information to scan for matching or exceptional cases, tries to second-guess behaviours. In what amounts to an 'informated form of stereotyping'[49] the profile is used as an advance notice of likely purchases – which in the case of electronic commerce will trigger advertising targeted at specific persons – or an advance warning of potential offences, in the case of police computer systems.

But, says Bogard, the informated stereotype is not merely a 'false image' used to justify power differences. It is more a self-fulfilling prophecy, as the reality comes to resemble the image. Verification may occur prior to identification, at least identification in the modern sense. With the right password, or code, life can continue as normal. Without it, the individual is served up as a suspect or as a marketing target. Is Bogard correct about this? I shall make further comments about his perspective below but at this point let us just note that it lacks empirical substance in an important respect. It is not necessarily wrong, but one area in which insufficient research has been done is on how 'realities come to resemble the image' in the surveillance context. A critical understanding of this process will make a considerable contribution to surveillance studies.[50]

Simulant surveillance technologies have some important features. They simulate factuality rather than documenting empirical events, thus reinforcing the uncertainty of subjects. They aim to deter and to prevent or to guide and enable certain behaviours. The more daily life is mediated by electronic technologies and the more the screen events substitute for experience, the less the working of these technologies is perceptible. For Foucault, discipline normalizes people to moral standards of behaviour or to institutional requirements. For Bogard, in 'telematic' societies, individuals are 'supernormalized' according to codes, managed as flows of data. Simulated surveillance may also be understood in relation to transparent surfaces, sterile zones, breaks and flows of images, and as technological imaginary.

Bogard comments on the paradox that whereas surveillance wishes to get beneath the surface, to see behind the world as it appears, simulation sees *across* the surface. What is visible is all that is visible. Perception itself becomes transparent, in this view, with the goal of eliminating the difference between the real and the illusion. Again, where modern surveillance aimed at creating clean, sterile environments of order, simulation aspires to take this further, towards perfect disinfection. Bogard connects this with biomedical surveillance, with its accompanying uncertainties about moments of death or the boundaries of the body.

Bogard also highlights the shift from surveillance to simulation by observing that the former is a means of recording, and, as such, it already shows signs of simulation. For in recording – an event, a word, a transaction – a copy has been made, and a break created in the flow, which in turn is the start of a fresh flow. Lastly, and this is the point towards which Bogard's other observations converge, simulation has to do with pure control, so much so that the 'imaginary annihilates the image'.[51] Simulation attempts to go beyond the limits of surveillance, to a virtual reality where the spaces and times to be controlled are manufactured ones. The environment can be perfectly controlled. Indeed, it no longer requires control; the environment *is* control.

The Bogardian perspective takes us unremittingly into the realm of the hyperreal. In so doing it tends to flatten the social world in ways that I try to avoid in this book. It is not that simulated surveillance does not occur on an increasing scale or that computer-generated identities based on data fragments do not actually circulate within surveillance databases with consequences for subjectivity and for social justice. The problem is rather that, in pursuing surveillance into the shadowy world of panoptic imaginary, the real world of embodied persons itself appears to have dissolved. We are thus left with a vision that is at once playful and paranoid. It is also paralysed politically.

New surveillance in theory

The two kinds of surveillance theory discussed here present what appear to be quite divergent accounts, especially if the exhortations are heeded to go 'beyond Marx and Weber'. At the same time, these theories have in common a desire to explain the electronic enhancement of surveillance since the late twentieth century. They also recognize that Foucault's studies, particularly those of the panopticon, are relevant to that explanation. In what follows, I argue that while going 'beyond' Marx, Weber and others may be required for an adequate theory of contemporary surveillance practices, 'going beyond' does not entail forsaking *in toto* the modes of analysis inspired by them. Indeed, important continuities exist between the different theoretical modes, and aspects of the newer theories can add nuance to the older, for their mutual benefit, and to the advantage of the quest for appropriate surveillance theory.

The classically orientated theories have in common a search for the social – and especially the institutional – roots of surveillance processes as they have developed, especially in the twentieth century. Thus military competition between nation states, the rationalization expressed in bureaucracy and the class imperatives of capitalism are viewed variously as the origins and the providers of the essential dynamics for modern surveillance. Each emphasizes aspects of surveillance that can readily be understood as magnifying the power of the institution employing the relevant practices to the relative disadvantage of individuals who are thus located, recorded, observed, monitored, classified and processed. Each also has excellent exemplars in discrete areas, such as in factory or office organization, urban planning or policing, and so on.

The shortcomings of the more conventional approaches, particularly when it comes to understanding the impact of new technologies on surveillance, may be summarized as follows. The strength of specific studies of institutional areas is a weakness when it comes to new technologies, which often have the effect of producing convergence.[52] Management functions of supervision and monitoring, for example, become blurred when electronic technologies are adopted.[53] Similarly, a focus on surveillance that seeks commonalities across institutional areas will note features such as the use of computer matching using different databases, which are found in areas such as marketing and policing. It is hard to imagine these two being uttered in the same breath in more conventional accounts.

This speaks to another concern. Technology often appears as an 'external' factor in earlier accounts rather than as a mode of mediating daily life. As such, technology may seem to exibit some essential features – such as rationalizing, or producing efficiency – rather than ones that are flexible, malleable, constructed, contestable. Lastly, when it comes to the relevance of theory to policy, the laudable concern for disadvantaged individuals (understandable in terms of a classic society/individual dualism) sometimes means that the systematic disadvantaging of whole populations is missed (though this is not true of Marxian approaches, of course). Thus privacy appears as the complementary item – the policy antidote – in the surveillance/privacy binary relation.

The newer theories commend themselves by focusing explicitly on the differences made by communication and information technologies. Poster's work attempts to recalibrate surveillance theory in terms of the language of computer databases and thus of discursive power. By showing what the database *does*, how its peculiar language *performs* certain functions, Poster indicates fresh avenues for surveillance inquiry, structured around the idea of the superpanopticon. How the data subject is positioned within the database's grid of specification reveals much about the domination involved as well, insists Poster, as how it might be countered. Similarly, Deleuze's isolation of the code, as discussed by Bogard, indicates further the means of power within surveillant simulation. Again, this sieve-like code is not fixed, but, as Christine Boyer says, transmutes, undulates and is constantly at work.[54] This is another insight into the specific differences made in surveillance by the use of computer-based technologies.

On their own, however, the newer theories also fail to satisfy completely. Poster's work, while highly suggestive, does not yet go far enough. While he acknowledges the interesting features of Marxian and Weberian theories, he does not return to them to say how they might still provide explanatory purchase on the problems of current surveillance. Rather, they are discarded as action-based theories, inappropriate to the world of database language and discourse. In addition, while Poster makes brief mention of 'biopower' – the concept at the heart of Foucault's *History of Sexuality* – and leans on it implicitly, he does not fully incorporate it into his account of surveillance.

One could argue that Poster's superpanopticon actually depends upon biopower for its operation. For Foucault, biopower originated in the dusty-sounding statistical study of populations. But it 'made knowledge-power an agent of transformation of human life'.[55] Counting bodies, argues Ian Hacking, had the subversive effect of creating 'new categories into which people had to fall, and so to create and render rigid new conceptualizations of the human being'.[56] Translate this into computer language and its signficance emerges. Note its massive expansion and automation in the contemporary surveillance and simulation of behaviours under the sign of mobility. Contrast this with the counting of relatively static bodies of earlier modernity and one can see that what began in the era of 'moral science' has precise ramifications for the codes that order social life today.

Bogard's work, on the other hand, goes too far. His extravagant prose, a trait not entirely absent from Baudrillard's output as well, serves to obscure rather than clarify. Though important and insightful, his probing of paradox and ambiguity leaves the impression of a highly determined, inescapable web of electronic impulses, the essentialist core of which is simulation, spinning off unchecked through the post-social spheres. Seemingly aware of this, Bogard concludes with a note on 'cyborgian boredom' as a mode of resistance. This will hardly do. One doubts that electronic ennui will catch on quickly as an alternative to liberal solutions of data protection and privacy law.

It is unfortunate but unsurprising that Bogard falls prey to just the same mistakes as his mentor, Baudrillard. The metaphors that inform his work take off on their own and he seems to deny that they refer to any reality except their own.[57] Digital codes are all that is left. But even Baudrillard notes the way that in contemporary simulation 'digitality is its metaphysical principle . . . and DNA its prophet'. In the genetic code the 'genesis of simulacra' finds its archtype.[58] As we have seen, the computer-assisted coding and sorting of DNA has both its arcane aspects and its all-too-concrete effects on embodied persons and on particular social groups. It is easy to slip into surface preoccupations and self-referentiality. Simulacra do indeed challenge the 'real'. But an alternative response is to pursue a sociology that acknowledges the instability of categories with a view to participating in their value-based transformations.

To justify my proposal that modern and postmodern theory may be mutually informing, however, I turn to two exemplars. One reconsiders the panopticon in relation to policing, and the other simulation in relation to urban management. In each case, the idiosyncratic effects of electronic technologies are discussed in ways that are open to Foucaldian and Baudrillardian insights, but are now articulated with the life chances of concrete individuals and with the practical shaping of material geographies respectively.

Ericson and Haggerty's *Policing the Risk Society* (1997) brings together perspectives often thought of as divergent: those of Michel Foucault on the one hand, and of Ulrich Beck on the other. Surveillance is understood in terms of responses to risk. Foucault's microphysics of power, seen in everyday police practices, connects governmentality with the management of risk. Within the network society, policing constitutes a vital node, through which data pertaining to risk assessment flow. The rising sense of insecurity, engendered by many means and encouraged by insurance companies, is countered by efforts to contain threats and deflect hazards to the social fabric. Institutions external to the police, including education, welfare, health, employment and, prominently and pervasively, insurance, require knowledge of risks, which the police garner and communicate. To do so, they renew and extend their intelligence networks, particularly through community policing, linked with the high technology mobile offices that appear on the street as patrol cars.[59]

This is exemplified in the consequences of the British Crime and Disorder Act of 1998. Not only do the police siphon off intelligence for other areas such as health care and municipal government. In addition, all areas seem to take on policing functions for crime reduction, whether municipal governments, probation services, education or health authorities. Groups such as the new 'Youth Offending Teams' are multi-agency entities with no one lead agency. Such inter-agency activity relating to policing is clearly enhanced by whatever data sharing is possible. But in the UK the Data Protection Act assumes that discrete agencies hold and process personal data. The consequences of this contradiction will surface sooner or later.

Policing the Risk Society says little about the panopticon. It is seen as less relevant to explaining policing than biopower, the key concept of Foucault's *History of Sexuality*. Still, Ericson and Haggerty's discussion of biopower connects neatly with Poster's discursive interpretation of the superpanopticon. Biopower operates in social spaces between the state and civil society, 'making up people' and fabricating them into the logic of the norm. But in contemporary police practices, suggest Ericson and Haggerty, the 'norm' has to do with risk assessments, with statistical probabilities and thus with observable (or simulated) behaviours. If the superpanopticon is correctly viewed as a form of discourse within which individuals are situated within 'grids of specification' then these seem to be instances of very similar if not identical phenomena. Indeed, despite his emphasis on the superpanopticon, Poster also acknowledges the connection with biopower. As he says, 'An important political effect of databases, as they have been disseminated in our societies, is to promote the "governmental" form of power, to make knowledge of the population available to coercive institutions at every level'.[60]

Unlike Poster, however, Ericson and Haggerty weave the actor back into their account. They claim that the electronic persona acts back on the subject but with the cooperation of that subject. Invoking Pierre Bourdieu's work, they argue that individuals may accept the classifications imposed upon them by biopowerful means, providing people with categorical scripts which are followed to a greater or lesser degree. Although not much evidence is given for this, the risk society and surveillance thesis is nevertheless borne out in many other respects, particularly in the thick descriptions offered of police patrol work. Much credence is thus given to the proposal that governmentality is a sort of risk management and thus that it operates increasingly a kind of amoral political arithmetic for governing populations at a distance. Surveillance in this theory is driven by the imperatives of risk management and is subject to the logic of the codes that such risk management generates.

In their *Telecommunications and the City: Electronic Spaces, Urban Places*, Stephen Graham and Simon Marvin show how new technologies are used to determine where businesses should be set up or closed down. In the former case, this also indicates who should receive particular encouragement to become a loyal customer and who will be effectively ignored by retailers.[61] In a later work, Graham picks up explicitly on the Bogardian 'surveillant simulation' phrase and applies it to the same situations of city planning. But he also charges Bogard with failing to 'explore how practices of surveillant simulation become embodied in the production of grounded sociospatial relations'.[62] While these authors accept some of the important insights of surveillant simulation they also weave them into a critical account of the contemporary city. By this means they demonstrate how simulations are implicated in the allocation of goods and services and in the attempted patterns of social control.

In the 1990s, retailers and banks in Europe as well as in North America used a growing array of geodemographic tools for making decisions about where to locate and invest. Geodemographic profiles cluster potential consumers into postcode and zipcode neighbourhood groups known by stereotypical nicknames such as 'graffitied ghettoes' and 'pools-and-patios'. They provide fine-grained dynamic maps of consumption and spending potential. Such simulations are then treated as if they were accurate representations of reality. An artificial image of the outside world is mapped inside the computer. There it is monitored and manipulated as if there were no ironic gap between the image and the reality, and is utilized to determine all too concrete plans for the material world of people and places.

The results are that patterns of discrimination are reinforced. Surveillant simulations produce practices that tend towards the withdrawal of banks and retail outlets from already disadvantaged areas and their installation within the economically preferable locations chosen from computer generated representations of the sociospatial grid. Graham and Marvin refer to this process as 'cherry-picking'. An example would be the fact that the main banks in the UK have used geographic information systems to select which branches will close in a general contraction of outlets by 25 per cent over less than 15 years. They also show that within privatized British utilities, restructuring processes have involved surveillant simulation to cherry-pick lucrative market segments and to withdraw from unprofitable social and spatial commitments.

Not only does categorical selection and rejection of individuals occur by virtue of which neighbourhoods they happen to live in, surveillant simulations are also implicated in more precise decision making about opportunities and life chances. Growing trends of electronically-enabled home-based consumption of goods and services permit a growing range of devices for monitoring the buying patterns and consumption rates of particular households.[63] The simulated digital consumer image is constructed for corporate purposes and used not only to trace and track the big spenders but also to create blacklists of bad credit risks. Once again, it is merely observable behaviours that count in constructing the image – the simulation. The fact that self-fulfilling prophesies might also be involved, or that disabling illness, breakdown of relationships or some other factor might be the proximate cause of poverty or inability to meet demands on time, does not enter the simulated equation.

In these two examples, then, insights are combined from theoretical sources which are, according to some of their proponents, incommensurate. These studies use Foucaldian and Baudrillardian ideas respectively but within frames of social analysis that derive from much more classical sources, especially those of Marx and Weber. Acknowledging the need to go beyond the latter does not necessitate their displacement by more poststructuralist approaches. Used in the ways suggested, they provide complementary insights into the urgent issues surrounding contemporary surveillance societies. One may agree with Gary T. Marx that a 'new' surveillance is enabled by information technologies but also with Mark Poster that the 'newness' has as much to do with discursive power expressed in computer databases as with the technological penetration of barriers, darkness and distance. Equally, one may concur with William Bogard that simulation is a key to contemporary surveillance practices, but also with Stephen Graham that this fact does not somehow propel us altogether out of real-world patterns of inclusion and exclusion in today's cities.

Returning the body

Any social theory worthy of the name will offer a mode of interpreting the processes that pattern today's world. In this case, the process in question is surveillance. We are right to expect theory to explain why some things happen in the way that they do in terms of both historical background and likely developments. Theory is constrained by empirical evidence, events and trends that can in some way be demonstrated. But theory is never produced by mere evidence. It is an argument, a process of rhetoric, that relies for its illuminatory power on metaphors and on commitments. These are the elements of theory that cannot be proved but cannot but be presupposed.

To understand surveillance today it is not enough to rely on classical sources of the sociological imagination. Marx, Weber, Simmel and others provide fascinating and essential insights but is it anachronistic to rummage in their theories for clues about emergent features of informational network societies. Equally, I have argued, some prominent social theories that take cognizance of the new technologies fail to do full justice to the problems raised by surveillance. In part, this is because they shelve the classical sociological heritage and its concerns with action, the material conditions of life, and the prospects for political engagement.

This is not just a plea for a patching together of theoretical pieces, although I do think that a disciplined eclecticism is a valid way forward. The pattern for the patchwork should be provided by a more coherent view of embodied persons, of the cultural obsession with omniperception, and of an ethic to guide the politics of surveillance. These elements are either underplayed or absent from the theoretical traditions discussed above.

First, embodied personhood should be kept central to surveillance (and to other) theory because it both grounds explanation in everyday life and offers ways of bridging classical and contemporary theory. Bodies may disappear from social relationships in a media-wrapped world but they still need friendship, food and meaningful activities in mundane local life. The disembodied relations of surveillance data do not entirely lose contact with the embodied lives of the persons from whose behaviour or bodies those data are extracted. Under today's surveillance conditions the uneven distribution of life chances and opportunities is increasingly subject to automation and thus to virtual reinforcement. The processes depend, crucially, upon digital stereotyping of groups and individuals, using codes derived from computer grids of specification, at least some of which are then transposed back into the real world of everyday life.

Other aspects of the dispersal and multiplication of identities may both enable and constrain individuals in ways that are as yet inadequately understood. These processes are not innocent or autonomous. Surveillant simulations do not arise in a political-economic vaccuum or operate merely according to some whimsical logic of arcade computer games. They are still driven by the dictates and the routines of the nation state, of large corporations and of bureaucratic organizations, even as personal data flows less discriminately within and between these sectors. Embodied persons and distinct social groups are still privileged or disadvantaged, online or switched off, enabled or constrained in ways that relate to their electronic classification by surveillance.

Second, the cultural obsession with omniperception must be further explored if an adequate theory of surveillance is sought. The rise of risk management and the vastly enhanced technical capacities of new surveillance technologies do not themselves explain the compulsion to account for everything and to capture all within the range of vision. Ellul exposes the dangerous power of derailed knowledge, embodied in artefacts, technical expertise and processes, and he even anticipates aspects of surveillance in its electronically-enabled, simulated phase. Just such aspects Bogard finds in surveillant simulations; the 'dream of perfect knowledge' as it were, in computer-enhanced form. What Ellul excoriates as idolatry, Bogard situates as social science fiction. It is, says Bogard, 'the fantastic dream of seeing everything capable of being seen, recording every fact capable of being recorded, and accomplishing these things, whenever and wherever possible, prior to the event itself'.[64]

How long can surveillance theory ignore the implications of this? It seems entirely appropriate to add to the surveillance impetuses of the nation state, capitalism and bureaucracy, the imperatives of an implicit cultural commitment to omniperception. It was already visible in Bentham's panoptic hubris and is now a persistent pulse that beats on through other social transformations and economic restructuring. To take it seriously adds both to the predictive power of theory – we may expect surveillance to expand according to its own technologic in addition to external demands made of it – and to its critical cutting edge. The driving desire to dragnet yet more detailed data is both as old and as ominous as the aspiration to be 'as God'.[65]

Third, theories and politics of surveillance should be yoked together. Today surveillance is a supercharged means of power in any and all societies dependent upon information infrastructures. It thus demands fresh political commitment to understand it and to challenge its negative aspects. What surveillance helps to produce is a form of social orchestration, where the scores are provided by those classically dominant formations, and where the melody is produced by musicians who participate by being aware of the score. The scores are computer coded and classifying, but they also allow for improvisations, so the music is less predictable than in 'classical' compositions.

The scores themselves may alter in some respects as characteristics of the musicians are fed into the loop, or indeed as musicians succeed in counterposing their rhythms and their tunes to the dominant ones. As synthesizers are brought in, so computing power extends the scope of the music, while at the same time setting new limits to it. This is not a static or rigid 'musical' production, but it does locate individuals. It also includes them or excludes them from full social and political participation by criteria that are not entirely of their choosing, criteria that do not transcend in any meaningful way the abstract and self-referring data embedded in the coded notation.

Political involvement is thus undertaken by those already implicated as participants in surveillance situations and processes. It calls, not for opposition to surveillance as such, but for a principled awareness of the tendencies of current practices and of their potential threats to social justice and personal dignity. In the next chapter I explore these politics of surveillance in terms of modes of resistance and their relative effectiveness. The ethics that pilot both theory and politics through the shoals of surveillance may again be appropriately based in embodied personhood.

Persons are intrinsically social and thus communication is vital. This has two implications. One, the notion of the face to face should be privileged in a communicative ethic. Voluntary self-disclosure in relations of trust may only be impugned reluctantly and with very good cause. Two, concern for the Other is a primal demand of humanness. When the society of strangers has been extended electronically to create categories of 'strangeness' in addition to those of classical racial or class stereotyping, that demand is accentuated, not abrogated. It also connects indissolubly the personal with the political.

The politics of surveillance

Few people, unless they are painfully shy, would miss the opportunity to collect an award for which they had been nominated. There could be another reason, though. Would you want to run the gamut of television cameras and reporters if you had just been named as the winner of this year's 'Big Brother' award for violating privacy? The first award, a bronze statuette of a boot on a human face, was presented by Privacy International in ceremonies in London and Washington in 1998 and 1999. Microsoft Corporation and the Federal Depository Insurance Corporation were among the 'Orwell' award winners. The politics of surveillance are certainly becoming more prominent although, as we shall see, their prospects are still far from bright.

Surveillance technologies and practices are proliferating, bred and cloned by electronic technologies. Security cameras, barcodes, personal identification numbers (PINs) and passwords exist as an unremarkable part of the fabric of daily life. Many are more subtle, discreet, routine and taken for granted than ever. But the decreasing visibility and overtness of some monitoring and observing devices does not mean that people are unaware of the contemporary expansion of surveillance. After all, cameras are usually mounted where they may be seen and signs often alert us to their gaze. And when it comes to biometrics, DNA and drug-testing, most surveillance is sensed by the body.

In the early 1970s Francis Ford Coppola's film *The Conversation* explored the moral and ethical dilemmas of wiretapping. But wiretapping was and is a 'special case' in most circumstances. In the film a surveillance expert starts to question the propriety of his profession but in an ironic twist becomes a victim himself. He ends by tearing up his apartment to find the hidden bugs. Only two decades later Tony Scott's *Enemy of the State* (1997) portrayed the victim as an innocent who just happened to be in the wrong place at the wrong time. He is hounded by a corrupt official within the National Security Agency, who plays the techno card for all it is worth, complete with GPS and closed-circuit television devices. But the other part of the plot is that the National Security Agency official would highjack the Telecommunication Privacy Bill if he could, thus bringing the politics of security and civil liberties right into centre screen. The politics of surveillance is much more generalized in the 1990s than in the 1970s picture.

So, far from surveillance simply happening behind our backs, leaving us perilously ignorant of how much is known about our daily doings, ordinary people are often aware at least of some of the ways their everyday lives are monitored. Why else would teenagers deliberately antagonize camera systems operatives by playing up to the cameras[1] or workers tear down a surveillance camera from the canteen wall?[2] Beyond the personal and the *ad hoc*, many media and movements also alert us to the fact, and sometimes to the extent, of our being monitored. Films, consumer groups, Internet campaigns and international watchdogs are just some of the ways that ongoing surveillance practices are brought to the surface of our consciousness, and thus overtly into the realm of ethical evaluation and political response.

Much surveillance, rightly or wrongly, is welcomed as benign and is complacently accepted. But some surveillance generates a sense of threat. A whole spectrum of possible responses to surveillance is manifest today, reflecting the range of contexts in which surveillance now occurs. Generally speaking, while routine administrative surveillance by government departments is taken for granted, errors and abuses within such systems generate alarm. They may be feared as endangering autonomy or liberty. Defensive responses include attempts to 'protect privacy', to ensure freedom from interference, or possibly to try to ensure maximum participation without fear of reprisals.

In the workplace the thinness of the line between legitimate and illegitimate monitoring is becoming increasingly apparent. The category of 'private' is increasingly invoked in disputes about the use of surveillance cameras in the workplace or about what kinds of email and Internet use are appropriate in worktime. The latter example also hints at the growing range of establishments within which such questions are raised. Increasing reliance on electronic communications within all kinds of workplace, professional as well as shopfloor, means that surveillance issues inevitably arise. In this case surveillance is treated as a matter to be negotiated and if necessary resisted. But as we shall see, resistance often tends to be limited to complaints about violations of rights.

With the ballooning of commercial surveillance, the field has broadened to include a desire to be left alone, seen for instance in opposition to junk mail or spamming, or to control the flow of personal data. So while some responses to surveillance refer to political liberties or workers' rights, others may concern our sense of identity and how to bring its consumer caricatures under control. Most of the time passivity seems to characterize consumer situations. Research is required on this point, to check for example the anecdotal evidence that many people fake details requested on registration forms unless they actually want to hear again from the company involved. But while the public awareness of consumer surveillance may be rising, it is undoubedly doing so at a rate far slower than the opportunities for consumer surveillance are being exploited.

The vast bulk of responses to surveillance come under the rubric of protecting privacy. This is very understandable, given the rush towards rights in current politics, and in some ways appropriate, given the invasive nature of many surveillance practices. It is also comprehensible in the light of political pressure to ease the way for electronic commerce. In his State of the Union address for 2000 President Clinton promised more privacy for all Americans using the Internet. In particular he was at pains to offer financial privacy, which of course is a key concern for those promoting and engaging in electronic commerce.[3] But the politics of privacy also misses the point in some significant respects.

The automation of inequality through digitized stereotypes and through categorical seduction and suspicion calls for responses of a more fundamentally social kind, ones that refer to a concept of justice. Even the politics of privacy has often lost sight of the social as well as the personal issues of human dignity that are raised when the capacity to disclose ourselves to others within relationships of trust is compromised. So although, in what follows, privacy is alluded to with some frequency, I wish also to stress its relation to broader issues.

What follows in this chapter is a review of various responses to surveillance that have emerged since the widespread computerization of the 1960s. These are multiplying at popular, policy and political levels. While many of these responses are to be welcomed, they often display a limited understanding of the social dimensions of privacy and of the deeper implications of surveillance for social orchestration. That said, some responses to surveillance have coalesced into social movements – my second major focus – that are serving to raise awareness of surveillance issues on a broader, international, scale.

This in turn raises the question of why these kinds of response have arisen at this time and what they mean in terms of changing political contexts. Are they instances of Ulrich Beck's 'subpolitics' in the risk society, for example, or of Alberto Melucci's 'challenging codes' in the information society? Finally, some judgement is required as to how far the responses discussed are making a difference. In particular, we must ask why resistance is often lacking and why it fails. Are the negative aspects of contemporary surveillance likely to be mitigated or eliminated if present trends continue?

Regulative responses

The computerization of personal data – its collection, storage, processing and dissemination – since the 1960s has engendered policy responses in all countries dependent on information infrastructures, with European countries taking the lead.[4] What usually goes under the name of privacy has quietly become a policy sector in its own right, even though it is seldom politicized. Although the ways of approaching the issues differ markedly in different countries, a general consensus did emerge in the last part of the twentieth century. So while the UK depends on a Data Protection Registry, Sweden on licensing data collectors, Germany on an ombudsman, Canada on Privacy Commissions, the USA on the courts, and so on, general agreement on fair information principles is growing across these different countries.

The principles enunciate how personal data should be handled. Those involved should be accountable for information entrusted to them, should be clear about the purposes of collecting information, and should ensure that it is collected with the knowledge and consent of those to whom it pertains. The harvesting of personal information should be limited to the stated purposes, according to the principles, and not disclosed to other parties without consent. It should not be kept longer than necessary, but when retained, should be accurate, complete and up to date. Security safeguards should be provided, information policies should be open and data subjects should have access to and the right to correct their personal information. Such general principles have found their way into legislation, voluntary codes, international agreements and standards, which in itself must be seen as a considerable achievement for the agencies, experts, advocates, pressure groups, lawyers, business persons and academics concerned.

Those advocating these principles have been quite clear that, while enshrining them in legislation is an important step, their broader dissemination is required if they are to have any hope of making a difference. Thus in several countries fair information principles have been adopted within voluntary codes and guidelines. In Canada, for example, the Direct Marketing Association encourages conformity with the principles. It did so before the passing of any law, outside Quebec, covering commercial databases. In 1995, moreover, the Canadian Standards Association published a national privacy standard, which was the first of its kind.[5] Many banks and other personal data processing agencies in Canada now publish their privacy policies, issuing them to all new customers.

Examples may be found in the USA, too. American Express has agreed with the New York state attorney to inform customers of tracking and of comparing personal data lists for sale. The publishing of codes and guide lines is seen by some as good public relations, analogous to the 'environmental friendliness' tag that has been sought by many companies since the 1980s. But whatever the reason, the consequence is that customer satisfaction is seen more and more as including a sense that personal data is being fairly and appropriately handled.[6]

Others have objected that this, too, is insufficient, given the corporate goals of those collecting and processing personal data. However much companies may wish to give an impression of caring for customers they are still insatiably hungry for personal data, the analysis of which is now a central means of marketing. Personal data has been commodified on a massive scale and trade in such details appears in many ways to be out of control. Particularly notable is the increasing resort to personal databases for medical insurance, credit allocation and employment and housing application purposes.

In the USA a number of consumer groups and individuals now promote the idea of what Kenneth Laudon calls 'a property right over the commercial exploitation of personal information'.[7] In this case, information could be used only with permission, it would not be released without the knowledge of the data subject, and the default position would be no release at all. Royalties would be charged on the exchange or sale of personal data and in addition, James Rule and Lawrence Hunter suggest, data rights agencies would oversee the operation of such a process.[8] No such proposal has been implemented to date but there is a rising tide of interest in it, at least in the USA.

The main difficulty, as I argue elsewhere[9] is that commercial solutions to commercial problems do nothing to raise awareness of the deeper connections of that data with human dignity and social justice. Market solutions, while they may have limited attraction, particularly for those whose data is worth a lot, do nothing to reduce the automation of inequality that is central to contemporary surveillance. In any case, the principle could hardly be extended to other realms such as digitized street camera images.

The individualism involved in such remedies has also been attacked by contemporary communitarians such as Amitai Etzioni. Arguing that there should be limits to privacy, Etzioni proposes a voluntary 'publicness' that would, he believes, 'curtail the need for governmental control and intrusion'.[10] In the 'third realm' of civil society – neither the state nor the market – some trust and reciprocity that is lost in the society of strangers may be regained. There is something inherently attractive in this view. Mutual care should indeed be nurtured wherever it is found. But Etzioni's remedies are only part of the picture and other key issues of contemporary surveillance must still be addressed. Such issues have to do with massive involvement of other agencies than the state on the one hand and with pre-emptive and anticipatory surveillance on the other.[11]

From the 1980s, it also became increasingly clear that the rapidly emerging networked world raised a number of other challenges for fair information principles and the forms of data protection that are based on them. Such principles might be expected to work well in situations of relative fixity, rather than flows, in discrete sectors, rather than in very porous data conduits and in situations where one finds only one species of data. What happens when data of different dimensions is involved, including biometric measures, DNA tests and screens, and digitally stored video images?

Attempting to find at least some solutions to this, various coalitions of computer scientists and consumer groups have developed innovations that technically enhance data protection, using advanced forms of encryption. Users of the Internet are now familiar with some of these, whose adoption is advocated for entering certain sites, or for performing certain kinds of financial transaction. Again, it has been the growth of electronic commerce above all that has prompted the quest for new modes of technical protection.

Privacy enhancing technologies made considerable strides during the 1990s. Like the idea of a property right in personal information, these techniques are designed to allow data subjects to regain control over circulation of data that pertains to them. David Chaum, one prominent advocate of privacy enchancing technologies, created the 'blind signature' as an anonymous proof of authenticity in electronic transactions. Separating the identity of the consumer from the transaction by means of a public and a private key is, according to Chaum, a means of avoiding 'Orwellian' situations in the marketplace.[12]

In addition, Chaum advocates the use of encrypted biometrics – especially fingerprints – in the service, not of the would-be data processor, but of the data subject. In this scenario, the fingerprint is used for authenticating eligibility, not as a unique identifier. By such means consumers may remain anonymous to organizations while organizations may verify that their customers are *bona fide*. The outstanding difficulty with this, once again, is that most organizations are keen, not only to know that their clients and customers are who they say they are and that they are creditworthy, but also to use that personal data for managing consumption.

Such legal, voluntary, market and technical remedies for the perceived problems of privacy comprise the best-known range of responses to surveillance. Each has its keen advocates and many of the schemes noted here have advantages for mitigating the worst effects of surveillance practices today. However, while 'privacy policy' and data protection themselves have not been widely politicized this does not mean that the issues behind them have no political momentum. Few involved in the four types of activity mentioned here imagine that their 'remedies' are settled solutions to the perceived problems. To continue the medical analogy, each proposed remedy lasts only as long as the organism remains invulnerable to new parasites, new bacteria. The latter are breeding constantly, and thus, to return to surveillance, the need for constant vigilance is met by various movements that attempt to challenge each new development whose negative aspects are recognized.

Mobilizing responses

Another way of looking at responses to the rapid expansion of surveillance is to examine popular non-government groups and movements that arise to challenge what they see as abuses and excesses within personal data processing. Such mobilizing responses engage a variety of strategies and tactics, exhibit a range of organizational styles and enjoy differing levels of success. Their activities may also be mapped against a backdrop of political and technological change since the 1960s. Thus, for example, the kinds of activism visible in the 1980s tended to be based around national movements – sometimes in opposition to a specific perceived threat such as the Australia Card[13] – whereas those of the 1990s shifted into electronic spaces which often spilled over national borders. In addition, the focus of dissent extended in the 1990s from an exclusive concern with government data processing to include that of commercial organizations.

The earliest movements, springing up after the establishment of the first computer databases in the 1960s, often operated in contexts where memories of Nazi or state socialist surveillance were still strong. These were also relatively successful in fostering climates in which legislative change could occur. It is thus no accident that in the once-occupied Netherlands' opposition to a national census was so strong in the 1970s that full scale data collection became impossible to achieve. Nor is it a surprise that the first federal privacy commissioner in Canada, Inge Hansen, had a Scandinavian background that informed her approach to surveillance issues. She argued that the wartime experiences of many European migrants and refugees in Canada left a legacy of wariness about any hints of state intrusion and control – especially those involving the garnering by government departments of personal data.[14]

Privacy and data protection organizations formed independently of government appeared in a number of countries in the 1970s and 1980s. Simon Davies lists some of these as follows: Argedaten (Austria), the Australian Privacy Foundation, the Canadian Privacy Network, the Electronic Privacy Information Center (USA), Infofilia (Hungary), the New Zealand Privacy Foundation, Stichting Waakzaamheid Persoonregistratie (the Netherlands) and the United States Privacy Council.[15] They came into being for a variety of reasons, from impatience with the limitations of privacy legislation (for example, the Canadian Privacy Network) to the coalescing of opposition to a specific symbolic challenge for example, the proposed Australia Card and Kiwi Card in the case of the Australian and the New Zealand Privacy Foundations, or Korean struggles against a proposed national electronic ID.[16] Such organizations were led by groups representing a coalition of interests, including civil libertarians, computer professionals, social scientists and journalists, as well as persons with specific concerns such as the consumer lobby or those worried about the security of medical records.

In the 1990s, however, social movements concerned about privacy and data protection shifted both their membership and operation increasingly into the electronic sphere. Computer professionals of various kinds became more prominent in advocacy groups and the medium of exchange and of mobilizing became the Internet. Thus some of the most celebrated cases have occurred through the networking of resources among those who are both users and designers of electronic systems. Opposition to the Marketplace:Households software from the Lotus Corporation in 1993, to Lexis-Nexis P-TRAK in 1996 and the Pentium III chip with its unique identifier in 1999, to take just three major examples, was all conducted largely on the Internet. The first two would have released to third parties the ability to glean large amounts of personal information on American households directly from databases and the third enhanced the traceability of personal computers whose uses could easily be connected with identifiable users.

At the same time the use of the Internet as a medium for political activity proliferated during the 1990s. The interests of those involved also broadened from the specifically surveillance focused ones of earlier privacy groups to include a defence of the medium – the Internet – as a free space. This had two effects: to strengthen the arm of Internet-based oppositional movements, and simultaneously to dilute discrete concerns about the surveillance capacities of electronic media. The Global Internet Liberty Campaign,[16] founded in Montreal in 1996, is one such group. It was formed of a coalition of interests, and promotes security, access and freedom from government restriction on the Internet. The latter issue centres on controversies about encryption. The big question is whether or not governments have the right to intercept everyday electronic communications for reasons of security or crime control.

Much now hangs on this issue and it will continue to be the locus of political activity. In 1993 the US government announced a plan for 'key escrow' that would both allow for the widespread use of secret codes to maintain the security and privacy of electronically based communications and for governments to hold keys to unlock such codes if the need should arise. This unleashed a storm of protest not least from the Electronic Privacy Information Center and Computer Professionals for Social Responsibility who circulated an electronic petition condemning this so-called 'Clipper Chip'. The business community also objected vociferously. They deplored the added cost to every product of including the chip and also worried that only the US government could gain access through the chip, thus reducing the exportability to other countries of products containing it.[17] This crucial war is not over but the point here is that Internet advocacy groups will continue to be key players in the ongoing battles.

Social movements dedicated to challenging surveillance have proliferated over the past 30 years. But they have also undergone a significant transformation of aims, objectives, methods and memberships. It remains to be seen whether the current core groups will continue to be so and whether the partial dilution of privacy and data protection concerns will be offset by the existence of international groups such as Privacy International, for whom those issues are central. The latter organization was founded in 1990 largely through the efforts of Simon Davies, a journalist who had himself become politicized regarding surveillance during the anti-Australia Card campaign in the mid-1980s. Among the 'Greenpeace'-type tactics used by Privacy International to gain media publicity are annual presentations of the 'Big Brother' awards to organizations that most flagrantly violate fair information practices.

At a grass roots level surveillance is frequently challenged by one or more of many different kinds of group with little or no connections with official privacy or data protection lobbies, depending on the specific issue. This reflects the ways in which surveillance is increasingly bound up with monitoring everyday life in a constantly expanding range of contexts. Thus consumer groups and civil liberties organizations may from time to time take up the cause, along with educational, medical or other professional groups. Anti-poverty campaigners have crossed swords with the designation of police hotspots in Toronto,[18] for example, and community groups protested the installation of closed-circuit television systems in Bradford and Manchester, UK.[19] There is also popular appreciation for the work of 'culture jammers' such as Adbusters who do much to call the bluff of commercial advertisers, not least in their association with the processing of personal data for profit.[20]

Resistance in context

Resistance to the negatively construed aspects of contemporary surveillance appears to confirm the studies of a number of theorists writing about current political transformations. For a number of reasons social movements have become more important for political life in all democratic societies. This may relate to disillusion with large-scale bureaucratic political parties, to identity politics that has narrowed the focus of many struggles to persons with more local interests, or to the recognition that in a globalizing world more rapid responses are required to issues than can be generated by more traditional means. Let me isolate three features of current debates on social movements – codes, tactics and sub-politics – as a means of connecting the discussion of resistance to surveillance with wider sociologies of contemporary politics.

For Deleuze (1992), today's societies are engaged less with discipline than with control. It is in the surveillance flows, with their constituent codes, that power is contested, rather than in physical spaces marked by barriers that constrain bodies. While questions might be raised about how far constraint within physical spaces is a thing of the past, the point is well taken. Codes are now crucial. It is by these means that the categories and classifications are made that trace and target populations for different purposes. Social movements, characterized by a similar fluidity, might be expected to offer appropriate resistance to such codes, as demonstrated here at least to some extent. Although he does not spend any time on the details of surveillance, Alberto Melucci makes a relevant case for this in his book, *Challenging Codes: Collective Action in the Information Age.*[21]

Melucci sees movements as signs. They perceive risks and dangers before their contours are clear and help to name them and thus to identify them as public issues. At the same time they form networks in order fully to be effective; networks with flexible cultural meanings. And these networks operate on an increasingly global plane, partly because the risks are perceived to be global ones, and partly 'because information flows have become central to the cultural processes by which we reproduce ourselves'. Power, says, Melucci, 'operates through the languages and codes which organize the flow of information'.[22] He believes that social movements, while they may address institutions on their own terms, also work at a level beyond instrumental rationality. They bring back everyday concerns. After all, questions about age, sex, culture, birth and death are the stuff of lived experience.

Melucci is exercised about the 'apparatuses which exact identification and consensus' that apply increasing control to persons in their daily lives. Why? Because they involve the 'definition of self in its biological, affective, and symbolic dimensions and in its relations with time, space, and the "other"'.[23] Melucci does not explicitly discuss surveillance or resistance to it, but it is striking how far his general analysis applies. He complains that while Marxian and Foucaldian perspectives tend to mislead by positing situations of total control, in the symbolic realm about which he writes there is always ambivalence on both sides. When information is central and symbols thus enter the constitution of the field, they render it open to multiple interpretations. Thus the situations concerned are never under full control. What matters, he insists, is the construction of a sufficiently open arena of public spaces where conflicts can be expressed. This is the task of social movements.

Such opening up of public spaces for democratic intervention is discussed by Michel de Certeau in his comments on political activities as 'games'.[24] Games have rules that define players' range of action without determining their moves. Applied to technology, suggests Andrew Feenberg,[25] technical codes are the most general rule of the game, that bias it towards the dominant contestant. The institutionalized controls embodied in social organizations – expressed in the present context as surveillance capacities – are de Certeau's 'strategies' through which power is accumulated and maintained. Those on the outside who are affected by these strategies engage certain 'tactics' that challenge the inescapable strategies. They may have no direct access to the strategic activities of the larger organization, but their tactics of subtle deviance, non compliance or overt protest may nevertheless alter the significance of the strategies. Again, this kind of analysis is played out in the situations described above, although a further feature may be noted. Computer professionals in particular play an ambiguous role here, operating both as 'outsiders' in joining protests and as 'insiders' whose actions may influence the construction of the codes.

Many of the strategies employed by powerful groups within the surveillance 'game' are placed within the realm of institutional politics. Here the chances of making a relevant difference are slim. However, as Ulrich Beck argues, within today's risk societies new avenues for social action are emerging at a 'sub-political' level.[26] Most social movements that challenge surveillance must surely be thought of as instances of sub-politics. Indeed, it is unlikely that in the case of resistance to surveillance items like data protection and privacy would ever become political 'hot button' issues (partly for the reasons mentioned below). Although the Clipper Chip and its descendants will continue to be politically significant at a central level, the intellectual sources of oppositional arguments are as likely to arise outside the realm of institutional politics as inside. Again, this is consistent with the risk society 'reinvention of politics' position.

Why resistance is limited

It sounds as if the politics of surveillance is wishful thinking. Negative responses to the colossal growth of surveillance over the past 20 years are minimal and frequently *ad hoc*. Spontaneous resistance should not be trivialized, of course. Indeed where it occurs it exudes the robustness of real-life engagement with the issues. Teenagers winding up surveillance camera operatives and workers using camera blind spots to screen themselves from the boss are not insignificant responses.

Another example comes from single mother responses to a state-of-the-art computer system – Ohio's Client Registry Information System-Enhanced, or CRIS-E. One woman complained, 'All the time you are on welfare, yeah, you are in prison. Someone is watching like a guard'. Yet they do not simply comply. Another woman holds bank accounts for family members even though they are detectable. 'I feel bad but pretty defiant about that' is her heartfelt comment. Others depend on a cash-based economy to get around restrictions placed upon them. Resistance is not organized but it does yield some benefits, a zone of autonomy, the 'sustenance of a shared identity and undermining the surveillance mission itself'.[27]

I do not wish to minimize the gains achieved in the legal realm of data protection and privacy law, but it has to be admitted that they have severe limitations. Also, considering the sub-political tactics of social movements that challenge the classificatory codes of surveillance societies sounds fine in theory but does not at present provide great grounds for hopefulness. The actual gains from such activities are far from earth-shaking and social movements in this area are up against considerable odds.

Why is this? It will be clear by now that I have little time for paranoid theories about the malevolent panoptic power of capitalist and bureaucratic organizations. But I do see great dangers in some unintended consequences of surveillance, especially as far as it is connected with risk management classifications. Surveillance power is often wielded in ways that systematically disadvantage some groups rather than others, but this can be a side-effect of policies meant to achieve other ends. The biggest obstacle in the path of re-sistance is the rather mundane fact that the benefits of surveillance are attractive to many, and well promoted. Surveillance always has two faces, and part of the problem of convincing people about the more worrisome and unsocial aspects is that they appear merely as the price one pays for the speed, safety and security apparently offered by the other 'face'. Needless to say, those government departments and corporations that stand to gain from surveil-lance are in a good position to make their case.

There are several reasons why such large organizations are in such a strong position. One, of course, is their sheer organizational and technological strength. They have the means at their disposal to pursue forms of personal data collection and processing that retain their potentially negative features even when privacy legislation is firmly in place. A further reason for their strong position, however, is the hegemonic power suffusing many contem-porary technologically advanced societies. By this I mean the consent given by most people to the general direction of social life as expressed by its more dominant groups.[28] Within such consent are two items. On the one hand there is an agreement that some level of surveillance is necessary in most areas of life, and on the other is a widespread assumption that rights to priv-acy comprise the appropriate language for questioning surveillance when necessary.

The agreement that some surveillance is necessary is easily seen in many contexts. Citizens want to take advantage of the benefits that accrue from having a correct tax file or unemployment benefit registration. Workers whose pay or promotion is dependent on some mode of monitoring to determine bonuses or achievements will assume they are better off with than without supervision. People strolling on city streets at night will be reassured to know that cameras and alarms are in place, and even new mothers in hospital may be glad of electronic tagging systems that protect their babies from abduction.[29] This is the positive and productive side of surveillance power. It should not be downplayed or discounted. When the new technologies are presented as protective and as preventative of harm or abuse then the kinds of social order that is assumed to be procured by them will be sought the more readily.

The language of privacy rights is the other side of the hegemonic coin. However well formulated the right to privacy and however well it may be enshrined in legal or voluntary codes, it is still limited. The advantage of privacy talk is that it yields a shared vocabulary, sometimes the help of expert groups and a venue for conflict. But it is still part of the hegemonic system of consent to the dominant liberal culture of law and the establishment. It will not go beyond these to question the very worldviews and power bases of those who have access to the surveillance switches. How far can a challenge be meaningful, asks John Gilliom, if it is 'advanced in the formal legal terms of the state?'[30]

Gilliom's studies concern drug testing in the workplace, so this is an area where surveillance is both anticipated and accepted. Yet as we have seen, drug testing does raise some questions that go beyond traditional modes of workplace monitoring. They involve body fluids and they relate to non-work aspects of the employees' lives. In addition, Gilliom says, what workers really feel – 'I will not pee in a jar so that you can analyse my life' – may be masked by the more abstract 'This violates my right to privacy'.[31] Yet only a tiny proportion of workers interviewed by Gilliom saw the issues in terms of broader questions of power or of the role of testing within wider surveillance trends.[32]

Another issue is how new technologies are construed, which again has two aspects. First, new technologies in one area may be taken more seriously than those in another for their potential hazards. Information technologies tend to be viewed as cleaner and less inherently risky than biotechnologies, for instance. Second, new technologies may be seen either as artefacts whose features are fixed or as malleable and redirectable. This too has consequences for the politics of surveillance.

Dorothy Nelkin makes some telling points about the relative failure to generate an adversarial culture against the negative face of surveillance by comparing the fortunes of resistance to biotechnology with those of information technology.[33] She refers to the downsides of communication and information technologies as the 'cursor' of our times, above all for their surveillance effects, as understood here, and also for their de-skilling effects, for the production of 'smart' weaponry, and for their apparent capacity to substitute for thoughtful curricular design in educational institutions. Yet where, she asks, is the opposition to these features? She compares this situation with that of biotechnology, arguing that this area has been the focus of persistent public opposition, replacing nuclear power as 'technology out of control'. Despite the benefits, such as higher crop yields, disease-resistance in plants, pharmaceutical products and therapeutic procedures, protests have been large and vocal. From the use of laboratory animals to growth hormones, to, most recently, cloning or genetically-engineered food products, biotechnology often has a bad press. Objectors include everyone from farm lobbies and animal rights activists to religious groups objecting to the transgression of 'natural' boundaries, or environmentalists warning of biohazards.

Nelkin suggests that culturally, in the USA, privacy is not seen as an issue worth fighting for (and its social dimensions are overlooked in an individual-istic culture). Social control issues associated with information technologies tend to be seen as marginal, or as temporary and fixable aberrations. Where corporate efficiency is prized as if it were an ultimate value, these other matters can safely be downplayed. Alleged threats to democratic values seem vague and unfocused.

With biotechnology, however, resistance has rested partly on already existing interests, such as those directly affected by a noxious facility in their neighbourhood, or on the well-organized animal rights movement. As Nelkin says, 'helpless animals, like beseiged farmers, or vulnerable fetuses become easy lightning rods for social movements'. Invisible health hazards also provide a potent source of support in societies obsessed with wellness and the perfect body. But biotechnology dissenters seem to have a trump card in claims that their opponents are tampering with nature or violating the sanctity of life.

It may be that the tide is turning, Nelkin's helpful analysis notwithstanding. Information technology is not necessarily becoming culturally unacceptable, although if it is anything to go by the number of negative film treatments of these technologies in their surveillance guise does seem to be growing at present. Rather, biotechnology may be gaining ground, especially, perhaps, through association with information technology. And biometrics raises questions that extend to other forms of surveillance as well. Ironically, those areas of technological interdependence, such as epidemiology, that offer rich benefits in isolating environmental and related causes of disease, also have deep surveillance dimensions associated with them.[34]

There are also more and less appropriate ways of bringing 'moral and reli-gious agendas' into technology debates. Biotechnological 'tampering with the body' may have attracted more ire than information technology's 'tamper-ing with the mind', but either way, critique cannot be excluded just because it is religious, especially when world religions have always been sought as the wellsprings of morality. At the end of the day, however, Nelkin is justifed in saying that, especially in the USA the 'issues most likely to generate resistance to a given technology have more to do with its potential risk to health, its impact on organized interests, and especially its effect on moral and religious agendas'.

The other factor associated with the construal of technologies is how soft or hard they appear to be. As we saw earlier, biometrics may in some contexts be seen as 'the enemy of privacy' and in others as 'privacy enchancing'. Irma van der Ploeg argues that the politics of a technology are bound up with the way that technology is construed or constructed in the public mind.[35] She shows how, if biometrics is seen to be 'in the making' and thus soft and malleable, it may be seen as something that can be shaped to appropriate ends or if necessary curbed. If on the other hand biometrics is seen as a stable object with given properties, it is accorded fixed meaning and significance irrespective of future potential users' actions and intended future applications.

The paradox is that the latter construal of biometrics is used as a means of alerting the public to the negative potentials, whereas the former may be used to justify the use of the technologies – for example in encryption devices. As van der Ploeg says, the first, reified version 'allows for a sharp and critical assessment of biometrics that the other, more elusive version cannot sustain; the latter version remains slippery to the grasp, because of a dispersed allocation of agency, properties and responsibility'.[36]

The sharp critique made possible by the first construal may generate opposition but little by way of constructive proposals as to how to modify it. Thus it will probably alienate powerful actors who would have to cooperate if the technology is to be shaped for more appropriate ends. If the soft version succeeds in getting them on board, however, they may well underestimate the immense difficulties involved in making biometrics into a 'friend of privacy' let alone in reducing its propensity to produce automated stereotyping and discrimination.

Numerous attempts are made to resist and to regulate the negative aspects of surveillance. Strong institutions promote and pay for the establishment of large scale surveillance systems, and there are numerous obstacles to realizing the importance of the issues. So it comes as no surprise that progress in confronting surveillance's negative aspects is piecemeal and patchy. But it is not altogether discouraging. Fair information practices are gaining a wider and wider hearing and are becoming embedded in both legislation and in voluntary codes of practice. These are important in creating a culture of awareness about surveillance issues. Whatever the weaknesses of the 'privacy' approaches, the term – along with cautions about Big Brother – will continue to be used. As such its qualified use should be supported by all who wish to open spaces for democratic debate regarding new technologies in their surveillance dimensions. If these are the concepts and metaphors that make sense to potential pockets of resistance, then it would be bloody-minded to ignore or bypass them.

Along with the negative, however, must come the positive. Any who would question and challenge technological systems must have a sense of the desirable sociotechnical arrangements that are preferred. Surveillance in technically advanced, globalizing societies is bound up with broad sociocultural transformations of modernity and has to be seen within that frame. Such an analysis is offered in the next chapter.

What persists into postmodern conditions is an abiding infrastructural dependence on communication and information technologies. They are undoubtedly viewed in the popular and political imagination as far more beneficial than baleful to humanity. That they will continue to expand their influence is beyond doubt, short of some global catastrophe. Their aid is actively sought as a means of ameliorating the human condition as well as of galvanizing the global economy. In their surveillance role they offer opportunities for risk management and for proving their purported potential to provide perfect knowledge. But they are ever profoundly ambivalent. As Herminio Martins warns, 'moral imagination and political courage of a high order will be needed to resist the tyranny of technological possibilities'.[37]

The future of surveillance

The title of this chapter is meant to be ambivalent. There is no one future of surveillance and even if there were I would make no claim to know it. This chapter places the discussion of surveillance in the context of the general social and cultural transformations taking place at the start of the twenty-first century. I think of this realigning in various ways, including under the term 'postmodernity'. All single descriptors are inadequate, so I hesitate to use any. But I do think that 'postmodernity' is the best on offer.[1] Before you put the book down, however, let me say that this is not 'postmodern*ism*' so much as a sociological way of looking at some contemporary cultural and social shifts. In this context, we can at least get a sociological sense of where surveillance is going.

The other task I have set myself here is to comment not only on where surveillance is going, but where it should go. Again, I hesitate because I can think of many things that disqualify me from being so bold. Yet as I have argued, surveillance is amenable to ethical and moral critique and it ought to be politically contested in many contexts. It is, after all, about power and about persons, two things that I care passionately about. So in the second half of this chapter I return to the key themes with which we began and hint at ways in which the ethical and political should be highlighted in discussions of surveillance. All I can do is act as a kind of witness informing those involved in surveillance as concerned citizens, software architects, policy-makers, political activists, computer experts and so on. None of us can claim that we are not affected by this. In the surveillance society all our everyday lives are monitored.

Modern and postmodern surveillance

Surveillance is so much an intrinsic part of everyday life today that it is sometimes hard to explain exactly what it is and how much it has changed in less than a generation. We unblinkingly produce passports for scanners to read at airports, feed plastic cards with personal identifiers into high street bank machines, fill out warranty forms when we buy appliances, key confidential data into online transactions, drive through automated toll sensors in inner cities or on highways, make cellphone calls, or use barcoded keys to enter offices and laboratories. How inefficient and inconvenient it would be if we were obliged to pay cash for everything, or to be interviewed by officials before we were permitted to enter a building or cross a border! The benefits of surveillance must be affirmed. Nonetheless, at each encounter we leave a trail of personal data that is tracked and processed in ways that influence our activities and our life chances. Surveillance is always Janus-faced.

Some surveillance practices have been a feature of modern life for a long time. Medical records, voting lists, housing registries, tax files and employee numbers are part of what everyday living is all about, at least in urban industrial societies. Indeed, they facilitate modern life by giving evidence of eligibility and entitlement to benefits and privileges, even though they simultaneously place power in the hands of the system processing the information. Modernity is in part constituted by surveillance practices and technologies and it should be stressed that some modern features of the social world do not go away in postmodern times. Postmodernity is superimposed on some aspects of modern conditions even as it replaces others. Computerization links the two together.

At first, computerizing surveillance simply made easier the processes of bureaucratic administration, thus reinforcing government and workplace surveillance as classic hallmarks of modernity. You could say that Max Weber's rational institutional ordering of the office was upgraded from an iron to an electronic cage, or that Frederick Taylor's detailed work-task monitoring system shifted from scientific to technological management. But as personal databases proliferated within government departments so the very idea of centralized control became less plausible in many sectors. And as capitalist enterprises turned their attention as much if not more towards managing consumption as to organizing workers, surveillance spilled into numerous other areas, further diffusing its patterns within the social fabric.

The sociological debate over postmodernity has leaned toward examining either the social aspects of new technologies, or the rise of consumerism, but a good case can be made for combining these two forms of analysis to consider postmodernity as an emergent social formation in its own right.[2] Surveillance technologies are vitally implicated in the processes of postmodernity, understood thus. Analysts of consumerism have tended to underestimate the extent to which surveillance is used for consumer management purposes, whereas those investigating the new technologies have often failed to note how they are driven by the imperatives of consumer capitalism.

The question of surveillance systems is in this view central to the tilt towards postmodernity. It highlights important questions, not only of the role of surveillance in constituting postmodernity, but also of how surveillance is best conceived in ethical and political terms. While discourses of privacy have become crucial to legislative and political efforts to deal with what is perceived to be the darker face of surveillance they frequently fail to reveal the extent to which surveillance is a site of larger social contests. If the following argument is correct, surveillance practices and technologies are becoming a key means of marking and reinforcing social divisions and thus an appropriate locus of political activity at several levels.

Early in this debate Roger Clarke used the helpful term 'dataveillance' to refer to the 'systematic monitoring of people's actions or communications through the application of information technology'.[3] He concluded that the rapid burgeoning of such dataveillance demanded urgent political and policy attention, given that it tends to feed on itself. In the same year, Gary T. Marx released his study of undercover police work in the USA,[4] which also warned of some broader social implications that he dubbed the 'new surveillance'. Among other things, he showed how computer-based surveillance was increasingly powerful, but by the same token decreasingly visible. He also noted the turn toward pre-emptive surveillance in which categorical suspicion plays a significant role. This refers to the ways that the computer matching of lists of names generates categories of persons likely to violate some rule. One's data image could thus be tarnished without cause.

Other kinds of consequence of computerized surveillance became evident during the 1980s and 1990s, including particularly the increasing tendency of personal data to flow across boundaries that were previously less porous. Data matching between government departments permitted cross-checking in a way hitherto undreamed of, and the supposed limits to such practices always seemed to contain clauses that permitted such leakage under 'routine' conditions. The outsourcing of services in more market-orientated government regimes, and the growing interplay between commercial and administrative sectors – in health care, for instance – meant that the flows of personal data grew to a flood in certain contexts. A centralized surveillance system such as Orwell feared is unnecessary when databases are networked. Any one of a number of identifiers will suffice to trace the location or activities of persons.

Despite the emphasis on how computerization made a difference to surveillance practices, the primary mode of questioning and critique occurred very much along modern lines. 'Orwellian' became the preferred adjective to refer to computerized administration that seemed in some way to overstep democratically established limits to government power. Thus the proposal for a nationally-based electronic identification card in Australia was defeated in 1986, and similar initiatives have met a similar fate elsewhere, such as in the UK, the USA and South Korea.[5] More mundanely, 'Big Brother' was found in the 'telescreens' of factory supervision or, by the 1980s, in stores and in street-level video surveillance systems.

Until the 1990s – consistently *with Nineteen Eighty Four* – it was still assumed that the greatest dangers of computerized surveillance lay in the augmented power of the nation state, with the capitalist corporation as a decidedly secondary source of risk. But this was also a period in which the politics of Reagan and Thatcher became dominant. Many state functions and utilities were sold off to become big business in the private sector. Such large-scale deregulation meant for instance that what once were public streets became private shopping malls. They were now surveilled and policed in different ways. It also meant that personal data moved between sectors as some services previously offered by national or state governments were devolved to commercial interests. At the same time, database marketing encouraged a mushrooming of trade in personal data. Postmodern conditions were in the making.

The strategies for resisting and limiting surveillance power have been mainly modern in style. Legislation relating to data protection (in Europe) or privacy (in North America) came to be seen as the effective muzzle on more menacing aspects or methods of surveillance.[6] They undoubtedly arose in direct response to the computerization of personal data handling, but were understandably slow to recognize the peculiar traits that computerization had added to modern surveillance. Only in the late 1990s, for instance, did Canadians outside Quebec start to take seriously the 'privacy' issues raised by the personal data gathering activities of private corporations. Orwell had no inkling of these!

Another notable feature of social and political life today is the raised profile of risk. This is relevant to surveillance in at least two ways. On the one hand, as more and more organizations turn their attention to the future, to capture market niches, to prevent crime and so on, the language of risk management steadily becomes supreme. Surveillance is seen increasingly as the means of obtaining the knowledge that aids risk management, with the models and strategies of insurance companies taking the lead.[7] On the other hand, surveillance itself has come to be viewed more as presenting risks, as itself an aspect of the risk society.[8]

At the same time, the scope of insurable or securable risks seems constantly to expand. Most if not all of the world's wealthy societies today use surveillance cameras to guard against theft, vandalism or violence in shopping malls, streets and sports stadia. Biometric methods such as thumbprints or retinal scans are adopted to check identities, and genetic tests are introduced to exclude the potentially diseased or disabled from the labour force. Risks may be managed by a panoply of technological means, each of which represents a fresh surveillance technique for collecting and communicating knowledge of risk. What is particularly striking about each of these, however, is their dependence on information infrastructures to realize their generalized surveillance potential.

In each case of technological scrutiny that goes beyond personal checking and dataveillance, information technologies still provide the means of collating and comparing records. Any video surveillance that attempts automatically to identify persons whose image has been captured will rely on digital methods to do so. Likewise, biometric and genetic surveillance depend for their data processing power on information technologies. It is computer power that enables voice recognition to classify travellers on the Saskatchewan-Montana border between the USA and Canada; computer power that allows researchers to screen employers or insurance applicants for tell-tale traits that indicate illicit drug use or early pregnancy.

Information technologies are also at the heart of another surveillance shift. Not only does surveillance now extend beyond the administrative reach of the nation state into corporate and especially consumer capitalist spheres, it also extends geographically and in virtual space. Surveillance, once restricted to the administration of bounded territories, is steadily experiencing globalization and virtualization. The growth of electronic commerce, whose surveillance consequences are huge and often almost imperceptible, introduces 'cybersurveillance'. One major Internet company, Doubleclick, collects surfing data from 6400 locations on the web, and a rival, Engage, has detailed surfing profiles on more than 30 million individuals in its database.[9]

By the 1990s, then, surveillance had become both more intensive and more extensive. Using biometric and genetic methods, it promises to bypass the communicating subject in quest of identificatory and diagnostic data obtained directly from the body. Using electronically enhanced cameras the optical gaze is reinserted into surveillance practices, which for a while relied only on the metaphor of watching to maintain their power. So what is new about these developments? At what point do quantitative changes cross the threshold to become qualitative alterations in social formations and social experiences?

At the beginning of the twenty-first century, that which helped constitute modernity is still present, as is modernity itself. Persons find themselves subject to scrutiny by agencies and organizations that are interested in influencing, guiding or even manipulating their daily lives. But the widespread adoption of information technologies for surveillance purposes has rendered that scrutiny ever less direct. Co-presence has become less and less necessary to the maintenance of control or to keep individuals within gravitational fields of influence. Not only are many relationships of a tertiary nature, where interactions occur between persons who never meet in the flesh, many are even of a quaternary character, between persons and machines.[10] Moreover, those relationships occur increasingly on the basis of a consumer identity rather than a citizen identity.[11]

The modes of social integration are shifting, subtly but surely, not only away from face-to-face relations relations involving trust (or its absence) and from integration based on institutions that extend those relations. Rather, today's modes of social integration are more and more electronically enabled, abstract and disembodied.[12] Surveillance, in the sense that it issues tokens of trust, is an aspect of that disembodied integration. In the later part of the twentieth century its most rapidly growing sphere was commercial, outstripping the capacities of the most advanced surveillance systems of nation states. And even within nation states, administrative surveillance came to be guided at least as much by the canons of consumption as those of citizenship, classically construed.[13]

At the start of the new century electronically enabled surveillance is networked, polycentric and multidimensional, including biometric and video technologies as well as more conventional dataveillance. These same technologies are the central means of time-space compression. Relationships are stretched in fresh ways involving remoteness and speed, but still sustained for particular purposes including those of influence and control. In some respects those influences and controls resemble previous, modern, conditions. But in others, especially in the consumer dimensions of surveillance, the influences involved are at once less coercive and more comprehensive than in modernity's classic, institutional, body-disciplining surveillance phase.

Both questions of meaning and political issues are raised by what might be called postmodern surveillance. But as yet little systematic work has appeared that draws these together. Indeed, some matters of meaning are discussed in ways that pay little attention to actual empirical realities, with the result that the political questions similarly fail to connect with the world we live in.[14] This relates back to a more general issue, that sociological accounts of the postmodern – with a few exceptions – pay scant attention to technological development as such.[15] Thus while there is a sprawling literature on postmodernity, insufficient stress is placed on the technological shifts that are central to it.

Surveillance operates in so many daily life spheres today that it is impossible to evade, should one wish to. We are indeed wrapped in media.[16] Most of our social encounters and almost all our economic transactions are subject to electronic recording, checking and authorization. From the Electronic Funds Transfer at Point of Sale (EFTPOS) machine for paying the supermarket bill or the request to show a barcoded driver's licence, to the cellphone call or the Internet search, numerous everyday tasks trigger some surveillance device. In these cases, it would be a check to determine that sufficient funds are available, a verification of car ownership and past record, a timed locator for the phone call, and data on sites visited drawn from the parasitical cookie on the hard drive in order more precisely to target advertising on your computer screen.

No one agency is behind this focused attention to our daily lives. Modernist centralized panoptic control is not so much in question as polycentric networks of surveillance, within which personal data flow fairly freely. In most countries the flows are more carefully channelled in government systems, where fair information principles are practised to varying degrees. By contrast, much commercial data flows with less inhibition. Personal data, gleaned from multifarious sources, is collected, sold and resold within the vast repositories of database marketing. These polycentric surveillance flows are as much a part of the so-called network society[17] as the flows of finance capital or of mass media signals that more frequently are considered as signs of the information age or of postmodernity. Zygmunt Bauman's stimulating analyses of postmodernity, which highlight its consumerist aspects, are remarkably silent about the surveillance technologies that are used to manage consumer behaviour.

The fact that one agency does not direct the flows of surveillance does not mean that the data gathered are random. The opportunities for cross-checking and for indirect verification through third party agencies are increased as networks act as conduits for diverse data. This means that it is easier for a prospective employer to learn about traits, proclivities and past records not included in the CV; taxation departments to know about personal credit ratings; or for Internet marketers to send precisely relevant advertising materials to each user's screen. Dykes between different sectors and institutional areas are eroded by such surveillance flows, leading to traffic between them that might not have been anticipated by the data subject. People's lives become more transparent to more agencies, undermining the hope that data disclosed for one purpose within one agency will not end up being used for another. The social and political implications of this are considerable.

Within modern surveillance systems it was generally assumed that some sort of symmetry exists between the record and the individual person; the one represents the other for administrative purposes. But with the proliferation of surveillance at all levels the very notion of a fixed identity, to which records correspond, has become more dubious. The vast and growing array of means of identification and classification that circulates within electronic databases has given rise to questions about how far the data image or the digital persona may be said to correspond to the embodied person who walks the downtown street.[18] Individuals are in a sense made up by their digital classification.

In terms of power, everyone is affected. At one end of the social spectrum, the carceral net has been spread more and more widely, though not necessarily as coercively.[19] It is true that prisons are extending their capacity at an alarming rate throughout the so-called advanced societies. But surveillance systems diffuse other less overt means of segregation and exclusion throughout society. Contemporary surveillance is both inclusive and exclusive of deviants.[20] Video surveillance, for instance, succeeds in prohibiting some teenagers from entering shopping malls or displaces them from certain city streets. This may mean that less shoplifting will occur but it could also mean that they will be unnoticed by those who care when they engage in dangerous activities. Electronic tagging of offenders, on the other hand, helps to keep them 'in the community'.[21] And at the other end of the spectrum, the rising crescendo of calls for credentials, and other tokens of trustworthiness, means that another range of discretionary and screening powers has grown up, largely distinct from those of government.

The idolatrous dream of omniperception embodied in the panopticon is present in contemporary surveillance. This is the minacious twinkle in the electronic eye. But it is now connected with a yet more ambitious goal of perfect knowledge, in which simulation steadily supercedes knowledge of past records. This is surveillance without limits, aspiring not only to see everything but to do so in advance. Simulation's seductive claim is that 'any image is observable, that any event is programmable, and thus, in a sense, foreseeable'.[22] This dream lends a vital thrust to the constant upgrading and extension of surveillance. It is not merely the technical refining of surveillance strategies but a fresh form of social ordering by computerized codes.

Much may be learned from accounts of the superpanopticon and simulated surveillance but two important qualifications must be made. One is that older methods of electronically enabled surveillance persist and expand. Social science fictions of simulation should not be allowed to detract from their ongoing significance. The other is that even where surveillant simulation occurs it does not operate on its own. The fact that individuals may be made up by their digital image, or that self-referential simulation seems to have intoxicated surveillance systems should not be taken to mean that the digital personae are somehow randomly constructed, or that all references have been removed from categories that sift and sort one group from another. Modes of control and influence are connected with deeper determinants of life chances and of social ordering. In such surveillance practices technological potential meets social pressure. It is still worth trying to penetrate '. . . the visible forms of the present in search of the concealed mechanisms that organize contemporary life'.[23]

High technology surveillance systems, however self-referential, are not self-financing either. They are set up by those with specific kinds of interest in control and influence. As mentioned earlier, varieties of risk management lie behind much expansion of surveillance facilitated by electronic technologies. Behind them, in both commercial and government sectors, one frequently finds 'market values', so-called. Police, for example, act as brokers of knowledge – personal data – that is used to satisfy the demands of institutions, especially those of insurance. Thus the making up of individuals according to certain categories useful to those institutions produces databases used in the effort to eliminate or at least to minimize criminal behaviour.[24] Police today are concerned less to apprehend criminals after the fact than to anticipate criminal behaviours, classify them on a risk calculus, and contain or pre-empt them.

Here in high profile may be seen just those processes of control by codes, and of self-referentiality, contextualized within specific settings in which the interests of actors are more effectively laid bare. In the setting of police work, the strengthening surveillance has meant establishing data gathering and processing systems that are more and more cut loose from previous rationales and goals of policing. Moral wrongdoing seems at best to have been pushed to the edge of the picture as has, at least for the majority of routine police work, the discovery and bringing to justice of lawbreakers.

This shift is not a function of the application of surveillance technologies as such. The relentless drive for efficiency noted in earlier critical studies, and now the quest of speed and of simulation, is an attitude, an obsession, perhaps even an idolatry.[25] That such attitudes become embedded in technology-dependent surveillance practices, thus giving the impression that the system produces these amoral, self-referential effects, is not in question.

Electronics-based surveillance, using databases to enable and support a whole panoply of practices, is complicit within the emerging peculiar conditions of postmodernity. This hints at new conduits of power and new modes of control. Dependence on information technologies, a basic trait of postmodernity, vastly upgrades biopower, the intimate, everyday knowledge of populations. Governmentality is exercised increasingly by other agencies than the welfare state in which at first it was practised. As in the case of policing, even agencies that once had legal power behind them are now as answerable, if not more so, to commercial organizations such as insurance companies. This connects surveillance directly with the second major trait of postmodernity, consumer enterprises and consumer experiences.

Toward a new approach

Computerized surveillance straddles the modern and the postmodern. As such, it illustrates well the mutual shaping and influence of technological developments and social processes. Modernity is characterized by an increasing reliance on bureaucratic apparatuses for social administration and control Once those systems are augmented by computerization, certain other features appear and are amplified through greater technological capacity. Automated cross-checking between databases is a very powerful tool, for example. As their power is realized, those features reappear in other contexts, thus gradually altering the social conditions in which the technologies are developed.

Surveillance practices that once relied on a generalized knowledge of populations garnered in paper documentation and classified within files now find themselves capable of simulating future situations and behaviours. This suits nicely the burgeoning enterprises of consumer capitalism, which now have the means more directly to manage their markets rather than merely the flows of raw materials or the activities of productive workers. With enhanced simulation capabilities, market criteria become more significant within decision-making, not only within commercial agencies but also within government organizations. Thus subtly and imperceptibly the shape of modernity morphs into the postmodern.

At this point it is worth recalling the key themes with which this book began: coordination, risk, privacy and power. Looking at these again serves as a reminder that the very contexts within which surveillance grows are changing. This means that the modern impetuses behind and solutions to surveillance may also be viewed in a fresh light. Risk and privacy as we think of them today in the West are very much a product of modernity and this accounts for many of their limitations as well as their broad appeal. It would be naive to suggest that postmodernity holds some better solutions. But I shall suggest that postmodern conditions offer some new openings for ethical and political engagement that are worth exploring.

In the first part of this chapter we have already examined extensively the new modes of coordination enabled by emerging surveillance techniques. They cope with the increasingly rapid disappearance of the body in our relationships and in social integration. The codes of classification that determine eligibility and access are means of coordinating social life in mobile, fast societies, where co-presence is seldom found. We take for granted from day to day that those administrative and commercial codes and networks will hold things together conveniently and efficiently. At the same time we rightly assume that surveillance will protect us, enhance our security and minimize the risks of daily life. And in many ways, reassuringly, it does.

The problem is that the very systems that have so painstakingly developed to try to minimize risk themselves create further risks. The risk society breeds risks. It is also involved in some subtle moral transformations. In order to operate best for risk-assessment purposes surveillance strips down the complex actions of self-conscious embodied persons to their basic behavioural components. An amoral approach supplants older notions of virtue or value.[26] A utilitarian calculus based on probabilities and a surveillant sort based on likely behaviours is all that risk knowledge requires. It is no coincidence, of course, that insurance companies have experienced their most dramatic rise to prominence in societies where fate and providence are at a lower premium.[27] The idea that human beings can control and colonize their own futures is of a piece with the demotion of serious moral critique.

This brings me to privacy. The risks created by surveillance may be met, some argue, by a focus on privacy. The sancrosanct self can be sheltered behind legal limits on the promiscuous processing of personal data. Now, this answers neatly the problem as it is often perceived by data subjects, and thus should be treated seriously. It also resonates in important ways with deep philosophical commitments, for example to the self as communicative, and as possessing inherent dignity. Moreover, the development of privacy policies has itself contributed at least tangentially to the shaping of surveillance systems.[28] Undeniably, it is an effective mobilizing slogan. In each of these ways, privacy is positive.

At the same time, privacy falls far short as a means of challenging contemporary surveillance. First, privacy answers, consistently but paradoxically, to personal fears of invasion, violation and disturbance. Having successfully prised each of us from our neighbours so that we could be individuated social atoms, amenable to classification and sorting as disembodied abstractions, privacy responses echo just such individuation. Second, privacy is frequently conceived as a residual means of compensating for human errors and computer failures. The systems themselves are deemed safe when policies protect against surveillance slippage or data leakiness. Third, privacy policy and legislation is notoriously cumbersome and unresponsive to the rapid changes taking place in surveillance. Also, few citizens and fewer consumers are even aware of regulations governing data collection or of the legal recourse available to them. In any case, they are left to protect themselves.

In each instance, privacy tends not to see surveillance as a social question[29] or one that has to do with power. Claims made for privacy are embraced by persons who feel instinctively that something is wrong when big government and large corporations seem to extract, process, exchange and even trade personal data with apparent impunity. This is the story their lives tell. But this sense of personal troubles needs to be matched with a conviction that this is a public issue to do with strong social forces. And the personal biography should be the means of holding together that person's past and its present network of social relations.[30]

Surveillance today is a means of sorting and classifying populations and not just of invading personal space or violating the privacy of individuals. In postmodernizing contexts surveillance is an increasingly powerful means of reinforcing social divisions, as the superpanoptic sort relentlessly screens, monitors and classifies to determine eligibility and access, to include and to exclude. The social fractures of modernity have not so much disappeared as softened, becoming fluid and malleable. Surveillance has become an indirect but potent means of affecting life chances and social destinies. As we have seen it can display unjust and antisocial features even when privacy policies are in place.

Technological developments and social processes interact to produce outcomes which, though not necessarily as stark as the rigid class divisions of early modernity, nevertheless raise analogous questions of fairness, mutuality and appropriate resistance. Beyond these are other issues, as yet far from fully understood. Privacy misses the point of the superpanopticon, for instance, which sees databases as discursive webs that locate and limit – even constitute – data subjects as such. Those dispersed and multiple identities that circulate within the superpanopticon cannot fully be grasped in terms of the singular, stable self of modernity. The part played by the control codes of surveillant simulation in reproducing and reinforcing social difference and divisions must also be explored as it extends and mutates familiar struggles of class, ethnicity and gender.

Re-embodying persons

To say that electronic technologies and consumer cultures contribute to the rise of postmodernity is not for a moment to say that the novelty of the circumstance entirely displaces all earlier concerns for human dignity or for social justice. Indeed, the inscribing of panoptic categories and of surveillant simulations on the practices and patterns of everyday life is a challenge to redouble analytical and political efforts to ensure that disadvantage is minimized, especially for the most vulnerable. Exploring the mutual shaping and influence of technological development and social process is to explore possibilities as much as it is to discover patterns of determination. As Judy Wajcman reminds us, if it is true that technology is socially shaped – as, indeed, social situations are also technically shaped – then it may also be reshaped for appropriate purposes.[31] The question is, how?

I want to suggest that 're-embodying persons' is a positive way forward. I mean this metaphorically, of course. It is not that I am disembodied as I write this or that you are as you read. Rather, the way in which surveillance systems work should be influenced by the conviction that we are embodied persons, as should the social theories within which we try to explain such things. In other words, re-embodied persons represents an ethical stance which should inform our being human in postmodern information societies. It is a value position intended to guide sociotechnical developments as much as the choice of appropriate theory.

Having argued so strenuously that surveillance raises questions of power that privacy can never address, am I falling back on some individualistic remedies after all? Emphatically not. For one thing, persons are inherently social creatures; modernist individualism is thus excluded from my account. For another, to assert the significance of embodiment is to reinsert our understanding of persons firmly in material life. This is not reductionism. To say that we need bread is not for a moment to say that we live by bread alone. And for a third, an ethic of embodied personhood gives birth to an earthed and relevant politics.

What kind of power are we up against when it comes to questions of surveillance? As I observed at the beginning, surveillance is a focused attention to personal life details with a view to managing or influencing those whose lives are monitored. It may involve care, and more often, control. It is, in other words, the power of classification, of social sorting. We are all participants in the process, hence the metaphor of social orchestration. The categories have material force, of course, because they include and exclude, declare eligible or not. This is why Baudrillard's cool memories of simulacra just won't do.[32] Surveillance has real enough effects especially when you're a poor single mother on welfare in the Appalachians.

So surveillance power is not directly or necessarily connected with coercion and violence, nor is it the power of tradition that would yield a sense of having to submit to authority. Still less is it the power of love, with its strong sense of obligation and even sacrifice for the other person or persons. As a classificatory power it engages in social sorting which may at the severe end be panoptic, but which may equally be productive. As I have reiterated several times, surveillance always has two faces. Even its social sorting strength runs the gamut from suspicion to seduction. The one induces fear and the other desire.

The stance taken to surveillance is that of participants and of witnesses. As I say, we are all involved, so there can be no pretending that we are somehow outside the situations described. What I offer is a perspective, an approach, a mode of engaging with the issues from within them, not some simplistic set of solutions adumbrated from without. This would bring appropriate values, assumptions and purposes into play,[33] against the hidden bases of surveillance and social sorting such as the utilitarian probability calculus. This approach offers no certainties, still less guarantees, but if it resonates with our experiences and explanations of the situations described here, then it holds some promise. Ethical involvement comes with its own risks, of course. It is contestable and entails negotiation.

Affirming the value of embodied persons helps put in focus what is wrong with some surveillance strategies today. An abstract data image has negative effects on one's life chances. Our autobiographies are diminished by the direct extraction of data from our bodies. Data-hungry agencies may resort to body modification into order to obtain the infallible identification. A photographic image may stand between our testimony and justice in court. A communicative ethic, derived from a sense of embodied personhood, begins

to redress the balance. As I suggested, voluntary self-disclosure within relations of trust should be the default position. Other forms of communication
my be judged in this light. In a world of disappearing bodies the abstract data
is privileged. Turning the tables, and assessing the communication in terms
of the expectations of face-to-face relationships of embodied personhood
would go a long way towards allowing the social to shape the technical rather
than vice versa.

The other key principle is care for the Other. In a society of strangers, a
situation whose negative aspects are exacerbated electronically by surveillance, care for the Other requires radical re-emphasis. At present, while some
surveillance systems do indeed contribute to care, the overwhelming tendency is towards control. In certain situations, of course, the technical system
can never substitute for local face-to-face care and that, rather than any closed-
circuit or remote sensing apparatus, should be the priority. To say that care
for the Other is a primal demand of humanness stems from the argument
that persons are inherently social.[34] To apply this to surveillance situations is
to attempt first to give the stranger a place, a welcome.[35] The current tendency, to exclude the ineligible on minimal criteria, stands in stark contrast to
such an approach. But it is cheaper.

Starting elsewhere, with the ethics of embodied personhood, puts surveillance practices in singularly bold relief. But these same ethics offer the means
of rethinking surveillance from the viewpoint of the citizen, the consumer,
the systems designer or the policy maker. Contemporary surveillance has a
bias towards control, suspicion, seduction and a utilitarian obsession with
the statistical norm. To ask what might happen if surveillance were guided
by an ontology of peace rather than of violence, an ethic of care rather than of
control, an orientation to forgiveness rather than to suspicion may appear as
a weak alternative. But weak in what sense? Is the only conceivable action to
counterpose dominative power with its equal? If not, then 'weak' solutions
might be worth a try.

It is ironic that Jeremy Bentham, with whom all this began,[36] ensured his
bodily preservation. He left his taxidermed body in a cupboard at University
College, London, where he sits to this day. This macabre and Disneyesque
inheritance is ironic because his actual legacy is one that steers right away
from embodied personhood to affirm as appropriate social relations based on
disembodied abstraction. Not only this, we inherit from his work a utilitarian calculus of probability that is only today coming to full flower, if botanic
metaphors are permitted in a world of electronic machines. Lacking significant social and cultural resistance, the actual practices of social ordering are
indeed coming to depend on auditing and actuarial principles.

The real irony, though, would be to discover that the world Bentham himself tried so hard to exclude as 'irrational' – the world of spiritual life and of
theological thought – actually provides elements of a vocabulary that could
assist us today. Without denying for a moment the importance of efforts at
voluntary or legal limits to personal data processing or of the struggle for
democratic control of technology it must be said that these do little to provide

a language for addressing the deeper issues of surveillance. It is the cultural grammar[37] of today's technologies that must be explored and contested. But we must look elsewhere for the means of confronting them than within the technologic of surveillance and its person-blind obsession with monitoring everyday life.

Such means exist beyond both technologic and the discourses of privacy in an ethics of surveillance that engages both with large scale issues of social justice and with other things that really matter to ordinary people. It begins with embodied personhood. To seek these ethics will entail uncovering again layers of language that have languished for too long. It will take a further book to elaborate this, but its basic message will be clear by now. Where humans are seen as embodied persons, where the face-to-face is privileged over abstract communication, justice over automated classification, and communal involvement over technical imperatives there are strong hints of hope.

Notes

Introduction

1 J. Glave (1999) 'Medical records exposed': <http://www.millernash.com>.
2 T. Hamilton (1999) 'Security breach exposes private Air Miles data', *The Globe and Mail* (Toronto), 22 January.
3 In this, I follow the same definition of surveillance as I used in D. Lyon (1994) *The Electronic Eye: The Rise of Surveillance Society*. Cambridge: Polity Press, p. ix.
4 For a preliminary discussion of this see A. Giddens (1999) *Runaway World*. London: Profile, pp. 22–5.
5 R. Ericson and K. Haggerty (1997) *Policing the Risk Society*. Toronto: University of Toronto Press, pp. 426–7.
6 See U. Beck (1992) *The Risk Society: Towards a New Modernity*. London: Sage.
7 Data sharing arrangements involving banks are currently coming under greater legal scrutiny in the USA. Chase Manhattan Bank, for instance, has been obliged to disclose no more financial information to other companies following a ruling by Attorney General Eliot Spitzer. See *The Age* (Melbourne), 1 February 2000, IT Supplement, p. 9.
8 A. Elger and C. Smith (1996) *Global Japanization: The Transnational Transformation of the Labour Process*. London: Routledge.

Chapter 1

1 The following discussion owes much to the work of Anthony Giddens on time-space distanciation, and David Harvey on time-space compression. But also, more specifically, to C. Calhoun (1994) The infrastructure of modernity: indirect relationships, information technology, and social integration, in H. Haferkamp and N. Smelser (eds) *Social Change and Modernity*. Berkeley, CA: University of California Press, and P. James (1996) *Nation Formation: Towards a Theory of Abstract Community*. London: Sage. It may also be connected with a broader debate over 'cyberspace'. See D. Lyon (1997) Cyberspace sociality: controversies over

computer-mediated communication in B. Loader (ed.) *The Governance of Cyberspace*. London: Routledge.

2 Philip Sampson (1994) discusses this, for instance in From dust to plastic, *Third Way*, January, pp. 17–22.

3 It is also the case that the body is returning to cultural prominence, for similar reasons, but this is not the topic of this present study. See, for example, discussions in the journal *Body and Society*.

4 The term 'structures of feeling' is Raymond Williams' but it is picked up in the context of space-time by N. Thrift (1996) *Spatial Formations*, London: Sage, p. 258ff.

5 H.A. Innis (1962) *The Bias of Communication*. Toronto: University of Toronto Press.

6 Thrift, op cit., pp. 279–84.

7 P. Virilio (1994) *The Vision Machine*. London: British Film Institute, cited in Thrift, ibid., p. 280.

8 R. Bray (1997) Smart cards help track passengers, *Financial Post*, 25 November.

9 See C. Calhoun, op cit. and D. Lyon, op cit.

10 G. Deleuze (1992) Postscript on the societies of control, *October*, 59: 3–7.

11 G. Duby (1987), foreword, in P. Veyne, *A History of Private Life*. London and Cambridge, MA: Harvard University Press.

12 See A. Giddens (1992) *Modernity and Self-Identity*. Cambridge: Polity Press, p. 152.

13 E. Shils (1975) Privacy and power, in *Center and Periphery: Essays in Macrosociology*. Chicago: University of Chicago Press.

14 N. Abercrombie, S. Hill and B. Turner (1986) *Sovereign Individuals of Capitalism*. London: Allen & Unwin, p. 189.

15 B. Russell (1912) *Problems of Philosophy*. Oxford: Oxford University Press.

16 C.B. Macpherson (1962) *The Political Theory of Possessive Individualism: Hobbes to Locke*. Oxford: Oxford University Press, p. 3.

17 S. Nock (1993) *The Costs of Privacy*. New York: Aldine de Gruyter.

18 Whether Nock is right about other matters, such as the changing role of the family, and surveillance among young people, is less clear. A further point about privacy is that it arises from a sense of surveillance risks, while at the same time surveillance itself is a response to the risk society. See on the former point, C.D. Raab and C.J. Bennett (1998) The distribution of privacy risks: who needs protection? *The Information Society*, 14: 263–74.

19 R. Samarajiva (1994) Privacy in electronic public space: emerging issues, *Canadian Journal of Communication*, 19(1): 90.

20 P. Regan (1996) Genetic testing and workplace surveillance: implications for privacy, in D. Lyon and E. Zureik (eds) *Computers, Surveillance, and Privacy*. Minneapolis, MN: University of Minnesota Press, p. 34. See also P. Regan (1995) *Legislating Privacy*. Chapel Hill, NC: University of North Carolina Press, p. 221.

21 P. Agre (1997) Introduction, in P. Agre and M. Rotenberg (eds) *Technology and Privacy: The New Landscape*. Cambridge, MA: MIT Press, p. 11.

22 See, for example, S. Brown (1998) What's the matter, girls? CCTV and the gendering of public safety, in C. Norris, J. Moran and G. Armstrong (eds) *Surveillance, Closed Circuit Television and Social Control*. Aldershot: Ashgate.

23 On this see C. Gotlieb (1996) Privacy: a concept whose time has come and gone, in Lyon and Zureik, op cit.

24 J. Carey and J. Quirk (1970) The mythos of the electronic revolution, *The American Scholar*, 39(2): 219–41; and 39(3): 395–424.

25 See D. Lyon (1986) *The Silicon Society*. Oxford: Lion, pp. 27–8.

26 See, for example, A. Feenberg (1999) *Questioning Technology*. London: Routledge.

27 N. Thrift (1996) New urban eras and old technological fears: reconfiguring the goodwill of electronic things, *Urban Studies*, 33: 1471.
28 D. Gelernter (1991) *Mirror Worlds, or the Day Software Puts the Universe in a Shoebox*. Oxford: Oxford University Press, p. 15.
29 See L. Winner (1986) *The Whale and the Reactor*. Chicago: University of Chicago Press, 22–5.
30 G.T. Marx (1988) *Undercover: Police Surveillance in America*. Berkeley CA: University of California Press.
31 The larger scale questions of infrastructure are examined in the following chapter.
32 J. Rule and P. Brantley (undated) 'Surveillance in the workplace: a new meaning to personal computing?' State University of New York at Stony Brook.
33 C. Norris and G. Armstrong (1999) *The Maximum Surveillance Society: The Rise of CCTV*. Oxford: Berg.
34 P. Agre (1997) Beyond the mirror world: privacy and the representational practices of computing, in Agre and Rotenberg, op cit., p. 49.
35 This is an indirect reference to the work of Michel Callon on 'actor-network theory'. See, for example, M. Callon (1991) Techno-economic networks and irreversibility, in J. Law (ed.) *A Sociology of Monsters: Essays on Power, Technology, and Domination*. London: Routledge.
36 See A. Feenberg (1991) *Critical Theory of Technology*. New York: Oxford University Press.

Chapter 2

1 Y. Ito (1993) How Japan modernized earlier and faster than other non-Western countries, *Journal of Development Communication*, 4: 2. S. Nora and A. Minc (1980) *The Computerisation of Society*. Cambridge MA: MIT Press.
2 The 'information superhighway' was an idea championed by US vice-president Al Gore.
3 The technological convergence of computer power with telecommunications is no alchemical magic, but rather the outcome of specific military imperatives, funding priorities and government policies. See D. Lyon (1988) *The Information Society: Issues and Illusions*. Cambridge: Polity Press. See also D. Winseck (1998) *Reconvergence: The Political Economy of Telecommunications in Canada*. Cresskill, NJ: Hampton Press.
4 The idea of 'knowledge-based' businesses and economies stresses the intellectual capital of organizations, which yields a capacity to create new technologies, not merely to use them. A premium is placed on technological development or on technologically advanced products. In Canada, for instance, the information technology sector (which is growing at 15 per cent per annum) is larger than Canada's traditional sectors of oil and gas, mining, pulp and paper, but those latter sectors are also utilizing new technologies. This would indicate that by some measures Canada is becoming a knowledge-based economy. 'Knowledge-based' ideas have been developed in Japan, and go beyond the idea that the only useful knowledge is 'hard data'. Tacit knowledge, teamwork, uncertainty and risk are all important. See, for example, I. Nonaka and H. Takeuchi (1995) *The Knowledge-Creating Company: How Japanese Companies Create the Dynamics of Innovation*. Oxford: Oxford University Press.
5 This phrase is taken from an unpublished draft paper on 'Infrastructure and Modernity' given at a workshop on technology and modernity at the University of Twente, the Netherlands, November 1999.

6 This is discussed in D. Lyon (1999) *Postmodernity*, 2nd edn. Buckingham: Open University Press, Ch. 1.
7 George Orwell's *Nineteen Eighty Four* was first published in London in 1948.
8 Castells (1996) *The Rise of the Network Society*. Oxford: Blackwell, pp. 403–9.
9 G.T. Marx (1985) The surveillance society: the threat of 1984-style techniques, *The Futurist*, June: 21–6.
10 D.H. Flaherty (1989) *Protecting Privacy in Surveillance Societies*. Chapel Hill, NC: University of North Carolina Press, p. 1.
11 C. Bennett (1992) *Regulating Privacy: Data Protection and Public Policy in Europe and the United States*. Ithaca, NY: Cornell University Press.
12 Flaherty, op cit., p. 375.
13 D. Burnham (1983) *The Rise of the Computer State*. New York: Vintage Books.
14 Manuel Castells rightly insists that 'surveillance society' is a better term than 'surveillance state'. But I think that he goes too far in claiming that 'today's state is more surveilled than surveillant'. See M. Castells (1997) *The Power of Identity*. Oxford: Blackwell, p. 302.
15 Big Brother: the all-seeing eye, *The Economist*, 11 January 1997, p. 53.
16 *Wired News*, 2 June 1999, and *Yomiuri Shimbun*, 7 June 1999, p. 2.
17 S. Strange (1996) *The Retreat of the State: The Diffusion of Power in the World Economy*. Cambridge, NY: Cambridge University Press, p. 122.
18 Ibid., p. 127.
19 Ibid., p. 133.
20 See M. Poster (1996) Databases as discourse, in D. Lyon and E. Zureik (eds) *Computers, Surveillance and Privacy*. Minneapolis, MN: University of Minnesota Press.
21 D. Lyon (1994) *The Electronic Eye: The Rise of Surveillance Society*. Cambridge: Polity Press, p. 126.

Chapter 3

1 N. Waters (1996) Street surveillance and privacy. Paper presented at the Privacy Issues Forum, Christchurch, New Zealand, 13 June.
2 Resistance to developing surveillance systems is discussed in a more focused way in Chapter 8 of this book.
3 This sectoral approach to surveillance is discussed in the four central chapters of D. Lyon (1994) *The Electronic Eye: The Rise of Surveillance Society*. Cambridge: Polity Press.
4 D. Campbell and Connor (1986) *On the Record: Surveillance, Computers, and Privacy: The Inside Story*. London: Michael Joseph.
5 H. Kunzru (1999) The police get more byte, *The Daily Telegraph*, 14 January, pp. 4–5.
6 Compare S. Cohen (1985) *Visions of Social Control*. London: Blackwell.
7 See R. Ericson and K. Haggerty (1997) *Policing the Risk Society*. Toronto: University of Toronto Press.
8 See, for example, F. de Coninck (1994) *Travail Integré, Société Eclaté*. Paris: PUF.
9 S. Greengard (1996) Privacy: entitlement or illusion? *Personnel Journal*, May: 75–87. Data mining is also used in consumer surveillance. Similar techniques are used in quite different sectors, though not necessarily with the same kinds of effects.
10 See the letter from Alison Wakefield in *The Times*, 30 November 1999.
11 Rights of privacy: technology has its eyes on you, *Scientific American*, November 1995: 36–7.

12 See T. Johnston (1999) Quit watching me! *The Globe and Mail* (Toronto), 29 January.
13 See the detailed study by M. McCahill and C. Norris (1999) Watching the workers: crime, CCTV and the workplace, in P. Davies, P. Francis and V. Jupp (eds) *Invisible Crimes: Their Victims and their Regulation*. London: MacMillan, pp. 208–31.
14 K. Wilson (1998) Who's been reading your e-mail? *Guardian*, 20 April, p. 54.
15 Alarming threat to workplace privacy. BBC News online, 18 February 1999, <http://news.bbc.co.uk/hi/english/uk/newsid_282000/282073.stm>.
16 For instance, the article by K. Wilson, cited in Note 15.
17 T. Johnston, op cit., p. 2.
18 'Sloanism' is a term used by F. Webster and K. Robins (1986) *Information Technology: A Luddite Analysis*. Norwood, NJ: Ablex, also discussed in Lyon, op cit.
19 See, for example, P. Agre and M. Rotenberg (1997) Introduction, in P. Agre and M. Rotenberg (eds) *Technology and Privacy: Emerging Landscapes*. Cambridge MA: MIT Press.
20 M.J. Culnan and R.J. Bies (1999) Managing privacy concerns strategically: the implications of fair information practices for marketing in the twenty-first century, in C.J. Bennett and R. Grant (eds) *Visions of Privacy: Policy Choices for a Digital Age*. Toronto: University of Toronto Press, p. 150.
21 H. Martins (1999) Technology, modernity, politics, in J. Good and I. Velody (eds) *The Politics of Postmodernity*. Cambridge: Cambridge University Press.
22 R. Laperrière (1999) The Quebec model of data protection, in Bennett and Grant, op cit., p. 183ff.
23 See M. Venne (1995) Une agence privé e pour gérer les données du réseau de la santé: les banques de données pourraint être vendues au secteur privé, *Le Devoir*, 5 April, cited in Laperrière, ibid.
24 B. Nicholson (1999) Alarm at Packer database scheme, *The Age*, 1 December, pp. 1–2.
25 U. Beck (1997) *The Reinvention of Politics: Rethinking Modernity in the Global Social Order*. Cambridge: Polity Press.
26 Ibid., p. 42.
27 Ericson and Haggerty (op cit., pp. 426–52) discuss this helpfully in relation to policing.

Chapter 4

1 'Social science fiction' is a term used by W. Bogard (1996) *The Simulation of Surveillance*, Cambridge: Cambridge University Press, p. 6ff., and R. Burrows (1997) Virtual culture, urban social polarization, and social science fiction, in B. Loader (ed.) *The Governance of Cyberspace*, London: Routledge, p. 38ff.
2 An example would be J. Bleecker (1994) Urban crisis: past, present, and virtual, *Socialist Review*, 24(1&2): 189–221.
3 R. Sennett (1996) *Flesh and Stone*. London: Faber & Faber, p. 113.
4 S. Cohen (1985) *Visions of Social Control*. Oxford: Blackwell, p. 206.
5 P. Virilio (1994) *The Vision Machine*. London: British Film Institute, p. 9.
6 See, for example, G. Simmel (1950) The metropolis and mental life, in K.H. Wolff (ed.) *The Sociology of Georg Simmel*. Glencoe, NY: Free Press.
7 S. Cohen (1985) *Visions of Social Control*. London: Blackwell.
8 J. Jacobs (1961) *The Death and Life of Great American Cities*. New York: Vintage.
9 Cohen, op cit., p. 215.

10 M. Davis (1992) *City of Quartz: Excavating the Future in Los Angeles*. New York: Vintage.
11 See R. Sennett (1970) *The Uses of Disorder: Personal Identity and City Life*. New York: Knopf.
12 The term 'informational city' comes from M. Castells (1989) *The Informational City: Information Technology, Economic Restructuring and the Urban-Regional Process*. Oxford: Blackwell.
13 Virilio, op cit., p. 75.
14 S. Graham (1997) Urban Planning in the Information Society, *Town and Country Planning*, November: 298.
15 Ibid., p. 299. See also S. Graham and S. Marvin (1996) *Telecommunications and the City: Electronic Spaces, Urban Places*. London: Routledge.
16 J.L. Wilson (1994) *The Official SimCity Planning Commission Handbook*. Berkeley, CA: Osborne McGraw-Hill.
17 Ibid., p. xxii.
18 T. Friedman (1995) Making sense of software: computer games and interactive texuality, in S.G. Jones (ed.) *Cybersociety*, p. 81. Thousand Oaks, CA: Sage.
19 Ibid., p. 85.
20 A. Bryman (1999) The Disneyization of society, *The Sociological Review*, February. It is interesting that Singapore has a 'smile' policy. See also W. Gibson (1995) Disneyland with the death penalty, *Wired*, 1(4). This is another instance of social science fiction.
21 S. Zukin (1995) *The Culture of Cities*, p. 77. Oxford: Blackwell.
22 Ibid., p. 52.
23 The relation of surveillance to Disneyland was noted in C. Shearing and P. Stenning (1985) From the Panopticon to Disneyworld: the development of discipline, in E. Doob and E.L. Greenspan (eds) *Perspectives in Criminal Law*. Aurora: Canada Law Books.
24 Cookies are computer codes sent to the user's hard drive when a website is visited. Once installed on the hard drive it allows the website operator to track how and when the site is accessed.
25 Castells, op cit.
26 M. Castells (1996) *The Rise of the Network Society*, p. 386. Oxford: Blackwell.
27 R. Crawford (1996) Computer assisted crises, in G. Gerbner, H. Mowlana and H. Schiller (eds) *Invisible Crises*, p. 57. Boulder, CO: Westview Press.
28 J. Douglas (1990) Reaching out with 2-way communications, *EPRI Journal*, 15(6): 4–13, cited in Crawford, ibid., p. 79.
29 G.W. Hart (1989) Residential energy monitoring and computerized surveillance via utility power flows, *IEEE Technology and Society Magazine*, June: 12–16.
30 N. Ellin (ed.) (1997) *Architecture of Fear*, pp. 44–5. New York: Princeton Architectural Press.
31 See the discussion in D. Lyon (1994) *The Electronic Eye: The Rise of Surveillance Society*. Cambridge: Polity Press.
32 Davis, op cit.
33 S. Zukin (1991) *Landscapes of Power: From Detroit to Disney World*, p. 321. Berkeley, CA: University of California Press.
34 F. Bell (1999) Victoria: unreal city, *The Ottawa Citizen*, 10 March.
35 D. Ley (1996) *The New Middle Class and the Remaking of the Central City*, p. 15. Oxford: Oxford University Press.
36 See C. Dandeker (1990) *Surveillance, Power, and Modernity*. Cambridge: Polity Press.
37 W. Bogard (1996) *The Simulation of Surveillance*, p. 38. Cambridge: Cambridge University Press.

38 R.V. Ericson and K. Haggerty (1997) *Policing the Risk Society*, p. 41. Toronto: University of Toronto Press.
39 D. Graham-Rowe (1999) Warning! Strange Behaviour, *New Scientist*, 11 December: 25–8.
40 N.R. Fyfe and J. Bannister (1996) City watching: closed-circuit television surveillance in public places, *Area*, 28(1): 40.
41 Ibid., pp. 40–1.
42 This argument is made strongly by Ericson and Haggerty, op cit.
43 S. Graham (1998) Towards the fifth utility? On the extension and normalization of public CCTV in C. Norris, J. Moran and G. Armstrong (eds) *Surveillance, Closed-Circuit Television and Social Control*. Aldershot: Ashgate.
44 N. Fyfe and J. Bannister (1996) City watching: closed-circuit television surveillance in public spaces, *Area*, 28: 1.
45 M. Crang (1996) Watching the city: video, resistance, and surveillance, *Environment and Planning A*, 28: 2102–3.
46 See J. Ditton, E. Short, S. Phillips, C. Norris and G. Armstrong (1999) *The Effect of Closed-Circuit Television on Recorded Crime Rates and Public Concern about Crime in Glasgow*, p. 17. Edinburgh: Stationery Office.
47 CCTV for Public Safety, *American City and County*, 113: 11.
48 Graham, op cit., 100–6.
49 D. Jones (1996) Candid cameras, *Report on Business Magazine*, April: 109–12.
50 T. Van Straaten (1998) VerifEye sets sights on taxicab market, *Financial Post*, 5 November.
51 Ericson and Haggerty, op cit., p. 135.
52 I. Amato (1999) God's eyes for sale, *Technology Review*, March/April: 37–41.
53 T. Grescoe (1996) Murder, he mapped, *Canadian Geographic*, September/October: 48–52.
54 S. Verma (1999) Police double crime 'hotspot' targets, *Toronto Star*, 23 July.
55 J. Plant (1998) Highways: warfare to tolls, *Canadian Consulting Engineer*, March/April: 22.
56 S. Graham (1998) Spaces of surveillant simulation: new technologies, digital representations, and material geographies, *Environment and Planning: Society and Space*, 16: 494.
57 A. Reeve (1998) The panopticization of shopping: CCTV and leisure consumption' in C. Norris, J. Moran and G. Armstrong (eds) *Surveillance, Closed Circuit Television and Social Control*. Aldershot: Ashgate.
58 O. Gandy (1993) *The Panoptic Sort: A Political Economy of Personal Information*. Boulder, CO: Westview Press.
59 See report in the (London) *Daily Mail*, 18 May 1999.
60 M. Kronby (1998) This man wants to program your life, *Shift>Magazine*, November: 43–50.
61 P. Pullella (1999) Vatican goes high tech, *Globe and Mail* (Toronto), 22 January.
62 See, for example, D. Lyon (1998) The world-wide-web of surveillance: the Internet and off-world power flows, *Information, Communication, and Society*, 1(1): 91–105.
63 S. Graham (1998) The end of geography or the explosion of place? Conceptualizing space, place, and information technology, *Progress in Human Geography*, 22: 165–85.
64 See Reeve, op cit.
65 Ericson and Haggerty, op cit., p. 450ff.
66 Burrows, op cit., p. 41.
67 The phrase is in J. Bannister, N.R. Fyfe and A. Kearns (1998) Closed-circuit television and the city in Norris (*et al.* eds), 22.
68 Simmel, op cit.

69 A. Aurigi and S. Graham (1998) The 'crisis' in the urban public realm, in B. Loader (ed.) *Cyberspace Divide*, pp. 73–5. London: Routledge.
70 Ericson and Haggerty, op cit., p. 451.
71 J. Jacobs (1961) *The Death and Life of the Great American Cities*, quoted in Norris (*et al.* eds) 23.
72 J. Seabrook (1993) The root of all evil, *New Statesman and Society*, 26 February: 12.

Chapter 5

1 M. Kalman (1999) Israelis use high-tech to track Palestinians, *The Globe and Mail* (Toronto), 30 March.
2 D. Lyon (1994) *The Electronic Eye: The Rise of Surveillance Society*. Cambridge: Polity Press.
3 See, for example, I. van der Ploeg (1999) Written on the body: biometrics and identity, *Computers and Society*, 29(1): 37–44.
4 A scheme like this one appears in D. Tapscott and A. Cavoukian (1995) *Who Knows? Safeguarding Your Privacy in a Networked World*. Toronto: Random House.
5 P. Mellor and C. Shilling (1997) *Reforming the Body: Religion, Community, and Modernity*, p. 147. London: Sage.
6 See Lyon, op cit., pp. 3–21.
7 US Public Interest Research Group (1996) *Theft of Identity: The Consumer X-Files*, 14 August, cited in A. Cavoukian (1997) *Identity Theft: Who's Using Your Name?* Toronto: IPC.
8 K. Pearsall (1998) This technology is eye-catching, *Computing Canada*, 24: 2.
9 G. Kirbyson (1996) The smart card goes to China, *Financial Post*, 9(103): 6.
10 C. Guly (1997) Digital security, *Financial Post*, 6 September: 23.
11 V. Beiser (1997) The keyless society, *McLean's*, 110: 34. 25 August: 40.
12 E. Goffman (1956) *The Presentation of Self in Everyday Life*. Garden City, NY: Doubleday.
13 N. Abercrombie, S. Hill and B. Turner (1986) *Sovereign Individuals of Capitalism*, p. 33. London: Allen & Unwin.
14 As Paul Ricoeur points out in *Oneself as Another* (Chicago: University of Chicago Press, 1992), this way of considering things places the discussion outside the limits of both rationalism and nihilism. The self-attesting body thus shows its responsibility for the Other: 'As credence without any guarantee, but also as trust greater than any suspicion, the hermeneutics of the self can claim to hold itself at an equal distance from the cogito exalted by Descartes and the cogito that Nietzsche claimed forfeit' (p. 23).
15 Abercrombie *et al.*, op cit., p. 189.
16 J. Rule, D. McAdam, L. Stearns and D. Uglow (1983) Documentary identification and mass surveillance in the United States, *Social Problems*, 31(2): 222–34.
17 Ibid., p. 233.
18 R. Clarke (1988) Information technology and dataveillance, *Communications of the ACM*, 31(5): 498–512.
19 C. Bennett (1996) The public surveillance of personal data: a cross-national analysis, in D. Lyon and E. Zureik (eds) *Computers, Surveillance, and Privacy*, p. 237. Minneapolis, MN: University of Minnesota Press.
20 This is argued in a related context in D. Lyon (1988) *The Information Society: Issues and Illusions*, Ch. 2. Cambridge: Polity Press. See also Dwayne Winseck (1998) *Reconvergence: The Political Economy of Telecommunications in Canada*. Cresskill, NJ: Hampton Press.
21 M. Castells (1996) *The Rise of the Network Society*. Oxford: Blackwell.

22 R.V. Ericson and K. Haggerty (1997) *Policing the Risk Society*, pp. 426–7. Toronto: University of Toronto Press.
23 This distinction between persons and individuals is similar to that appearing in the work of P. James (1996) *Nation Formation: Towards a Theory of Abstract Community*, pp. 170–1. London: Sage.
24 See A. Davis (1997) The body as password, *Wired*, 5(7): 132–40.
25 Ibid., p. 132.
26 S. Nock (1993) *The Costs of Privacy: Surveillance and Reputation in America*, p. 76. New York: Aldine de Gruyter.
27 The polygraph is not admissible in Canadian courts, although police may use it to sort out suspicions of criminality. See Ericson and Haggerty, op cit., p. 247. The polygraph is also unacceptable to the American Psychological Association because it turns up 'an unacceptable number of false positives'. See G. Marx (1988) *Undercover: Police Surveillance in America*. Berkeley, CA: University of California Press.
28 The term is Gary Marx's, ibid.
29 M. Crang (1996) Watching the city: video, surveillance, and resistance, *Environment and Planning A*, 28: 2099–104.
30 *New York Times*, 12 November 1993.
31 Castells, op cit., p. 30, considers biological and genetic sciences within the 'information revolution'.
32 Genomics, *The Sunday Times* (Singapore), 12 September 1999: 42–3.
33 P. Regan (1995) *Legislating Privacy: Technology, Social Values, and Public Policy*, p. 170. Chapel Hill, NC: University of North Carolina Press.
34 A. Furr (1999) Social status and attitudes towards organizational control of genetic data, *Sociological Focus*, 32(4): 371–82.
35 See D. Spurgeon (1999) 'Thrifty gene' identified in Manitoba Indians, *British Medical Journal*, 318: 828.
36 See Davis, op cit.
37 The Social Assistance Reform Act attempted to address perceived deficiencies in the Family Benefits Act and the General Welfare Assistance Act, in particular those that seemed to permit double-dipping.
38 D.N. Gage (1997) Body language, *Computerworld Canada*, 13: 25, 32.
39 I. Ross (1997) IDs at fingertip, Harris predicts, *The Globe and Mail* (Toronto), 14 May: A1, A7.
40 R. Clarke (1997) Five most vital privacy issues, http://www.anu.edu.au/people/Roger.Clarke/DV/VitalPriv.html, 31 July.
41 K. Cottrill (1997) Reading between the lines, *Guardian*, 6 November: 6.
42 T. Keenan, cited in Gage op cit., p. 32.
43 Davis, op cit.
44 C. Norris *et al.* (1996) Algorithmic surveillance: the future of automated visual surveillance, in C. Norris, J. Moran and G. Armstrong (eds) *Surveillance, Closed Circuit Television and Social Control*, p. 265. Aldershot: Ashgate.
45 Ibid., p. 267.
46 Ericson and Haggerty, op cit., p. 248.
47 J. Gilliom (1994) *Surveillance, Privacy and the Law: Employee Drug Testing and the Politics of Social Control*. Ann Arbor, MI: University of Michigan Press.
48 D. Wagner (1987) The new temperance movement and social control at the workplace, *Contemporary Drug Problems*, Winter: 540–1.
49 C. Boyes-Watson (1997) Corporations as drug warriors: the symbolic significance of employee drug testing, *Studies in Law, Politics, and Society*, 17: 185–223. See also T.D. Hartwell, P.D. Steele, M.T. French and N.F. Rodman (1996) Prevalance of drug-testing in the workplace, *Monthly Labour Review*, November: 35–42, who argue that it is drug abuse rather than the larger employment problem, alcohol

abuse, for which employees are more frequently tested (two times as much, in fact) in the USA. Alcohol use is not in itself illegal or against company policies.

50 M. Mineham (1998) The growing debate over genetic testing, *HRM Magazine*, April: 208.

51 S.L. Smith (1998) Gene testing and work: not a good fit, *Occupational Hazards*, 60 (7): 38.

52 L. Surtees (1996) Spy tech set to thwart card fraud, *The Globe and Mail* (Toronto), 12 June: B4.

53 V. Beiser (1997) The keyless society, *McLean's*, 110: 34. 25 August: 40.

54 Davis, op cit., p. 132.

55 Beiser, op cit., p. 40.

56 C. Guly (1997) Digit-al security, *The Financial Post*, 6 September: 23.

57 J. Powell (1997) Eye-dentification, *The Financial Post*, 27 September: E1, E11.

58 A. Giddens (1990) *The Consequences of Modernity*. Cambridge: Polity Press.

59 P. Virilio (1991) *The Lost Dimension*, p. 13. New York: Semiotext(e).

60 A. Cavoukian (1999) The promise of privacy-enhancing technologies: applications in health information networks, in C. Bennett and R. Grant (eds) *Visions of Privacy: Policy Choices for the Digital Age*, p. 117. Toronto: University of Toronto Press.

61 U. Beck (1992) *Risk Society: Towards a New Modernity*, p. 34. London: Sage.

62 National Genome Project Research Institute (1998) Genetic information and the workplace, www.nhgri.nih.gov:80/HGP/Reports/genetics_workplace.html 3.

63 Ericson and Haggerty, op cit., p. 448.

64 Clarke, op cit., p. 2.

65 C. Reed (1998) Lack of fingerprints puts man under thumb of bureaucracy, *The Globe and Mail* (Toronto), 23 April.

66 Gage, op cit., p. 32.

67 E. Alma Draper (1997) Social Issues of genome innovation and intellectual property, *Risk*, 7 (Summer): 11.

68 See Gilliom, op cit., pp. 95–100.

69 Davis, op cit., p. 6.

70 Cited in Davis, ibid., p. 4.

71 See N.K. Hayles (1999) *How We Became Posthuman: Virtual Bodies in Cybernetics, Literature, and Informatics*, pp. 84–5. Chicago: University of Chicago Press.

72 See, for example, D. Haraway (1997) *Modest Witness@Second_Millennium. FemaleMan_Meets_Oncomouse: Feminism and Technoscience*. London: Routledge.

73 S. Plant (1995) The future looms: weaving women and cybernetics, in M. Featherstone and R. Burrows (eds) *Cyberspace/Cyberbodies/Cyberpunk: Culture of Technological Embodiment*. London: Sage.

74 Revelation, 13: 16–17.

75 E. Schüssler Fiorenza (1998) *The Book of Revelation: Justice and Judgement*. Minneapolis, MN: Fortress, 124. J. Sweet (1979) *Revelation*. London: SCM, pp. 213–19. M. Wilcock (1975) *I Saw Heaven Opened*. Leicester: Inter-Varsity press, p. 127.

76 This is a key theme of W. Bogard's (1996) *The Simulation of Surveillance*. New York: Cambridge University Press. One need not accept all aspects of his 'social science fiction' to see that this present point is well made by him.

77 D. Lyon (1991) Bentham's panopticon: from moral architecture to electronic surveillance, *Queen's Quarterly*, 98.

78 Kevin Warwick, professor of cybernetics at Reading University, UK, voluntarily implanted a chip under his skin in August 1998, in order more fully to control his surrounding environment. Needless to say the same kind of chip has potential to be used in ways that monitor and influence the person in whose body the chip is mounted.

Chapter 6

1 In 1991 Granada Television (UK) exposed the fact that all telexes, including birthday greetings, passing in or out of the City of London are routinely intercepted and passed through the GCHQ Dictionary. N. Hager (1996) *Secret Power*. Nelson, NZ: Craig Potton Publishing, p. 51.

2 See the article by J. Merrit in the *Observer* (London), 28 June 1992.

3 'Doing things at a distance' is how globalization is characterized by A. Giddens (1990) *The Consequences of Modernity*. Cambridge: Polity.

4 See the useful commentary in I. Wallace (1998) A Christian reading of the global economy, in H. Aay and S. Griffioen (eds) *Geography and Worldview*. New York: University of America Press, pp. 37–48.

5 Race and ethnicity are almost bound to be significant surveillance categories in globalizing contexts, but this does not mean that sexuality, gender and religion are unimportant.

6 It is also important to note that electronic mediation has not somehow displaced all face-to-face contacts. In fact, the most significant business decisions still tend to be made in face-to-face situations. But nonetheless many others, such as on the increasingly automated stock exchanges, require no such contact.

7 J. Pickles (1995) Representations in an electronic age: geography, GIS, and democracy, in J. Pickles (ed.) *Ground Truth*. New York: Guilford Press, p. 22.

8 M.R. Curry (1997) The digital individual and the private realm, *Annals of the Association of American Geographers*, 87(4): 681.

9 M. Castells (1996) *The Rise of the Network Society*. Oxford: Blackwell, p. 92.

10 Ibid., p. 93.

11 These categories are suggested in the excellent paper by C. Bennett (1999) What happens when you buy an airline ticket? Surveillance, globalization, and the regulation of international communications networks, presented at the Canadian Political Science Association, Sherbrooke, PQ, 6 June.

12 Ibid., p. 6.

13 Leslie Sklair (1995) *Sociology of the Global System*. London: Prentice Hall/Harvester Wheatsheaf, p. 6.

14 Ibid., p. 95.

15 See D. Chaney (1995) *Lifestyles*. London: Routledge.

16 What is actually done with these images in differing cultural contexts is, of course, an empirical matter. Even the consumption of images does not guarantee the consumption of the goods and services they refer to. But it is naive to imagine that the proliferation of such images has no effect on their recipients!

17 M. Poster (1996) Databases as discourse, in D. Lyon and E. Zureik (eds) *Computers, Surveillance, and Privacy*. Minneapolis, MN: University of Minnesota Press, pp. 190–1.

18 T. Mathieson (1997) The viewer society: Foucault's 'Panopticon' revisited, *Theoretical Criminology*, 1: 215–34.

19 Z. Bauman (1998) *Globalization: The Human Consequences*. Oxford: Polity Press.

20 See A. Bryman (1999) The Disneyization of society, *Sociological Review*, 47(1): 25–47.

21 R. Roberston (1995) Glocalization: time-space and homogeneity-heterogeneity, in M. Featherstone *et al.* (eds) *Global Modernities*. London: Sage.

22 See G. Therborn (1995) Routes to/through modernity, in Featherstone *et al.*, ibid.

23 These are discussed in D. Lyon (1994) *The Electronic Eye: The Rise of Surveillance Society*. Cambridge: Polity Press, Ch. 7.

24 H. Benyon (1984) *Working for Ford*. Harmondsworth: Penguin, p. 356.

25 P. Turnbull (1987) The 'Japanization' of production and industrial relations at Lucas Electrical, *Industrial Relations Journal*, 17(3): 193–206.
26 J.T. Womack, *et al.* (1990) *The Machine that Changed the World*. New York: Rawson Macmillan.
27 T. Elger and C. Smith (eds) (1994) *Global Japanization? The Transnational Transformation of the Labour Process*. London: Routledge.
28 Turnbull, op cit., p. 203.
29 Hager, op cit.
30 Hager, ibid., pp. 237–8.
31 Information about Comint is derived from a report by D. Campbell (May 1999) for the Science and Technological Options Assessment (STOA) section of the European Parliament. Entitled *Interception Capabilities 2000*, it is available electronically at www.cyber-rights.org/interception/stoa/ic2report.htm. The Studeman quotation is from page 6.
32 Ibid., p. 15.
33 W. Madsen (1995) Puzzle palace conducting Internet surveillance, *Computer Fraud and Security Bulletin*, June.
34 Campbell, op cit., p. 23.
35 M. Frost, quoted in D. Campbell, ibid., Careful, they might hear you, *The Age* (Melbourne), 23 May, noted this point. Sam de Silva drew this to my attention.
36 D. Bigo (1996) Larchipel des polices, *Le Monde Diplomatique*, 9 October.
37 G.T. Marx (1998) Social control across borders, in W. McDonald (ed.) *Crime and Law Enforcement in the Global Village*. Highland Heights, KY: Anderson.
38 M. Castells (1998) *The End Of Millennium*. Oxford: Blackwell, pp. 166–7.
39 Bigo, op cit., p. 9.
40 C. Raab (1994) Police cooperation: the prospects for privacy, in M. Anderson and M. Den Boer (eds) *Policing Across National Boundaries*. London: Pinter.
41 M. Baldwin Edwards and B. Hebenton (1994) Will SIS be Europe's Big Brother?, in Anderson and Den Boer, ibid., p. 155.
42 C. Fijnaut and G.T. Marx (eds) (1995) *Undercover: Police Surveillance in Comparative Perspective*. The Hague: Kluwer, p. 14.
43 G.T. Marx in Fijnaut and Marx, ibid., p. 337.
44 I. van der Ploeg (1999) The illegal body: 'Eurodac' and the politics of biometric identification, *Ethics and Information Technology*, 1(4): 295–302.
45 M. Weiner (1997) Ethics, national sovereignty, and the control of immigration, *International Migration Review*, 30(1): 177.
46 Ibid., p. 181.
47 D. Campbell (1994) Foreign investment, labour immobility and the quality of employment, *International Labour Review*, 2: 185–203. Cited in Castells (1996), op cit., p. 232.
48 Weiner, op cit., p. 184.
49 T. Espenshade (1994) Does the threat of border apprehension deter undocumented US immigration? *Population and Development Review*, 20(4): 889.
50 D. Bigo (1996) *Polices en Réseaux*. Paris: Presses de Sciences Po, pp. 327–39.
51 Ibid., p. 334, my translation.
52 Ibid., p. 333.
53 R. Samarajiva (1994) Privacy in electronic public space: emerging issues, *Canadian Journal of Communication*, 19: 87–99.
54 See O. Gandy (1993) *The Panoptic Sort: A Political Economy of Personal Information*. Boulder, CO: Westview Press.
55 An early argument along these line is found in F. Webster and K. Robins (1986) *Information Technology: A Luddite Analysis*. Norwood, NJ: Ablex.

56 D. Lyon (1998) The world wide web of surveillance: the Internet and off-world power flows, *Information, Communication, and Society*, 1(1): 91–105, reprinted in H. MacKay *et al.* (eds) (1999) *The Media Reader*. Milton Keynes: The Open University.

57 R. Stagliano (1996) Publicité du troisième type, in *L'Internet: L'ecstase et L'effroi*. Paris: Le Monde Diplomatique.

58 P. McGrath (1999) Knowing you all too well, *Newsweek*, 22 March.

59 Intel and the PSN, http://www.bigbrotherinside.com, accessed 12 February 1999.

60 Chapter 2 of this book discusses digital and biometric-based workplace surveillance.

61 This is not a critique of globalization as such. Useful distinctions such as that between 'globalization from above' and 'globalization from below' help to suggest different modes of globalization than that based merely on the transnational capitalist model. The latter views the global from a local perspective, respecting cultural difference. This yields other contrasts in international activities; offshore campuses versus student exchanges, tourism versus travelling and so on.

Chapter 7

1 The themes of *Until the End of the World* are manifold and I only mention one of them in the text. In an illuminating commentary on this film, Norbert Grob makes the point that '. . . the more images dominate our experience the less autonomy people will have in their access to images'. See (1997) Life sneaks out of stories: *Until the End of the World*, in R.F. Cook and G. Gemünden (eds) *The Cinema of Wim Wenders: Image, Narrative, and the Postmodern Condition*. Detroit, MI: Wayne State University Press, p. 171.

2 See, for example, A. Giddens (1985) *The Nation-State and Violence*. Cambridge: Polity Press. C. Gill (1985) *Work, Employment, and the New Technology*. Cambridge: Polity Press. D. Lyon (1988) *The Information Society: Issues and Illusions*. Cambridge: Polity Press.

3 Giddens, ibid., p. 175. G.T. Marx (1988) *Police Surveillance in America*. Berkeley, CA: University of California Press, p. 206ff.

4 Leaving the more futurological accounts on one side, one might mention the work of M. Castells (1996) *The Rise of the Network Society* (vol. 1 of *The Information Age*). Oxford: Blackwell. K. Kumar (1995) *From Post-Industrial to Post-Modern Society*, Cambridge, MA: Blackwell. Or D. Lyon (1999) *Postmodernity*, 2nd edn. Buckingham: Open University Press.

5 M. Poster (1996) Databases as discourse, in D. Lyon and E. Zureik (eds) *Computers, Surveillance, and Privacy*, Minneapolis MN: University of Minnesota Press; also in Poster's (1997) *The Second Media Age*. Cambridge: Polity Press.

6 W. Bogard (1996) *The Simulation of Surveillance: Hypercontrol in Telematic Societies*. Cambridge: Cambridge University Press.

7 M. Foucault, in G. Burchell, C. Gordon and P. Miller (1991) *The Foucault Effect: Studies in Governmentality*. London: Harvester Wheatsheaf, cited in Poster (1996), op cit., p. 180.

8 On the more conventional (and critical) side, the panopticon is utilized effectively by O. Gandy (1993) in his *The Panoptic Sort: A Political Economy of Personal Information*. Boulder, CO: Westview Press.

9 This view of surveillance owes much to the work of J. Rule. See Rule *et al.* (1983) Documentary identification and mass surveillance in the United States, *Social Problems*, 31(2): 222–34.

10 No special transdisciplinary sub-field of surveillance studies exists as yet. One strong implication of this book's argument, however, is that the establishment of such a sub-field is highly desirable.

11 C. Dandeker (1990) *Surveillance, Power, and Modernity*. Cambridge: Polity Press.

12 'Internal pacification' is the term used by Giddens (1985), op cit.

13 F. Kafka (1937) *The Trial*. New York: Knopf.

14 J. Rule (1973) *Private Lives, Public Surveillance*, Harmondsworth: Allen Lane.

15 D. Burnham (1983) *The Rise of the Computer State*. New York: Random House.

16 The reasons for Ellul's apparent marginality, especially to English-speaking sociology, include what some saw as his cavalier approach to citation (he is clearly dependent on Weber, for instance, but this is seldom if ever mentioned by him); the fact that he wrote in French; and his, for many, eccentric insistence that *la technique* represents a deeply spiritual malaise in western culture. He had – and has – champions in North America, along with theorists such as Langdon Winner, who have been at pains to dismantle what the latter sees as Ellul's determinism. See Winner (1977) *Autonomous Technology: Technics Out of Control as a Theme in Human Thought*. Cambridge, MA: MIT Press.

17 J. Ellul (1964) *The Technological Society*. New York: Vintage Books.

18 Marx, op cit. R. Ericson and K. Haggerty (1997) *Policing the Risk Society*. Toronto: University of Toronto Press.

19 Winner, op cit.

20 Gandy (1996), op cit. in Lyon and Zureik, op cit., p. 137.

21 See Ericson and Haggerty, op cit.

22 Giddens, op cit.

23 Contrast this with the work of A. Feenberg (1999) *Questioning Technology*. London: Routledge. He takes the view that Ellul, along with Heidegger, has essentialist views of technology. Ellul's (1980) *The Technological System* (New York: Continuum) for example, offers a seemingly pessimistic conclusion: 'The human being who uses technology today is by that very fact the human being who serves it' (p. 325). But Ellul chose to write about his political strategies in other books, such as his (1991) *Anarchy and Christianity*. Grand Rapids, MI: Eerdmans.

24 H. Braverman (1980) *Labour and Monopoly Capital*. New York: Monthly Review Press.

25 This is discussed, *inter alia*, in A. Francis (1984) *New Technology at Work*. New York: Oxford University Press. Also, in relation to surveillance studies particularly, in D. Lyon (1994) *The Electronic Eye: The Rise of Surveillance Society*. Cambridge: Polity Press.

26 F. Webster and K. Robins (1986) *Information Technology: A Luddite Analysis*. Newark, NJ: Ablex.

27 Gandy (1993), op cit.

28 Gandy (1996) Coming to terms with the panoptic sort in Lyon and Zureik, op cit., p. 152.

29 A useful critique of technological essentialism is A. Feenberg (1999) *Questioning Technology*. London: Routledge.

30 Personal email from Clive Norris, January 2000.

31 While Oscar Gandy, for example, made excellent use of the panoptic metaphor in *The Panoptic Sort*, his is not a discursive account. Sociologically, it is much more conventional, drawing especially on Marxian and Weberian categories.

32 Poster (1996), 176.

33 A similar point, that in the information age symbols become centrally important in social organization – and especially in social movements – is made by Alberto Melucci in his (1996) *Challenging Codes*. Cambridge and New York: Cambridge University Press. What Melucci takes from this, however, is,

unlike Poster, the notion of the unstability and contestability of symbolic communications.

34 Poster, op cit., p. 180.

35 Ibid., p. 181.

36 See D. Lyon (1991) Bentham's panopticon: from moral architecture to electronic surveillance, *Queen's Quarterly*, 98(3).

37 A similar argument is made, earlier, by G. Deleuze (1992) Postscript on the societies of control, *October*, 59 (Winter): 3–7.

38 Poster, op cit., p. 184.

39 Ibid., p. 186.

40 This is discussed in N. Abercrombie *et al.* (1983) *Sovereign Individuals of Capitalism*. London: Allen & Unwin. And also in Lyon (1994), op cit.

41 Poster, op cit., p. 188.

42 Bogard, op cit., p. 3. Bogard retains quotation marks around words like 'reality', believing as he does that such notions are destabilized by the processes he describes. I remove the marks as a means of indicating not that such realities have inflexible characteristics so much as that the category of the real nonetheless has some reliable referents, even though they may not be understood by us. See the discussions of realism in for example, T. May and M. Williams (eds) (1998) *Knowing the Social World*. Buckingham: Open University Press.

43 Bogard, op cit., p. 10.

44 J. Baudrillard (1983) *Simulations*. New York: Semiotext(e), p. 83.

45 See the discussion of Cromatica in Chapter 4.

46 Bogard, op cit., p. 18.

47 P. Virilio (1986) *Speed and Politics*. New York: Semiotext(e), p. 15. See also Bogard, ibid., p. 26.

48 See Lyon (1994), op cit., p. 65.

49 Bogard, op cit., p. 27.

50 The background to this issue is on the one hand, labelling theory, and on the other, Foucaldian notions of biopower (see below). To my mind, neither nominalism nor unqualified realism is theoretically adequate to the question. A good way forward may well lie in what Ian Hacking calls 'dynamic nominalism', which neither sinks into the absurdities of nominalism nor pretends that images and categories play no part in 'making up' people. See Hacking (1986) Making up people, in T.C. Heller, M. Sosna and D.E. Wellerby (eds) *Reconstructing Individualism: Autonomy, Individuality, and the Self in Western Thought*. Stanford, CA: Stanford University Press, p. 228.

51 Bogard, op cit., p. 46.

52 Technological convergence, which produces convergent 'effects', is not innocent, of course. A political economy perspective rightly stresses the ways in which technological convergence is itself the product of a complex of decisions and social circumstances. See D. Winseck (1998) *Reconvergence: The Political Economy of Telecommunications in Canada*. Cresskill, NJ: Hampton Press. See also D. Lyon (1988) *The Information Society: Issues and Illusions*. Cambridge: Polity Press, Ch. 2.

53 See Lyon (1994), op cit., Chapter seven.

54 C. Boyer (1996) *Cybercities: Visual Perception in an Age of Electronic Communication*. New York: Princeton Architectural Press, p. 18.

55 M. Foucault (1978) *The History of Sexuality*, vol. 1. New York: Random House, p. 138.

56 I. Hacking (1982) Biopower and the avalanche of printed numbers, *Humanities in Society*, 5: 279–95.

57 J. Baudrillard (1988) argues that the referent has disappeared in *The Evil Demon of Images*. Sydney: Power Institute Publications (no. 3) p. 21.

58 J. Baudrillard (1983) *In the Shadow of the Silent Majorities . . . or The End of the Social and Other Essays*. New York: Semiotext(e), pp. 103–4.
59 It might be remarked that already we see two features of significance here. Communication and information technologies enable convergence between conventional separate sectors of (private) insurance and (public) policing. And the process of computerization goes hand in hand with an intensification of face-to-face contacts, as community policing and high technology data management converge.
60 Poster, op cit., p. 189.
61 S. Graham and S. Marvin (1996) *Telecommunications and the City: Electronic Spaces, Urban Places*. London: Routledge.
62 S. Graham (1998) Spaces of surveillant simulation: new technologies, digital representations, and material geographies, *Environment and Planning D: Society and Space*, 16: 486.
63 See also A. Mowshowitz (1996) Social control and the network marketplace, in Lyon and Zureik, op cit.
64 Bogard, op cit., pp. 4–5.
65 Genesis, 3: 4.

Chapter 8

1 C. Norris and G. Armstrong (1999) *The Maximum Surveillance Society: The Rise of CCTV*. Oxford: Berg.
2 M. McCahill and C. Norris (1999) Watching the workers: crime, CCTV and the workplace, in P. Davies, P. Francis and J. Jupp (eds) *Invisible Crimes: Their Victims and their Regulation*. London: Macmillan, p. 229.
3 President Clinton offered financial privacy as a means of strengthening the Financial Services Modernization Bill that was passed, notably, with Republican support. See *The Age* (Melbourne), 1 February 2000, Information Technology Supplement, p. 13.
4 See, for example, C. Bennett and R. Grant (eds) (1999) *Visions of Privacy: Policy Choices for the Digital Age*. Toronto: University of Toronto Press, p. 5.
5 Canadian Standards Association (1995) *Model Code for the Protection of Personal Information*. Rexdale: CSA.
6 M.J. Culnan and R.J. Bies (1999) Managing privacy concerns strategically: the implications of fair information practices for marketing in the twenty-first century, in Bennett and Grant, op cit., p. 162.
7 K. Laudon (1996) Markets and privacy, *Communications of the ACM*, 9 (September): 92–104.
8 J. Rule and L. Hunter (1999) Property rights in personal data, in Bennett and Grant, op cit., p. 172.
9 D. Lyon (1994) *The Electronic Eye: The Rise of Surveillance Society*. Cambridge: Polity Press, p. 188.
10 A. Etzioni (1999) *The Limits of Privacy*. New York: Basic Books, p. 213.
11 Etzioni even makes the point that '. . . in free societies, the state does not scan homes preemptively to ensure that no child abuse is taking place' (1999: 211). While this specific example may be correct, in all sectors a central surveillance trend is precisely towards simulation, anticipation and preemption.
12 D. Chaum (1992) Achieving electronic privacy, *Scientific American*, August: 101.
13 See R. Clarke (1992) The resistable rise of the national personal data system, *Software Law Journal*, 5(1): 29–59. The story of the Australia Card is told in David Lyon, op cit.

14 I. Hansen (1981) *Report of the Privacy Commissioner on the Use of the Social Insurance Number.* Ottawa: Canadian Human Rights Commission.
15 Simon Davies (1999) The challenge of Big Brother, in Bennett and Grant, op cit., p. 246.
16 Global Internet Liberty Campaign, http:www.gilc.org/privacy
17 W. Diffie and S. Landau (1999) *Privacy on the Line: The Politics of Wiretapping and Encryption.* Cambridge, MA: MIT Press, p. 7.
18 S. Verma (1999) Police double criminal 'hotspot' targets, *Toronto Star,* 23 July; 21.
19 Davies, op cit., p. 254.
20 See the Canadian organization Adbuster's website, http:www.cmpa.ca/adbust.html
21 A. Melucci (1996) *Challenging Codes: Collective Action in the Information Age.* Cambridge: Cambridge University Press.
22 Ibid., p. 8.
23 Ibid., p. 9.
24 M. de Certeau (1980) *L'Invention du Quotidien.* Paris: UGE.
25 A. Feenberg (1999) *Questioning Technology.* London: Routledge, p. 112.
26 U. Beck (1997) *The Reinvention of Politics: Rethinking Modernity in the Global Social Order.* Cambridge: Polity Press.
27 J. Gilliom (1997) Everyday surveillance, everyday resistance: computer monitoring in the lives of the Appalachian poor, *Studies in Law, Politics and Society,* 16: 275–97.
28 This is a gloss on A. Gramsci (1985) *Selections from the Prison Notebooks,* Q. Hoare and G. Smith (eds). New York: International Publishers, p. 12.
29 The article about a maternity unit in an Edinburgh (Scotland) hospital appeared in *the Independent* (London), 5 July 1994.
30 J. Gilliom (1994) *Surveillance, Privacy and the Law: Employee Drug Testing and the Politics of Social Control.* Ann Arbor MI: University of Michigan Press, p. 13.
31 Ibid., p. 14.
32 Ibid., pp. 82–3.
33 D. Nelkin (1995) Forms of intrusion: comparing resistance to information technology and biotechnology in America, in M. Bauer (ed.) *Resistance to New Technology.* Cambridge and New York: Cambridge University Press.
34 R. James (1996) Data protection and epidemiological research, *The Science of the Total Environment,* 184: 25–32.
35 I. van der Ploeg (1999) Biometrics and privacy: a note on the politics of theorizing technology, presented at the Ethicomp conference, Rome, 6–8 October.
36 Ibid., p. 10.
37 H. Martins (1998) Technology, modernity, politics, in J. Good and I. Velody (eds) *The Politics of Postmodernity.* Cambridge: Cambridge University Press, p. 174.

Chapter 9

1 'Postmodernity' may be used to designate situations where some aspects of modernity have been inflated to such an extent that modernity becomes less recognizable as such. So it can be argued sociologically that postmodernity poses queries regarding novel social formations. It is thus not the same as the debates over intellectual trends, aesthetics and architecture that go under the rubric of postmodernism, and nor it is exactly the same as *anti*-modernism.
2 See D. Lyon (1999) *Postmodernity* 2nd edn. Buckingham: Open University Press. The analysis of postmodernity as an emergent social formation with its own

sociologic derives above all from the work of Z. Bauman (1992) *Intimations of Postmodernity*. London: Routledge.

3 R. Clarke (1988) Information technology and dataveillance, *Communications of the ACM*, 31(5) (May): 498–512.

4 G.T. Marx (1988) *Undercover: Police Surveillance in America*. Berkeley, CA: University of California Press.

5 I do not know much about the Korean situation, and doubt whether the 'Orwellian' epithet would have had much leverage there. But 'Orwellian' fears certainly lie behind opposition to national electronic identifiers in parts of Europe and North America.

6 Leading treatments of this theme, on a comparative basis, may be found in D. Flaherty (1989) *Protecting Privacy in Surveillance Societies*. Chapel Hill, NC: University of North Carolina Press; and C. Bennett (1992) *Regulating Privacy*. Ithaca, MI: Cornell University Press.

7 This is discussed with respect to policing in R. Ericson and K. Haggerty (1997) *Policing the Risk Society*. Toronto: University of Toronto Press.

8 Ulrich Beck has in mind the way that the modern industrial production of 'goods' seems to carry with it a less obvious production of 'bads' in unforeseen side effects and in environmental despoilation. But his description of how the risk society arises in '. . . autonomised modernization processes which are blind and deaf to their own effects and threats' certainly resonates with the expansion of computerized surveillance since the 1960s. See U. Beck, A. Giddens and S. Lash (1994) *Reflexive Modernization: Politics, Tradition and Aesthetics in the Modern Social Order*. Cambridge: Polity Press, p. 6.

9 S. Ellis (1999) Beware what you leave on the net . . . someone's watching, *The Australian*, 14 October, p. 30.

10 See C. Calhoun (1994) The infrastructure of modernity: indirect social relationships, information technology, and social integration, in H. Haferkamp and N. Smelser (eds) *Social Change and Modernity*. Berkeley, CA: University of California Press. This is also discussed in D. Lyon (1997) Cyberspace sociality: controversies over computer-mediated communication, in B. Loader (ed.) *The Governance of Cyberspace*. London: Routledge.

11 The tension between citizen and consumer identities is also one that is evident in earlier modernities, as Graham Murdock argues in his (1993) Communications and the constitution of modernity, *Media, Culture, and Society*, 15: 537. But there are reasons for arguing that by the end of the twentieth century consumer identities were ascendant in the technologically advanced societies.

12 P. James (1996) *Nation Formation: Towards a Theory of Abstract Community*. London: Sage, Ch. 1.

13 Modernity involved mainly institutionally-extended agency, rather than the increasingly abstract mode of social integration enabled by information technologies today. Hence postmodernity as a modest descriptor for novel circumstances. It retains a certain ambivalence and lack of fixity appropriate to the circumstances, while still depending on modernity for its cogency.

14 This is an oblique reference to a piece by K. Robins (1995) Cyberspace and the world we live in, *Body and Society*, 1(3–4): 135–55.

15 See D. Lyon (1997) Bringing technology back in: CITs in social theories of postmodernity, in M. Berra (ed.) *Ripensare la Tecnologia: Informatica, Informatzione e Sviluppo Regionale*. Torinto: Bollati Boringheieri.

16 William Gibson says that cyberspace is the condition of being 'wrapped in media' which I take to be a very insightful and instructive definition. See his (1984) *Neuromancer*. New York: Ace Books.

17 I refer indirectly to M. Castell's (1996) title *The Rise of the Network Society*. New York: Blackwell. He discusses surveillance networks in Volume 2 of *The Information Age* trilogy, *The Power of Identity* (New York: Blackwell, 1997).

18 See the work, *inter alia*, of Roger Clarke (1994) The digital persona and its application to data surveillance, *The Information Society*, 10: 2, or Kenneth Landon (1986) *The Dossier Society*. New York: Columbia University Press.

19 See S. Cohen (1985) *Visions of Social Control*. Oxford: Blackwell.

20 It seems mistaken to suggest as some do that today's surveillance is more inclusive than exclusive of deviants. See, for example, W. Staples (1997) *The Culture of Surveillance*. Cambridge: Cambridge University Press.

21 This is discussed in David Lyon (1994) *The Electronic Eye: The Rise of Surveillance Society*. Cambridge: Polity Press.

22 W. Bogard (1996) *The Simulation of Surveillance*. Cambridge: Cambridge University Press, p. 68.

23 R. Boyne and A. Rattansi (eds) (1990) *Postmodernism and Society*. London: Macmillan, p. 8.

24 Ericson and Haggerty, op cit., *passim*.

25 On this, and the critique of essentialist views of technology, see A. Feenberg (1999) *Questioning Technology*. London: Routledge. See also M. Shallis (1984) *The Silicon Idol: The Micro Revolution and its Social Implications*. Oxford: Oxford University Press.

26 Z. Bauman (1993) *Postmodern Ethics*. Oxford: Blackwell.

27 This is discussed in A. Giddens (1998) Risk society: the context of British politics, in J. Franklin (ed.) *The Politics of the Risk Society*. Cambridge: Polity Press.

28 See, for example, Bennett, op cit.; C. Bennett and R. Grant (eds) (1999) *Visions of Privacy in the Twenty-First Century*. Toronto: University of Toronto Press; and P. Agre and M. Rotenberg (eds) (1998) *Technology and Privacy: Changing Landscapes*. Cambridge, MA: MIT Press.

29 One noble exception to this is Priscilla Regan's work. See her (1996) Genetic testing and workplace surveillance: implications for privacy, in D. Lyon and E. Zureik (eds) *Computers, Surveillance, and Privacy*. Minneapolis, MN: University of Minnesota Press. See also her (1995) *Legislating Privacy Technology, Social Values, and Public Policy*. Chapel Hill, NC: University of North Carolina Press.

30 Sociologists will recognize the shadow of C. Wright Mills falling across my text at this point. He discussed how personal troubles become social issues. And he argued that the biography should be the nexus of history and biography. See (1962) *The Sociological Imagination*. Harmondsworth: Penguin.

31 J. Wajcman (1994) *Feminism confronts Technology*. Cambridge: Polity Press.

32 See the critique of Baudrillard, in G.C. Bowker and S. Leigh Star (1999) *Sorting Things Out: Classification and its Consequences*. Cambridge, MA: MIT Press.

33 See Z. Bauman (1992), op cit.

34 Theologically, the notion of persons-as-social originates in the doctrine of Trinity. Humans as the *imago dei* – the image of God – reflect the inherently social character of their source. See C. Gunton (1996) *The One, the Three and the Many*. Cambridge: Cambridge University Press.

35 On this, Jacques Derrida's analysis of Emmmanuel Lévinas' work is insightful. See (1999) *Adieu to Emmanuel Lévinas*. Stanford, CA: Stanford University Press, p. 68.

36 I assume for the sake of the argument that Foucault was right about this.

37 See I. Barns (1999) Technology and Citizenship, in A. Petersen, I. Barns, J. Dudley and P. Harris (eds) *Poststructuralism, Citizenship and Social Policy*. London: Routledge.

Bibliography

Abercrombie, N., Hill, S. and Turner, B. (1986) *Sovereign Individuals of Capitalism.* London: Allen & Unwin.

Agre, P. and Rotenburg, M. (eds) (1997) *Technology and Privacy: The New Landscape.* Cambridge, MA: MIT Press.

Ariès, P. and Duby, G. (1990) *A History of Private Life.* Cambridge, MA: Harvard University Press.

Aurigi, A. and Graham, S. (1998) The 'crisis' in the urban political realm, in B. Loader (ed.) *Cyberspace Divide.* London: Routledge.

Baudrillard, J. (1983) *Simulations.* New York: Semiotext(e).

Baudrillard, J. (1983) *In the Shadow of the Silent Majorities . . . or The End of the Social and Other Essays.* New York: Semiotext(e).

Baudrillard, J. (1988) *The Evil Demon of Images.* Sydney: Power Institute Publications.

Bauman, Z. (1992) *Intimations of Postmodernity.* London: Routledge.

Bauman, Z. (1993) *Postmodern Ethics.* Oxford and Cambridge, MA: Blackwell.

Beck, U. (1992) *Risk Society: Towards a New Modernity.* London: Sage.

Beck, U. (1997) *The Reinvention of Politics: Rethinking Modernity in the Global Social Order.* Cambridge: Polity Press.

Beck, U., Giddens, A. and Lash, S. (eds) (1994) *Reflexive Modernization: Politics, Tradition and Aesthetics in the Modern Social Order.* Cambridge: Polity Press.

Bennett, C. (1992) *Regulating Privacy: Data Protection and Public Policy in Europe and the United States.* Ithaca, MI: Cornell University Press.

Bennet, C. and Grant, R. (eds) (1999) *Visions of Privacy: Policy Choices for the Digital Age.* Toronto: University of Toronto Press.

Bigo, D. (1996) L'archipel des polices, *Le Monde Diplomatique,* 9 October.

Bigo, D. (1996) *Polices en Réseaux.* Paris: Presses de Sciences Po.

Bleecker, J. (1994) Urban crisis: past, present, and virtual, *Socialist Review,* 24(1&2): 189–221.

Bogard, W. (1996) *The Simulation of Surveillance.* Cambridge: Cambridge University Press.

Bowker, G.C. and Star, S.L. (1999) *Sorting Things Out: Classification and its Consequences.* Cambridge, MA: MIT Press.

Boyer, C. (1996) *Cybercities: Visual Perception in an Age of Electronic Communication*. New York: Princeton Architectural Press.

Boyes-Watson, C. (1997) Corporations as drug warriors: the symbolic significance of employee drug testing, *Studies in Law, Politics, and Society*, 17: 185–223.

Boyne, R. and Rattansi, A. (eds) (1990) *Postmodernism and Society*. London: Macmillan.

Braverman, H. (1980) *Labour and Monopoly Capital*. New York: Monthly Review Press.

Brown, S. (1998) What's the matter, girls? CCTV and the gendering of public safety, in C. Norris, J. Moran and G. Armstrong (eds) *Surveillance, Closed Circuit Television and Social Control*. Aldershot: Ashgate.

Bryman, A. (1999) The Disneyization of society, *The Sociological Review*, 47(1): 25–47.

Burnham, D. (1983) *The Rise of the Computer State*. New York: Vintage Books.

Burrows, R. (1997) Virtual culture, urban social polarization, and social science fiction, in B. Loader (ed.) *The Governance of Cyberspace*. London: Routledge.

Calhoun, C. (1994) The infrastructure of modernity: indirect relationships, information technology and social integration, in H. Haferkamp and N. Smelser (eds) *Social Change and Modernity*. Berkeley, CA: University of California Press.

Callon, M. (1991) Techno-economic networks and irreversibility, in J. Law (ed.) *A Sociology of Monsters: Essays on Power, Technology, and Domination*. London: Routledge.

Campbell, D. (1994) Foreign investment, labour immobility and the quality of employment, *International Labour Review*, 2: 185–203.

Campbell, D. and Connor, S. (1986) *On the Record: Surveillance, Computers, and Privacy: The Inside Story*. London: Michael Joseph.

Caplan, J. and Torpey, J. (forthcoming) *Documenting Individual Identity: The Development of State Practices Since the French Revolution*. Eiring, NJ: Princeton University Press.

Carey, J. and Quirk, J. (1970) The mythos of the electronic revolution, *The American Scholar*, 39(2): 219–41 and 39(3): 395–424.

Castells, M. (1989) *The Informational City: Information Technology, Economic Restructuring, and the Urban-Regional Process*. Oxford: Blackwell.

Castells, M. (1996) *The Rise of the Network Society*. Oxford: Blackwell.

Castells, M. (1997) *The Power of Identity*. Oxford: Blackwell.

Castells, M. (1998) *The End Of Millennium*. Oxford: Blackwell.

Certeau, M. de (1980) *L'Invention du Quotidien*. Paris: UGE.

Chaney, D. (1995) *Lifestyles*. London: Routledge.

Chaum, D. (1992) Achieving Electronic Privacy, *Scientific American*, August: 101.

Clarke, R. (1988) Information technology and dataveillance, *Communications of the ACM*, 31(5): 498–512.

Clarke, R. (1992) The resistable rise of the national personal data system, *Software Law Journal*, 5(1): 25–59.

Cohen, S. (1985) *Visions of Social Control*. London: Blackwell.

Coninck, F. de (1994) *Travail Integré, Société Eclaté*. Paris: Presses Universitaires de France.

Crang, M. (1996) Watching the city: video, resistance and surveillance, *Environment and Planning A*, 28: 2102–3.

Crawford, R. (1996) Computer assisted crises, in G. Gerbner, H. Mowlana and H. Schiller (eds) *Invisible Crises*. Boulder, CO: Westview Press.

Curry, M.R. (1997) The digital individual and the private realm, *Annals of the Association of American Geographers*, 87(4): 681.

Dandeker, C. (1990) *Surveillance, Power and Modernity*. Cambridge: Cambridge University Press.

Davis, A. (1997) The body as a password, *Wired*, 5(7): 132–40.

Davis, M. (1992) *City of Quartz: Excavating the Future in Los Angeles*. New York: Vintage Books.

de Tocqueville, A. (1945) *Democracy in America* (trans. Henry Reeves). New York: Alfred A Knopf.

Deleuze, G. (1992) Postscript on the societies of control, *October*, 59: 3–7.

Derrida, J. (1999) *Adieu to Emmanuel Lévinas*. Stanford, CA: Stanford University Press.

Diffie, W. and Landau, S. (1999) *Privacy on the Line: The Politics of Wiretapping and Encryption*. Cambridge, MA: MIT Press.

Ditton, J., Short, E., Philips, S., Norris, C. and Armstrong, G. (1999) *The Effect of Closed Circuit Television on Recorded Crime Rates and Public Concern about Crime in Glasgow*. Edinburgh: Stationery Office.

Elger, A. and Smith, C. (eds) (1994) *Global Japanization? The Transnational Transformation of the Labour Process*. London: Routledge.

Ellin, N. (ed.) (1997) *Architecture of Fear*. New York: Princeton Architectural Press.

Ellul, J. (1980) *The Technological System*. New York: Continuum.

Ericson, R. and Haggerty, K. (1997) *Policing the Risk Society*. Toronto: University of Toronto Press.

Etzioni, A. (1999) *The Limits of Privacy*. New York: Basic Books.

Feenberg, A. (1991) *Critical Theory of Technology*. New York: Oxford University Press.

Feenberg, A. (1999) *Questioning Technology*. London: Routledge.

Fijnaut, C. and Marx, G.T. (eds) (1995) *Undercover: Police Surveillance in Comparative Perspective*. The Hague: Kluwer.

Fiorenza, E.S. (1998) *The Book of Revelation: Justice and Judgement*. Minneapolis, MN: Fortress.

Flaherty, D.H. (1989) *Protecting Privacy in Surveillance Societies*. Chapel Hill, NC: University of North Carolina Press.

Foucault, M. (1978) *The History of Sexuality*, vol 1. New York: Random House.

Foucault, M. (1991) in G. Burchell, C. Gordon and P. Miller (1991) *The Foucault Effect: Studies in Governmentality*. London: Harvester Wheatsheaf.

Francis, A. (1984) *New Technology at Work*. New York: Oxford University Press.

Friedman, T. (1995) Making sense of software: computer games and interactive textuality, in S.G. Jones (ed.) *Cybersociety*. Thousand Oaks CA: Sage.

Furr, A. (1999) Social status and attitudes towards organizational control of genetic data, *Sociological Focus*, 32(4): 371–82.

Fyfe, N.R. and Bannister, J. (1996) City watching: closed circuit television surveillance in public places, *Area*, 28(1): 37.

Gandy, O. (1993) *The Panoptic Sort: A Political Economy of Personal Information*. Boulder, CO: Westview Press.

Gerlenter, D. (1991) *Mirror Worlds, or The Day Software puts the Universe in a Shoebox*. Oxford: Oxford University Press.

Gibson, W. (1984) *Neuromancer*. New York: Ace Books.

Gibson, W. (1995) Disneyland with the death penalty, *Wired*, 1(4).

Giddens, A. (1985) *The Nation State and Violence*. Cambridge: Polity Press.

Giddens, A. (1990) *The Consequences of Modernity*. Cambridge: Polity Press.

Giddens, A. (1992) *Modernity and Self-Identity*. Cambridge: Polity Press.

Giddens, A. (1998) Risk society: the context of British politics, in J. Franklin (ed.) *The Politics of the Risk Society*. Cambridge: Polity Press.

Giddens, A. (1999) *Runaway World*. London: Profile.

Gill, C. (1985) *Work, Employment and the New Technology*. Cambridge: Polity Press.

Gilliom, J. (1994) *Surveillance, Privacy and the Law: Employee Drug Testing and the Politics of Social Control*. Ann Arbor, MI: University of Michigan Press.

Gilliom, J. (1994) Everyday surveillance, everyday resistance: computer monitoring in the lives of Appalachian poor, *Studies in Law, Politics and Society*, 19.

Goffman, E. (1956) *The Presentation of Self in Everyday Life*. Garden City, NY: Doubleday.

Graham, S. (1997) Urban planning in the information society, *Town and Country Planning*, November: 298.

Graham, S. (1998) Spaces of surveillant simulation: new technologies, digital representations, and material geographies, *Environment and Planning: Society and Space*, 16: 494.

Graham, S. (1998) Towards the fifth utility? On the extension and normalization of public CCTV, in C. Norris, J. Moran and G. Armstrong (eds) *Surveillance, Closed Circuit Television and Social Control*. Aldershot: Ashgate.

Graham, S. (1998) The end of geography or the explosion of place? Conceptualizing space, place, and information technology, *Progress in Human Geography*, 22(2): 165–85.

Graham, S. and Marvin, S. (1996) *Telecommunication and the City: Electronic Spaces, Urban Places*. London: Routledge.

Graham-Rowe, D. (1999) Warning! Strange behaviour, *New Scientist*, 11 December: 25–8.

Grob, N. (1997) Life sneaks out of stories: *Until the End of the World*, in R.F. Cook and G. Gemünden (eds) *The Cinema of Wim Wenders: Image, Narrative, and the Postmodern Condition*. Detroit MI: Wayne State University Press.

Gunton, C. (1996) *The One, the Three and the Many*. Cambridge: Cambridge University Press.

Hacking, I. (1986) Making up people, in T.C. Heller, M. Sosna and D.E. Wellerby (eds) *Reconstructing Individualism: Autonomy, Individuality, and the Self in Western Thought*. Stanford, CA: Stanford University Press.

Hacking, I. (1982) Biopower and the avalanche of printed numbers, *Humanities in Society*, 5: 279–95.

Hager, N. (1996) *Secret Power: New Zealand's Role in the International Spy Network*. Nelson, NZ: Craig Potton Publishing.

Haraway, D. (1997) *Modest_Witness@Second_Millenium.FemaleMan_Meets_Oncomouse: Feminism and Technoscience*. London: Routledge.

Hart, G.W. (1989) Residential energy monitoring and computerized surveillance via utility power flows, *IEEE Technology and Society Magazine*, June: 12–16.

Hayles, N.K. (1999) *How We Become Posthuman: Virtual Bodies in Cybernetics, Literature and Informatics*. Chicago: University of Chicago Press.

Innis, H.A. (1962) *The Bias of Communication*. Toronto: University of Toronto Press.

Ito, Y. (1993) How Japan modernised earlier and faster than other non-Western countries, *Journal of Development Communication*, 4(2): 60–78.

Jacobs, J. (1961) *The Death and Life of the Great American Cities*. New York: Random House.

James, P. (1996) *Nation Formation: Towards a Theory of Abstract Community*. London: Sage.

Jürgens, U., Malsch, T. and Dohse, K. (1993) *Breaking from Taylorism: Changing Forms of Work in the Automobile Industry*. Cambridge: Cambridge University Press.

Kumar, K. (1995) *From Post-Industrial to Post-Modern Society: New theories of the Contemporary World*. Cambridge, MA: Blackwell.

Laudon, K. (1996) Markets and privacy, *Communications of the ACM*, 9 (September): 92–104.

Ley, D. (1996) *The New Middle Class and the Remaking of the Central City*. Oxford: Oxford University Press.

Lyon, D. (1986) *The Silicon Society*. Oxford: Lion.

Lyon, D. (1988) *The Information Society: Issues and Illusions*. Cambridge: Polity Press.

Lyon, D. (1991) Bentham's panopticon: from moral architecture to electronic surveillance, *Queen's Quarterly*, 98(3): 596–617.

Lyon, D. (1994) *The Electronic Eye: The Rise of Surveillance Society*. Cambridge: Polity Press.

Lyon, D. (1997) Cyberspace sociality: controversies over computer mediated communication, in B. Loader (ed.) *The Governance of Cyberspace*. London: Routledge.

Lyon, D. (1998) The World-Wide-Web of surveillance: the Internet and off-world power flows, *Information, Communication, and Society*, 1(1): 91–105.

Lyon, D. (1999) *Postmodernity*, 2nd edn. Buckingham: Open University Press.

Mackay, H. and T. O'Sullivan (eds) (1999) *The Media Reader*. London: Sage.

Macpherson, C.B. (1962) *The Political Theory of Possessive Individualism: Hobbes to Locke*. Oxford: Oxford University Press.

Martins, H. (1999) Technology, modernity, politics, in J. Good and I. Velody (eds) *The Politics of Postmodernity*. Cambridge: Cambridge University Press.

Marx, G.T. (1985) The surveillance society: the threat of 1984-style techniques, *The Futurist*, June: 21–6.

Marx, G.T. (1988) *Undercover: Police Surveillance in America*. Berkeley, CA: University of California Press.

Marx, G.T. (1998) Social control across borders, in W. McDonald (ed.) *Crime and Law Enforcement in the Global Village*. Cincinnati, OH: Anderson.

Mathieson, T. (1997) The viewer society: Foucault's 'Panopticon' revisited, *Theoretical Criminology*, 1: 215–34.

May, T. and Williams, M. (eds) (1998) *Knowing the Social World*. Buckingham: Open University Press.

Mellor, P. and Shilling, C. (1997) *Reforming the Body: Religion, Community, and Modernity*. London: Sage.

Melucci, A. (1996) *Challenging Codes: Collective Action in the Information Age*. Cambridge: Cambridge University Press.

Mills, C. Wright (1962) *The Sociological Imagination*. Harmondsworth: Penguin.

Mineham, M. (1998) The growing debate over genetic testing, *HRM Magazine*, April: 208.

Murdock, G. (1883) Communications and the constitution of modernity, *Media, Culture and Society*, 15: 537.

Nelkin, D. (1995) Forms of intrusion: comparing resistance to information technology and biotechnology in America, in M. Bauer (ed.) *Resistance to New Technology*. Cambridge: Cambridge University Press.

Nock, S. (1993) *The Cost of Privacy: Surveillance and Reputation in America*. New York: Aldine de Gruyter.

Nonoka, I. and Takeuchi, H. (1995) *The Knowledge-Creating Company: How Japanese Companies Create the Dynamics of Innovation*. New York: Oxford University Press.

Nora, S. and Minc, A. (1980) *The Computerization of Society*. Cambridge, MA: MIT Press.

Norris, C. and Armstrong, G. (1999) *The Maximum Surveillance Society: The Rise of CCTV*. Oxford: Berg.

Norris, C. and McCahill, M. (1999) Watching the workers: crime, CCTV and the workplace, in P. Davies, P. Francis and V. Jupp (eds) *Invisible Crimes: Their Victims and Their Regulation*. London: Macmillan.

Norris, C. *et al.* (1996) Algorithmic surveillance: the future of automated visual surveillance, in C. Norris, J. Moran and G. Armstrong (eds) *Surveillance, Closed Circuit Television and Social Control*. Aldershot: Ashgate.

Oliver, N. and Wilkinson, B. (1992) *The Japanization of British Industry*. Oxford: Blackwell.

Pickles, J. (1995) Representations in an electronic age: geography, GIS, and democracy, in J. Pickles (ed.) *Ground Truth*. New York: Guilford Press.

Plant, S. (1995) The future looms: weaving women and cybernetics, in M. Featherstone and R. Burrows (eds) *Cyberspace/Cyberbodies/Cyberpunk: Culture of Technological Embodiment*. London: Sage.

Poster, M. (1997) *The Second Media Age*. Cambridge: Polity Press.

Raab, C.D. (1994) Police cooperation: the prospect for privacy, in M. Anderson and M. Den Boer (eds) *Policing Across National Boundaries*. London: Pinter.

Raab, C.D. and Bennett, C.J. (1998) The distribution of privacy risks: who needs protection? *The Information Society*, 14: 263–74.

Regan, P. (1995) *Legislating Privacy: Technology, Social Values, and Public Policy*. Chapel Hill, NC: University of North Carolina Press.

Regan, P. (1996) Genetic testing and workplace surveillance: implications for privacy, in D. Lyon and E. Zureik (eds) *Computers, Surveillance, and Privacy*. Minneapolis, MN: University of Minnesota Press.

Ricoeur, P. (1992) *Oneself as Another*. Chicago: University of Chicago Press.

Robins, K. (1995) Cyberspace and the world we live in, *Body and Society*, 1(3–4): 135–55.

Rule, J. (1973) *Private Lives, Public Surveillance*. Harmondsworth: Allen Lane.

Rule, J. and Brantley, P. (cited as unpublished in Lyon 1994) *'Surveillance in the workplace: a new meaning to personal computing'*.

Rule, J., McAdam, D., Stearns, L. and Uglow, D. (1983) Documentary identification and mass surveillance in the United States, *Social Problems*, 32(1): 222–34.

Russell, B. (1912) *Problems of Philosophy*. Oxford: Oxford University Press.

Samarajiva, R. (1994) Privacy in electronic public space: emerging issues, *Canadian Journal of Communication*, 19(1): 87–99.

Sampson, P. (1994) From dust to plastic, *Third Way*, January: 17–22.

Seabrook, J. (1993) The root of all evil, *New Statesman and Society*, 26 February: 12.

Sennett, R. (1970) *The Uses of Disorder: Personal Identity and City Life*. New York: Knopf.

Sennett, R. (1996) *Flesh and Stone*. London: Faber & Faber.

Sewell, G. and Wilkinson, B. (1992) Someone to watch over me: surveillance, discipline, and the just-in-time labour process, *Sociology*, 26(2): 271–89.

Shallis, M. (1984) *The Silicon Idol: The Micro Revolution and its Social Implications*. Oxford: Oxford University Press.

Shearing, C. and Stenning, P. (1985) From the Panopticon to Disneyworld: the development of discipline, in E. Doob and E.L. Greenspan (eds) *Perspectives in Criminal Law*. Aurora: Canada Law Books.

Shils, E. (1975) Privacy and power, in *Centre and Periphery: Essays in Macrosociology*. Chicago: University of Chicago Press.

Simmel, G. (1950) The metropolis and mental Life, in K.H. Wolff (ed.) *The Sociology of Georg Simmel*. Glencoe, NY: Free Press.

Simmel, G. (1971) Freedom and the Individual, in D. Levine (ed.) *On Individual and Social Forms*. Chicago: University of Chicago Press.

Sklair, L. (1995) *Sociology of the Global System*. London: Harvester Wheatsheaf.

Smith, S.L. (1998) Gene testing and work: not a good fit, *Occupational Hazards*, 60(7): 38.

Stagliano, R. (1996) Publicité du troisième type, in *L'Internet: l'Ecstase et l'Effroi*. Paris: Le Monde Diplomatique.

Staples, W. (1997) *The Culture of Surveillance*. Cambridge: Cambridge University Press.

Strange, S. (1996) *The Retreat of the State: The Diffusion of Power in the World Economy*. Cambridge: Cambridge University Press.

Sweet, J. (1979) *Revelation*. London: SCM.

Tapscott, D. and Cavoukian, A. (1995) *Who Knows?: Safeguarding Your Privacy in a Networked World*. Toronto: Random House.

Thrift, N. (1996) *Spatial Formations*. London: Sage.

Thrift, N. (1996) New urban eras and old technological fears: reconfiguring the goodwill of electronic things, *Urban Studies*, 33: 1471.

Turnbull, P. (1987) The 'Japanization' of production and industrial relations at Lucas Electrical, *Industrial Relations Journal*, 17(3): 193–206.

van der Ploeg, I. (1999) Written on the body: biometrics and identity, *Computers and Society*, 29(1): 37–44.

van der Ploeg, I. (1999) The illegal body: 'Eurodac' and the politics of biometric identification, *Ethics and Information Technology*, 1(4): 295–302.

Virilio, P. (1986) *Speed and Politics*. New York: Semiotext(e).

Virilio, P. (1991) *The Lost Dimension*. New York: Semiotext(e).

Virilio, P. (1994) *The Vision Machine*. London: The British Film Institute.

Wagner, D. (1987) The new temperance movement and social control at the workplace, *Contemporary Drug Problems*, Winter: 540–1.

Wajcman, J. (1994) *Feminism Confronts Technology*. Cambridge: Polity Press.

Wallace, I. (1998) A Christian reading of the global economy, in A. Henk and S. Griffioen (eds) *Geography and Worldview: A Christian Reconnaissance*. Lanham MD: University of America Press.

Webster, F. and Robins, K. (1986) *Information Technology: A Luddite Analysis*. Norwood, NJ: Ablex.

Weiner, M. (1997) Ethics, national sovereignty and the control of immigration, *International Migration Review*, 30(1): 177.

Whitaker, R. (1999) *The End of Privacy*. New York: The New Press.

Wilcock, M. (1975) *I Saw Heaven Opened*. Leicester: Inter-Varsity Press.

Winner, L. (1977) *Autonomous Technology: Technics out of Control as a Theme in Human Thought*. Cambridge, MA: MIT Press.

Winseck, D. (1998) *Reconvergence: The Political Economy of Telecommunications in Canada*. Cresskill, NJ: Hampton Press.

Womack, J.P., Roos, D. and Jones, D.T. (1990) *The Machine that Changed the World*. New York: Rawson Macmillan.

Zukin, S. (1991) *Landscapes of Power: From Detroit to Disney World*. Berkeley, CA: University of California Press.

Zukin, S. (1995) *The Culture of Cities*. Oxford: Blackwell.

Index

Abercrombie, Nicholas, 73
active badges, 41
Adbusters, 81, 133
Africa, 93, 96
Agre, Phillip, 22, 37
Airbus Industrie, 96
airlines, 91
Air Miles, 2, 6
airport, 6, 62, 79, 142
American Express, 129
American Management Association, 41
Amnesty International, 88
anthropometry, criminal, 70
Aristotle, 52
Armstrong, Gary, 25
Asian-Pacific Economic Conference, 96
Aum Shinrikyo, 33
Australia, 8, 33, 45, 95, 143
Australia Card, 33, 131–2, 143
Austria, 132
automated bank machines, 81
automated toll road, 64, 142
Automatic Number-Plate Recognition System, 39
Axicom, 45

Bangalore, 54
banks
   machines, 72, 86, 142
   and privacy, 129
barcodes, 27, 52, 54, 75, 126, 142, 146

Baudrillard, Jean, 55, 108, 116, 120, 123, 152
Bauman, Zygmunt, 10, 59
Beck, Ulrich, 46, 83, 121, 128, 135
Bennett, Colin, 32, 74, 91
Bentham, Jeremy, 86, 109, 114, 115, 125, 153
Bies, Robert, 44
Big Brother, 110, 139, 143
   award, 126, 133
Bigo, Didier, 100, 101
biometrics, 4, 8, 9, 10, 21, 28, 29, 39, 52, 58, 69–70, 72, 75, 77, 80, 83, 85, 99, 104, 126, 139, 144–5
   encryption as privacy protection, 83
BioMouse, 72
biopower, 119, 121, 148
biotechnologies, 76, 137–8
birth certificates, 73
Blade Runner, 52
blind signature, 131
body, 8, 10, 15–19, 26, 27, 50, 63, 71, 72, 74, 79, 82–3, 85–9, 120, 134, 138
   data, 81, 145
   disappearance of, 15, 17, 27, 38, 40, 47, 49–50, 70, 107, 115, 124, 149, 153
   language, 15
   material
   modification, 84
   nomadic, 35

passwords, 77
source and site of surveillance, 70–1, 81
text, 75, 77, 82
Bogard, William, 116–18, 119–20, 122, 123, 124
border
  control, 99
  policing, 90
  security, 101
boundaries, blurring of, 61
Boyer, Christine, 119
Brantley, Peter, 25
Braverman, Harry, 112
Brazil, 94
British Airways, 19
bureaucracy, 109, 110, 118, 125, 136
Burnham, David, 33, 111
Burrows, Roger, 67

call centres, 41, 44
cameras, closed circuit television and video, 3, 5, 8–9, 21, 28, 33, 38, 42, 44, 51–4, 56, 57–62, 65, 78, 113, 126–7, 133, 135, 144, 147
Campbell, Duncan, 96
Canada, 2, 8, 32–4, 37, 44, 59, 63–4, 73, 75, 77–9, 81, 83, 95, 99, 132–3, 144
Canadian Airlines, 91
Canadian Privacy Network, 132
capitalism, 20, 41, 77, 91, 118, 125
  consumer, 112
  corporations, 80, 112
  entrepreneurialism, 6
  restructuring of, 103
  social classes, 92
  societies, 74
  transnational, 104
care, 130, 141, 152, 153
  and surveillance 3
Carey, James, 24
Caribbean, 99
Castells, Manuel, 57, 90, 91
categorical seduction and suspicion, 25, 128
categories, social, 65, 125
Catlett, Jason, 103
Cavoukian, Ann, 83
cellular mobile radio phones, 96, 142, 146
central aliens register, 100
Certeau, Michel de, 135

Chaum, David, 131
Chicago Tribute Company, 102
China, 32, 72, 95, 98
chip implants, 85
Christian Aid, 88
Christie, Linford, 85
CIA (Central Intelligence Agency), 81
Citicorp, 78
city, 24–5, 52–3, 67
  global, 57
  hyperreal, 59
  informational, 53
City of Quartz, 53
Clarke, Roger, 84, 143
classification, social, 86
Clickstream, 102, 103
Client Registry Information System-Enhanced (CRIS-E) (Ohio), 136
Clipper Chip, 96, 133, 135
Clinton, Bill, 128
closed circuit television, *see* cameras, closed circuit television and video
Coca-Cola, 81, 89
codes, 26, 75, 111, 116–17, 119, 122, 128–9, 133–4, 136–7, 148, 151
CODIS (Combined DNA Index System), 79
Cohen, Stanley, 53
collaborative filtering, 102–3
Colombia, 98
colonialism, 93
Comint, *see* Communications Intelligence
communication
  embodied, 23
  indirect, 19
  and information technologies (CIT) 1, 2, 15–17, 23, 27, 28, 32, 38, 71, 98, 107–8, 116, 139, 199
Communications Intelligence (Comint), 94–7
Communism, 31
Compuserve, 102
computerization, 39, 71–3, 108, 112–13, 128, 142, 143
consumer, 55, 93
  behaviour, 18
  capitalism, 112, 142, 149
  culture, 92
  freedom, 2
  information, 102
  management, 43
  surveillance, 43, 44, 103, 127

consumerism, 92–3, 142
contact management, 42
control, 4, 6, 17, 20, 26, 31, 35, 46, 49,
    60, 73, 79, 82, 85, 112, 115–16,
    118, 127, 134, 145–6, 148, 152–3
  centralized, 113
  by codes, 148, 151
  commercial, 46
  global power, 92
  hypersurveillant, 116
  social, 32, 53, 76, 80, 82, 108, 113,
    138, 149
  state, 132
  totalitarian, 38
Conversation, The, 126
cookies, 43, 56, 66, 102, 146
  definition of, 43, 102
co-presence, 16, 20, 145
Corda, Petra, 86
Crawford, Rick, 37
credit cards, 43, 65, 69–70, 73, 80, 82, 86
credit ratings, 147
crime networks, 97–8
Criminal Records Bureau, 41
Cromatica, 60
cross system enforcement, 37, 74, 143
cryptography, 96
Culnan, Mary, 44
Curry, Michael, 91
customized advertising, 102
cyberspace, 22, 24, 49, 54, 66, 82, 96,
    97, 101
cybersurveillance, 145
cyborgs, 52, 85, 87

Dandeker, Christopher, 110
data
  collection 32, 38, 43–4, 64
  discrimination, 76, 91
  flows, 10, 19, 24, 37, 44, 47, 49, 54,
    82, 88, 124, 127, 143, 146
  images, 26, 86–7, 143, 152
  interception, 33
  matching, 25, 143
  merging, 26
  mining techniques, 41, 102
  population, 10
  processing, 45
  protection, 120–1, 131–3, 135–6, 144
  security, 24
  subjects, 44, 129–31
Data Protection Act (UK), 121
Data Protection Registry, 129

databases, 92, 119
  marketing, 29, 101, 111
dataveillance, 74, 143–5
Davies, Simon, 132, 133
Davis, Mike, 53, 59, 75
Deleuze, Gilles, 19, 35, 119, 134
Denmark, 101
deregulation, 37, 39, 44–7, 77, 144
determinism, 23–4, 112
dictionary, 96
digital
  classification, 147
  consumer image, 123, 148
  mapping, 67
  personae, 35
direct checking, 73, 74
  targeting, 92
Direct Marketing Association, 129
disciplinary society, 35
Disneyization, 55, 59, 93
Disneyland, 56, 65
disorganized surveillance, 35
Ditton, Jason, 52
DNA, 70–1, 80, 82–4, 86, 120, 126,
    130
  codes, 2
  data, 69
  records, 30
  samples, 79
  traces, 9, 50
Doubleclick, 145
drivers licences, 73, 78, 82
dromology, 117
drug
  testing, 85, 126
  trafficking, 95, 97–8, 104
Duby, Georges, 20

ECHELON, 3, 96–7
ecology of fear, 89
Edwards, Paul, 29
EFTPOS (Electronic Funds Transfer at
    Point of Sale), 146
electrical power monitoring, 88
electricity (power), 17, 28
electronic
  commerce (e-commerce), 24, 43, 58,
    66, 80, 111, 127–8, 130, 145
  environments, 21–3
  identification card, 143
  signature, 81
  space, 17
  tagging, 147

Electronic Privacy Information Centre (EPIC), 133
elegibility, 149
Ellin, Nan, 58
Ellul, Jacques, 111, 113, 124
El Paso Intelligence Center (USA), 100
email, 3, 5, 8, 15–16, 33, 33, 40–2, 64, 71, 88, 97, 101
  monitoring of, 42, 127
emotional labour, 55
encryption, 4, 26, 85, 130, 133, 139
End of Violence, 28
Enemy of the State, 126
Ericson, Richard, 6, 83, 120–1
Espenshade, Thomas, 100
ethnic categories, 98
Etzioni, Amitai, 130
Eurodac, 98
Europe, 18, 20, 22, 65, 90, 93–4, 97–9, 122, 128, 144
European Intelligence System, 98
Europol, 98–100
exclusion, 34, 46, 67, 76, 83, 84, 86, 90, 92, 98, 122–3, 125, 128, 142, 144, 149–50, 153
expandable mutability, 25

face-to-face, 8, 16, 18, 29, 54, 105, 125, 149, 153, 154
facial recognition, 59, 63, 70, 78, 84
Fair Information Practices, 23, 38, 130, 133
fax, 5, 33, 96
FBI (Federal Bureau of Investigation), 75, 78
fear, 58, 67, 150, 152
  of crime, 98
Feenburg, Andrew, 135
feminism, 85
fibre-optics, 105
Fiji, 95
fingerprints, 19, 50, 72, 74–7, 80–1, 84, 99
finger scanning, 128
First Nations (Canada), 77
Flaherty, David H., 32
flexibility, 57
flows, 90, 91, 94, 99, 103, 105, 117, 134
  of consumption, 103
  of images, 117
  of information, 134
  of personal data, *see* data, flows
  of raw materials, 149

Ford, 94
Foucault, Michel, 57, 108, 109, 112, 144–8, 120, 123, 134
France, 28, 32, 52, 95, 96, 99, 101
frequent flyer clubs, 91
Friedman, Ted, 55
FTC (Federal Telecommunications Commission), 102
function creep, 111
fundamentalism, 85–6

Gandy, Oscar, 65, 111–13
Gardner, Norm, 64
GATT (General Agreement on Tariffs and Trade), 96
GATTACA, 9, 69
Gelenter, David, 24
gender, 20, 22, 85
General Communications Headquarters (GCHQ), 96
genetic, 81, 76, 81, 86, 145
  apartheid, 77
  code, 120
  determinism, 77
  discrimination, 79
  engineering of food products, 138
  identification, 85
  information, 84
  screening, 41, 76, 79
  surveillance methods, 29
  testing, 76–7, 79, 80, 87, 144
genomics, 76
GeoCities, 102
geo-demographic profiles, 122
Geographic Information Systems, 63, 91, 122
geographic profiling, 63
Germany, 20, 30, 33, 94, 99–100, 129
Giddens, Anthony, 17, 90, 108, 110, 111
Gilliom, John, 137
Global Position Satellite (GPS), 58, 153
global village, 99, 108
globalization, 50, 58, 89–90, 91–3, 100, 103, 107
  of data flows, 94, 101, 105
  of labour, 99
  of the market, 99, 104
  restructuring, 30
  and risk, 134
  and surveillance, 5, 9–10, 87, 89, 90, 94, 103, 145

Global Internet Liberty Campaign, 133
Global Positioning Satellite (GPS), 37,
    91, 126
globalization, 93
Goffman, Erving, 72
governance, 6
Graham, Stephen, 54, 62, 122–3
Greenpeace, 10, 88, 95, 133
Gropius, Walter, 55

Hacking, Ian, 120
Hager, Nicky, 95
Haggerty, Kevin, 6, 111, 120–1
Halford, Alison, 42
hand scanners, 72, 80, 82
handkey, 81
Hansen, Inge, 132
Harris, Mike, 78
health cards, 78
history, 18
Hong Kong, 32
human face, 40
Human Genome Project, 76
Hungary, 132
Hunter, Lawrence, 130
hyperreality, 116, 118

IBM (International Business machines),
    45
identity, 4, 9, 16, 20, 26, 31, 53, 65,
    69–72, 74, 75, 78, 81–3, 99, 107–8,
    127, 144, 147
  consumer, 145
  multiplication, 115
  papers, 33, 82
  politics, 72, 134
  verification, 117
identity theft, 71
image database, 69
Incyte Pharmaceuticals, 76
India, 54, 95
individualism, 20, 23, 93, 130
Indonesia, 32
industrialism, 91
information
  age, 22, 74, 116, 146
  flows of, 57
  highways, 92
  infrastructures, 4, 8, 28, 29, 34, 37–8,
      39, 40, 43, 47, 49–50, 53–4, 58,
      105, 108, 125, 128
  society, 24, 28, 34, 151
    definition, 30

superhighway, 28, 32
  technology, 57, 137–8
Information and Privacy Commision
    (Toronto), 64
informational cities, 53
informatisation, 28
Innis, Harold Adams, 18
Institute for Employment Rights (UK),
    42
insurance, 6, 11, 33–5, 46, 60, 76–7, 83,
    111, 115, 121, 144–5, 148, 150
Intel, 9, 43, 102–3
intelligence gathering, 38–9
intelligent agents, 102
Intelligent Island (Singapore), 28
international intelligence, 88
Internet, 5, 10, 18, 22, 39, 42, 44, 51,
    54, 57, 65–6, 71, 89, 90, 96–7,
    101–5, 108, 115, 127–8, 130,
    132–3, 145, 146–7
Internet Profiles (I/Pro), 102
interpellation, 115
Interpol, 98
Iperbole system (Italy), 67
Ireland, 33, 40, 54
Irish Republican Army, 39
Israel, 32–3, 69, 95, 99
Italy, 67, 94, 99, 101

Jacobs, Jane, 53, 68
Jamaica, 98
Japan, 7, 20, 33, 81, 93–4, 96, 98, 99,
    103, 105
  Ministry of International Trade and
      Industry (MITI), 32
  privacy in, 17
Japanization, 93–4, 103–4
justice, 50–5, 60, 75, 83–4, 86, 128,
    154
just-in-time management, 43, 93

Kafka, Franz, 110
key escrow, 133
keystroke counting, 42
KGB, 110
King, Rodney, 59
Kiwi Card, 132
knowledge-based economies, 5, 29
Korea, 32, 143

labour flows, 99
Lange, David, 95
Laudon, Kenneth, 130

Lexis-Nexis, 132
Ley, David, 59
libertarians, 85
life-chances, 17
Livescan, 39
local, 50, 58, 90, 105
London, City of, 33
Lotus, 80, 97, 132
loyalty clubs, 43
Lundy, Kate, 45

Macpherson, C.B., 21
magnetic stripe, 3, 74, 105
Mailcop, 40
mailshots, 43
Malaysia, 28, 32
Mandrake (facial recognition), 59
mark of the beast, 85–6
market research, 39, 46
marketing, 43, 44, 89, 90, 103, 119
Marks & Spencer's, 79
Martins, Herminio, 44, 140
Marvin, Simon, 122
Marx, Gary T., 25, 32, 35, 98, 100, 108,
    111, 114, 123, 143
Marx, Karl, 9, 116, 118, 123
Marxian, 112, 119, 134
mass media, 92, 103
MasterCard, 78, 80
material bodies, 24
Mathieson, Thomas, 59, 92
mediation, electronic, 16
Melucci, Alberto, 128, 134
memory, 72, 74–5, 82
Mexico, 63, 94, 98, 99
Michels, Roberto, 109
Microsoft Corporation, 43, 97, 126
Middle East, 95, 99
military origins of computers, 29, 43
mirror worlds, 26
mobility, 2, 5, 16, 18–19, 20, 35, 49, 57,
    67, 82, 120
  and modes of social integration, 27
Modahl, Diane, 85
modern, 5, 10, 16, 17, 31, 35, 53, 81,
    95, 105, 116–17
modernity, 2, 15, 20, 29, 31, 37–8, 49,
    56, 71, 73, 91, 93, 108–9, 111, 139,
    142, 149
  social fractures of, 151
money laundering, 95
Moses, Robert, 25
Multimedia Super Corridor, 28

nation-state, 20, 30, 33, 38, 71, 89, 92,
    93, 108–10, 118, 124, 143, 145
National Automated Fingerprint
    Identification System, 39
National Criminal Intelligence Service,
    79
national identity papers, 33, 100
National Security Agency (NSA), 3, 95,
    97, 127
Nazism, 132
Nelkin, Dorothy, 137–8
Net, The, 107
Netherlands, 132
Netscape, 97, 101
networking, 26, 39, 77, 86, 90, 92, 97,
    100, 105, 121, 134, 147, 149
  of resources, 132
  social-technological, 26
New York, 29, 105
New Zealand, 33, 63, 95, 132
Nigeria, 98
Nineteen Eighty Four, 31
Nock, Steven, 21, 75
Norris, Clive, 25
North America, 18, 20, 22, 28, 65, 90,
    93, 98, 122, 143–4

Oceania, 96
omniperception, 124, 147
One World, 91
online, 1, 142
ontology of peace, 153
order, 35
organized crime, 95
Orwell, George, 7, 31, 33, 35, 110, 126,
    131, 143–4
Other, 125, 152

Pacific Asia, 32, 90, 93, 95
pagers, 96
Pakistan, 95
panopticon, 7, 90, 92, 100, 109, 112,
    114, 115–18, 120, 147, 152
panoptic power, 136
panoptic sort, 65
Pareto, Vilfredo, 109
Paris (France), 52
passports, 73, 82
passwords, 117, 126
Payne, Robert, 84
Pentium, 43, 102, 132
personal identification number (PIN),
    16, 27, 70, 126

personhood, embodied, 9, 11, 26, 37, 49, 53, 86, 124, 147, 150, 151–4
place, 19, 35
Plant, Sadie, 85
Plato, 52
police, 8, 29, 34, 37–40, 45, 59, 60, 63–4, 74, 78–9, 83, 89, 90, 94, 97, 98, 100, 103, 105, 108, 111, 119–21, 133, 143, 148–9
police archipelago, 97
Police National Computer (PNC) (UK), 39, 40, 62
political economy, 109, 112
Poster, Mark, 92, 108, 114–17, 119, 120, 123
postmodern, 4, 20, 55, 105, 109, 114, 139, 141, 149
postmodernity, 141–2, 146–8
poststructuralism, 9, 123
poverty, 59
power, 5, 10, 16, 20, 31, 34, 46, 49, 62, 77, 82, 89–90, 91–2, 109, 115, 119, 141, 148, 149
  bureaucratic, 60, 110
  classificatory, 101
  and codes, 134
  global, 89–92, 104
  hegemonic, 136–7
  insurance and, 34, 46
  microphysics of, 121
  in spaces of flows, 57–9
  of the state, 30, 111
power-knowledge, 109
Prantl, Herbert, 46
privacy, 4, 5, 7, 9, 10, 20–3, 25, 27, 32, 63, 66, 128–9, 136–9, 144, 149–50
  definition of (Rohan Samarajiva), 22
  financial, 128
  informational, 22
  legislation, 44, 120, 136
  personal, 7, 32
  policy, 131
  politics of, 128
  protection, 127
  rights, 137
privacy-enhancing technologies (PETS), 23, 26, 71, 82, 130
Privacy International (PI), 10, 90, 126, 133
private, 7, 17, 19–23, 33, 35, 42, 44, 46, 61, 72, 84, 127
  communications, 97

Processor Serial Number (PSN), 102
progress, 31, 106
providence, 31
public, 7, 10, 17, 19–21, 23, 33, 44, 46, 61, 72

Qantas Airlines, 91
Quebec, private sector databases in, 45

rationalization, 112
Regan, Priscilla, 22
relationship marketing, 44
remote
  control, 89, 100
  sensing, 91
retinal scans, 19, 50, 56, 75, 78, 84, 144
ring of steel (London), 33, 39
risk, 6–7, 38, 46, 47, 60–1, 66, 74, 81, 83, 85–6, 104, 144, 149–50
  calculation, 49
  communication, 34, 46, 83
  management, 6, 10, 25, 26, 34, 39, 40, 46, 56, 60, 61, 66, 68, 72, 74, 77, 80, 84, 104, 120, 122, 124, 136, 144, 148
  profile, 74
  society, 128, 135, 144, 150
Robertson, Pat, 85
Robertson, Roland, 93
Robins, Kevin, 112–13
Rome, 65
Rule, James, 25, 73–4, 110, 130
Russell, Bertrand, 20
Russia, 95–8

Samarajiva, Rohan, 22
Sapphire, 91
satellites, 28, 52, 96, 105
Saudi Arabia, 96
Scandinavia, 93
scanner, 69, 75
Schengen Information System, 98
Scotland, 62
Seabrook, Jeremy, 68
security, 2, 6, 61, 66, 68, 78, 83, 86, 90, 104, 126, 129, 133, 136, 150
Sennett, Richard, 52
Sicily, 98
Sigint (Signals Intelligence), 95
Silent Witness, 63
SimCity, 9, 52–3, 55–6, 60, 66–8
Simmel, Georg, 20, 67, 82, 123

simulation, 26, 64, 67, 86, 113, 116–18, 122, 124, 147–8, 151
    sorting, 49, 51, 53
    urban management, 120
Singapore, 28, 93
Sklair, Leslie, 91–3, 97
Sloanism, 43, 112
smart cards, 52, 69, 72, 85
smart meters, 58, 84
Smith, Winston, 110
sniffer software, 96
Snoop Collection, 102
soccer violence, 79
social
    divisions, 10, 24, 67
    integration, 149
    justice, 11, 23, 27, 67–8, 118, 125, 130, 151, 154
    orchestration, 8–9, 27, 30, 36, 46, 47, 56, 68, 82, 88, 120, 124, 128, 147–8, 152–3
    science fictions, 148
    security card, 73
    sorting, 25, 47, 51, 61, 66, 69, 87, 92, 103–4, 108, 111–12, 148, 150, 152
Social Assistance Reform Act (Canada), 78
Social Insurance Numbers (SIN), 115
societies of control, 35
society of strangers, 20–1, 27, 67, 82, 125, 130, 153
Sorel, Georges, 109
South Africa, 32
South America, 96
South Korea, 143
Soviet Union, 31
space, 134
    gendered, 20
    public, 4, 135
spaces of flows, 57–9
Spain, 99
speed, 18, 35, 49, 57, 116, 136, 146, 148
spiders, 102
Stasi, 110
Strange, Susan, 34
Studeman, William, 95
subpolitics, 134
superpanopticon, 92, 108, 114–15, 120, 121, 151
surveillance, 3, 90, 109
    anticipatory, 130, 149
    compliance with, 7

    definition, 2
    and discrimination, 46, 90
    disembodied, 33
    pre-emptive, 103, 143
    postmodern, 146
    as a product of rationalization, 110
    as productive, 53, 137
    and risk, 121
Sweden, 32, 94, 129
synopticon, 92, 103

targeted advertising, 43, 58, 65, 102, 117, 146
Tasmania, 53
Taylor, Frederick (and Taylorism), 101, 112, 142
technique, 115
technological determinism, 24, 77
technological sublime, 33
telecommuting, 57
telematic societies, 116–17
telephone, 5, 16, 42, 56, 88, 96, 105, 108
    mobile, 54, 115
teleshopping, 57
television, 30, 108
Telex, 96
Telstra (Australia), 45
terrorism, 95–104
Thrift, Nigel, 18–19, 24
thumbprints
    see also fingerprints, 9, 144
time and space, 3, 7, 17, 18, 19, 30, 57, 64, 72, 82, 84, 134
    binding of, 18, 23
timetables, 18
Tocqueville, Alexis de, 31
Tokyo, 33, 105
totalitarian, 35, 38, 108, 110
Total Quality Control, 93
tradition, 18
trust, 22
    tokens of, 8, 16, 21, 27, 49, 66, 82, 145, 147
Turnbull, Peter, 94

Until the End of the World, 107
urban, 9, 51, 52, 58
UKUSA (UK–USA agreement), 95
utilitarian, 11, 46, 68, 83, 109, 153

van der Ploeg, Irma, 99, 139
video conference, 15

video surveillance, *see* cameras, closed
    circuit television and video
Virilio, Paul, 54, 82, 117
visibility, 62
voice recognition, 9, 81, 84, 96, 144

Wajcman, Judy, 151
webcams, 41
Weber, Max, 8, 108–9, 112, 114–15,
    118–19, 123, 142
Webster, Frank, 113
welfare, 78, 84, 86
Wenders, Wim, 28, 107
Winner, Langdon, 111
wiretaps, 33, 38, 126

work, flexible, 5
worker
    mobility, 40
    performance, 42
workplace
    drug testing, 85, 137
    monitoring/surveillance, 25, 39,
        40–3, 64, 94, 127, 137, 142
wrapped in media, 124, 146
Wright, Will, 55

Yahoo!, 102
yakuza, 33, 98

Zukin, Sharon, 59

CITIZENSHIP IN A GLOBAL AGE
SOCIETY, CULTURE, POLITICS
Gerard Delanty

- What is citizenship?
- Is global citizenship possible?
- Can cosmopolitanism provide an alternative to globalization?

Citizenship in a Global Age provides a comprehensive and concise overview of the main debates on citizenship and the implications of globalization. It argues that citizenship is no longer defined by nationality and the nation state, but has become de-territorialized and fragmented into the separate discourses of rights, participation, responsibility and identity. Gerard Delanty claims that cosmopolitanism is increasingly becoming a significant force in the global world due to new expressions of cultural identity, civic ties, human rights, technological innovations, ecological sustainability and political mobilization. Citizenship is no longer exclusively about the struggle for social equality but has become a major site of battles over cultural identity and demands for the recognition of group difference. Delanty argues that globalization both threatens and supports cosmopolitan citizenship. Critical of the prospects for a global civil society, he defends the alternative idea of a more limited cosmopolitan public sphere as a basis for new kinds of citizenship that have emerged in a global age.

Contents
Introduction – Part 1: Models of citizenship – The liberal theory of citizenship: rights and duties – Communitarian theories of citizenship: participation and identity – The radical theories of politics: citizenship and democracy – Part 2: The cosmopolitan challenge – Cosmopolitan citizenship: beyond the nation state – Human rights and citizenship: the emergence of the embodied self – Globalization and the deterritorialization of space: between order and chaos – The transformation of the nation state: nationalism, the city, migration and muliticulturalism – European integration and post-national citizenship: four kinds of post-nationalization – Part 3: Rethinking citizenship – The reconfiguration of citizenship: post-national governance in the multi-levelled polity – Conclusion: the idea of civic cosmopolitanism – Bibliography – Index.

c. 184pp   0 335 20489 9   (Paperback)   0 335 20490 2   (Hardback)

SOCIAL EXCLUSION
David Byrne

- What does the term 'social exclusion' mean and who are the 'socially excluded'?
- Why has there been such a significant increase in 'social exclusion'?
- How can we attempt to tackle this and the problems associated with it?

'Social exclusion' is the buzz phrase for the complex range of social problems which derive from the substantial increase in social inequality in Western societies. This timely and engaging volume examines these problems in societies where manufacturing industry is no longer the main basis for employment and the universal welfare states established after the Second World War are under attack. It reviews theories of social exclusion, including the Christian democratic and social democratic assertions of solidarity with which the term originated, Marxist accounts of the recreation of the reserve army of labour, and neo-liberal assertions of the sovereignty of the market in which the blame for exclusion is assigned to the excluded themselves.

Drawing on a wide variety of empirical evidence, the author concludes that the origins of social exclusion lie with the creation of a new post-industrial order founded on the exploitation of low paid workers within western capitalism, and that social policies have actually helped to create an unequal social order as opposed to simply reacting to economic forces. This controversial but accessible text will be essential reading for undergraduate courses on social exclusion within sociology, politics, economics, geography and social policy, as well as students on professional courses and practitioners in social work, community work, urban planning and management, health and housing.

Contents
Introduction – Part one – The possessive individualists: blaming the poor – Order and solidarity: collectivist approaches – Exploitation matters: Marxist approaches to exclusion – Part two – Dynamic society – dynamic lives – The dynamics of income inequality – Divided spaces: social divisions in the post-industrial city – Conclusion: what is and what is to be done about it – Notes – Bibliography – Index.

176pp   0 335 19974 7 (Paperback)   0 335 19975 5 (Hardback)

THE GOVERNANCE OF SCIENCE
Steve Fuller

- What does social and political theory have to say about the role of science in society?
- Do scientists and other professional enquirers have an unlimited 'right to be wrong'?
- What are the implications of capitalism and multiculturalism for the future of the university?

This ground-breaking text offers a fresh perspective on the governance of science from the standpoint of social and political theory. Science has often been seen as the only institution that embodies the elusive democratic ideal of the 'open society'. Yet, science remains an elite activity that commands much more public trust than understanding, even though science has become increasingly entangled with larger political and economic issues. Fuller proceeds by rejecting liberal and communitarian ideologies of science, in favour of a 'republican' approach centred on 'the right to be wrong'. He shows how the recent scaling up of scientific activity has undermined the republican ideal.

The centrepiece of the book, a social history of the struggle to render the university a 'republic of science', focuses on the potential challenges posed by multiculturalism and capitalism. Finally, drawing on the science policy of the US New Deal, Fuller proposes nothing short of a new social contract for 'secularizing' science.

Contents
Introduction – Part I: The political and material conditions of scientific inquiry – Science as the open society and its ideological deformations – The role of scale in the scope of scientific governance – Part II: The university as a site for the governance of science – The historical interdependence of the university and knowledge production – Multiculturalism's challenge to academic integrity – or a tale of two churches – The university as capitalism's final frontier – or the fading hope of enlightenment in a complex world – Part III: The secularization of science and a new deal for science policy – The road not taken: revisiting the original new deal – Elements for a new constitution of science – References – Index.

192pp   0 335 20234 9   (Paperback)   0 335 20235 7   (Hardback)

WORK, CONSUMERISM AND THE NEW POOR

Zygmunt Bauman

- Can poverty be fought and conquered by orthodox means?
- Should we seek new solutions like 'decoupling' the right to livelihood from the selling of labour and extending the socially recognized concept of work?
- How urgent is it to confront these social questions and find practical answers?

It is one thing to be poor in a society of producers and universal employment; it is quite a different thing to be poor in a society of consumers, in which life projects are built around consumer choice rather than work, professional skills or jobs. If 'being poor' once derived its meaning from the condition of being unemployed, today it draws its meaning primarily from the plight of a flawed consumer. This is one difference which truly makes a difference – in the way living in poverty is experienced and in the chances and prospects to redeem its misery.

This absorbing book attempts to trace this change, which has been taking place over the duration of modern history, and to make an inventory of its social consequences. On the way, it tries also to consider to what extent the well remembered and tested means of fighting back advancing poverty and mitigating its hardships are fit (or unfit) to grasp and tackle the problems of poverty in its present form. Students of sociology, politics and social policy will find this to be an invaluable text on the changing significance and implications of an enduring social problem.

Contents
Introduction – Part one – The meaning of work: producing the work ethic – From the work ethic to the aesthetic of consumption – Part two – The rise and fall – The work ethic and the new Poor – Part three – Prospects for the new poor – Notes – Index.

128pp   0 335 20155 5   (Paperback)   0 335 20156 3   (Hardback)

Guildford College
Learning Resource Centre

Please return on or before the last date shown.
No further issues or renewals if any items are overdue.
"7 Day" loans are **NOT** renewable.

Class: 303·483 LYO

Title: Surveillance society

Author: Lyon, David.